LENIN, HITLER, and ME

Boris J. Kochanowsky

Contents

Introduction
by Vera Kochanowsky

When I was a child my father loved to tell me stories about his youth. He would always speak dramatically, telling and re-telling each story with great relish and fervor. He was over fifty years old when I was born, so most of the events he spoke of had happened long before my birth. To me it seemed as if he were talking about someone else—a friend or a relative, who lived long ago in a foreign land, under circumstances totally alien to our life together. It was difficult for me to imagine my father, who even in my earliest recollections was over-weight and slow-moving, facing the dangers and hardships he described.

My father's narrative style was disjointed. His stories always came out in bits and pieces, without a clear context or regard for chronological order. I could never get a sense of the sequence of his life's events until I read his memoirs myself for the first time when I was in high school. Even then, he would not allow me to read certain sections, shielding me from certain passages he thought too racy for my innocent eyes. Now, years later, it has been a special pleasure for me to go back and experience his story again in its entirety, and to recall how each of his favorite vignettes fits in with the rest. Throughout, he focuses on himself and his view of the world, often neglecting to describe the people he encountered, or the places he visited, with much precision. This lack of detail, on the one hand, is unfortunate. But from a story-telling perspective, it may offer a kind of benefit by leaving more to the imagination and propelling the reader forward, headlong into the action of the tale.

The memoir, which he completed in 1971, the year following his retirement from the Pennsylvania State University, consists of 220 type-written pages. All but eighteen pages deal with the period spanning from his early youth until the end of World War II. The remaining twenty-four years receive cursory treatment in comparison. He wrote his memoirs entirely from memory, having never kept a journal or diary. His oral recollections, told to me and many others, may have helped keep his memories fresh through the years, the light-hearted anecdotes being among his favorites.

Soon after completing his memoirs, my father tried to have them published, in hopes that his story might be considered for a Hollywood film. But because he had begun his study of English relatively late in life—it was his fifth language—his writing style was less than literary, being fraught with grammatical and idiomatic errors. There were also problems with flow and organization, as well as a certain awkwardness of expression. The manuscript therefore met with some criticism. Realizing that he had omitted much historical detail as well, my father spent considerable time in the early 1980's researching Russian and German history, with the intention of adding more background to his story, but these improvements never materialized. His health was declining by this time, and the many pages of illegibly scrawled historical notes he amassed sat in a pile and were never reviewed or incorporated into the book.

In 1989, fully aware of his deteriorating health, I read the memoirs again, making careful note of specific questions I had. Using a simple hand-held cassette tape recorder, I interviewed my father for several days in May of that year, trying to pry any lingering memories from him that had not made it into his memoirs. In some cases, he could not remember anything more, but in other cases, I was able to glean additional information, particularly about his early years in Siberia.

After my father's death late in 1992, my husband, Gregory Hutton, set himself the task of editing the memoirs, making major improvements in organization and style. He completed the job in 1995. It had always been my intention to carefully review the work as well, to improve it to my satisfaction, and to add whatever material I could from the interview tapes, from my own memory, and from any additional resources available. Preoccupied with my family and career, I delayed this project for many years, until the fall of 2008, when my son left home to attend college. This delay, although in some ways regrettable, afforded me some additional insights. Of course, the Internet has proven useful in researching historical background information. Even more helpful, however, has been the unexpected establishment of a connection with a relative from my father's side of the family, Larysa Kapushchevska-Mazuren, the granddaughter of my father's older sister, Berta. Larysa's input has provided me with some valuable insights and a new perspective.

Until 2008, I had not yet reviewed the five hours of taped interviews I had made with my father in 1989, believing it would be painful to do so. Yet, once I resolved to listen to them, the experience turned out to be strangely soothing, as well as remarkably inspiring. It reminded me that his life's story, so familiar to me, was really quite unique and worthy of re-telling.

My father was a distinctive individual with strong ideas and even stronger ideals. Undoubtedly, these qualities helped him survive the many obstacles he faced in his life. Whether his character was formed by the particular circumstances he encountered, or whether he was "born" the way he was, is impossible to determine. The precise roles of "nature versus nurture" are still being debated. However he managed to survive, through sheer luck, personal determination, by knowing the right people, or by being in the right place at the right time, it is a miracle that he made it through so much adversity in one piece. His indomitable spirit and the great love he held for my mother and me have inspired me all my life.

My grateful thanks go, first of all, to my husband, for his initial work on the manuscript, and for his advice and patient support of this project. My thanks also go to those who read the first drafts of the book and gave me their comments and enthusiastic encouragement: Edmund and Marianne Bowles, Alice Breon, Barbara Costik, Marian Gormley, Carol Ireland, Marion Jetton, Lydia Johnson, Martha Jones, and Thomas MacCracken.

Foreword

I would not be who I am, nor would my life have been what it was, had I not lived during a time of great upheaval. Revolution and war brought an abrupt end to my sheltered, privileged existence, and I was thrust into a world filled with loss, struggle, and danger. Between 1922 and 1943 I escaped death twenty times. Of course, at that time escaping death, even twenty times, was not in itself particularly noteworthy. In those days, soldiers in combat—combat I only heard from a distance—faced death twenty times or more in a single battle. Prisoners in Nazi concentration camps—camps I was able to avoid—faced death continually at the hands of jailers who killed under orders or on whim. These stories are powerfully moving, and I honor those experiences far above my own. Yet it seems to me that there has been something special about my life, something unique about my struggle.

My brushes with death were isolated instances occurring over the course of many years, and they were personal. I met each of my adversaries face to face, and could see fear and hatred in their eyes. At the same time, I knew that I was no threat to them. I was never armed and had no power over them. I knew that their fear and hatred were senseless, the result of tragically misguided judgment. The persecutions I suffered, like the horrific mass murders I witnessed all around me, were all simply mistakes—unspeakably horrible mistakes.

I have written these pages because I want the world to see the atrocities and injustices of war as I saw them—not as grand military strategies or mass sociopolitical movements, but as a terrifying, deadly force directed at individual human beings such as me. Also, I want to bear witness to the valor of those who risked their lives to save me, to prove that true heroes still exist, even in our time. In that regard, I want to pose the question of whether it was by coincidence alone that I happened to know these heroes, and that they willingly came to my aid, or was there some divine intervention or plan afoot? The odds against my survival were absolutely absurd, yet here I am. Finally, I hope my story will demonstrate the incredible power of dreams. All my life I have been called a dreamer, an idealist, even a "moral athlete" because of how tenaciously I held on to my ideals and dreams. Perhaps this story will inspire others to hold onto their dreams, to strive for the highest human ideals, and, against all odds and obstacles, to courageously defend that which is deepest in their hearts.

Boris J. Kochanowsky
State College, Pennsylvania, 1972

Chapter 1

A SPECIAL KIND OF CHILDHOOD

The childhood shows the man, as the morning shows the day.

—John Milton, *Paradise Regained*

I was born in Krasnoyarsk, Siberia on May 4, 1905. In those days, this area—the town, the surrounding mountains, and the mighty Yenisei River—were magnificently beautiful. Here the Trans-Siberian railroad crossed the Yenisei, which made Krasnoyarsk an important center for commerce and travel. Famous itinerant authors, such as Anton Chekhov, described the region in glowing terms:

> *Never in my life have I seen a river more magnificent than the Yenisei.... While the Volga is a dressy, modest, pensive beauty, the Yenisei is a powerful, turbulent giant which does not know what to do with its enormous power and its youth...Man of the Volga started out with daring, and ended up with a moan, which he calls a song; his bright golden hopes have been replaced by hopelessness which is popularly known as Russian pessimism; on the contrary the Yenisei has started out with a moan, and will end up with such glory the likes of which we can't even dream about.... This is at least what I thought standing on the bank of the wide Yenisei and eagerly looking at its water which with incredible speed*

1

> *and power rushed towards the severe Arctic Ocean. There is*
> *not enough room for the Yenisei in its banks. Rolling waves*
> *are chasing one another, forming mighty whirlpools, and it*
> *seems strange that this powerful giant has not yet broken its*
> *banks, and has not drilled through its rocky bed.... On this*
> *bank stands Krasnoyarsk, the best and most beautiful of all*
> *Siberian towns, and on the opposite, there rise mountains*
> *which remind me of the Caucasus, misty and dreamlike.... I*
> *stood there and I thought: what a full, intelligent and brave*
> *life will some day illuminate these shores![1]*

From an early age, I felt deeply influenced by the natural beauty that surrounded me. In many ways, my love for its vastness, its noble beauty, and its invincible power molded my life, shaped my character, and nurtured a deep pride in my Russian heritage. I was such a zealous patriot as a student that it made me proud to learn of Russia's previous expansions and past conquests. I remain a Siberian patriot to this day. Yet I, like most Russians, was also eager to gain as much knowledge as I could about the outside world.

Many think of Siberia as an uncivilized wasteland inhabited only by criminals and political prisoners. Yet Krasnoyarsk, a town of a respectable size (pop. 80,000 at that time), was brimming with culture. It had its own opera house, theater, and symphony hall. Famous touring artists frequently visited and gave performances.[2]

---

[1] From Chekhov's travel notes of 1890, as transcribed by George St. George in his book *Siberia: The New Frontier,* New York: David McKay Company, Inc., 1969, p. 102.

[2] George Kennan, traveling through Krasnoyarsk during the last years of the nineteenth century, was himself taken by surprise to find such a wealth of culture in a place so remote (*Siberia & the Exile System,* New York: The Century Company, 1891, vol. 1, pp. 357-359.):

We arrived in Krasnoyarsk late on the evening of Wednesday, September 2nd....Thursday afternoon we called upon Mr. Leo Petróvitch Kuznetsóf, a wealthy gold-mining proprietor to whom we had brought a letter of introduction from St. Petersburg. We little anticipated the luxurious comfort of the house and the delightful social atmosphere of the home circle to which this letter would admit us. The servant who came to the door in response to our ring showed us into one of the most beautiful and

Another powerful force of my childhood was the infamous Siberian winter. Temperatures of seventy degrees below zero Fahrenheit were typical. The severity of our winters would freeze the powerful, mile-wide Yenisei solid enough for trucks to drive across it. It happened with amazing speed. In only a matter of days the visibly flowing river would become as solid as a rock.

All animals in Siberia are barrel-shaped, an evolutionary trait which promotes the conservation of internal body heat and minimizes relative surface area. The horses, particularly the smaller Siberian ponies, developed barrel-shaped bodies. Dogs, too, were barrel-shaped. Even the people, myself included, tended to have big round chests. Any skinny creature

---

tastefully furnished drawing-rooms that we had seen in Russia. It was fully fifty feet in length by thirty-five feet in width and twenty feet high; its inlaid floor of polished oak was hidden here and there by soft oriental rugs; palms, luxuriant ferns, and pots of blossoming plants occupied the lower portions of the high, richly curtained windows; the apparent size of the spacious apartment was increased by long pier-glasses interposed between the masses of greenery and flowers; a cheerful fire of birch wood was burning in an open fireplace under a massive mantel of carved marble; cabinets of polished cherry, filled with rare old china, delicate ivory carvings, bronze Buddhist idols, and all sorts of bric-à-brac, stood here and there against the walls; large oil-paintings by well-known Russian, French, and English artists occupied places of honor at the ends of the room; and at our right, as we entered, was a grand piano, flanked by a carved stand piled high with books and music.

We had hardly had time to recover from the state of astonishment into which we were thrown by the sight of so many unexpected evidences of wealth, culture, and refinement in this remote East Siberian town when a slender, dark-haired, pale-faced young man in correct afternoon dress entered the drawing-room, introduced himself as Mr. Innokénti Kuznetsóf, and welcomed us in good English to Krasnoyarsk. We were soon made acquainted with the whole Kuznetsóf family, which consisted of three brothers and two sisters, all unmarried, and all living together in this luxurious house. Mr. Innokénti Kuznetsóf and his sisters spoke English fluently; they had traveled in America, and had spent more or less time in New York, Philadelphia, Washington, Saratoga, Chicago, Salt Lake City, and San Francisco. Mr. Innokénti Kuznetsóf's personal acquaintance with the United States was more extensive, indeed, than my own, inasmuch as he had twice crossed the continent; had hunted buffalo on our Western prairies; had met General Sheridan, Buffalo Bill, Captain Jack, and other frontier notables, and had even visited regions as remote as Yellowstone Park and the "Staked Plains."

would freeze right through and have little chance of surviving the Siberian cold.

In winter, milk was sold in frozen chunks. The dairyman would fill a pail with milk into which he would immerse a heavy stick. The milk froze quickly into giant pail-shaped ice cubes, which people would carry home by the stick. We Siberians consumed enormous quantities of food in the winter to maintain our body temperature. Five meals a day were the norm, including steak for lunch and a heavy afternoon snack served at school. Five thousand calories a day—at least twice the normal adult intake—was the standard winter diet. I liked to eat butter by the stick, an especially refreshing treat when frozen.

A mighty river, the harsh winter, the beautiful majestic mountains, huge meals, and an endlessly vast country—in every respect, life in Siberia was impressive. Certainly, the environment in which I spent my early years, the beauties and extremes of nature, the people and traditions, had a great impact on my character and my way of thinking. I was a proud Siberian, and I believed that I lived in the largest, richest, most powerful and invincible country in the world. I was also proud of the Russian people for their generous hospitality, their love for music and the arts, and for their enterprising creative power demonstrated in art, science, and technology.

My father, Julius Kochanowsky, was about 5'6" in height. Broad and powerfully built, he had a thick, full head of reddish-blond hair in his youth. He had started out with nothing and, through hard work and ingenuity, had become a successful multi-millionaire. At the turn of the twentieth century Siberia was in the midst of an economic boom and my father's career had flourished as a result. He was an industrialist specializing in paper—everything from growing the timber to printing onto the final product. At the height of his career he was realizing a 400% annual profit. I remember that my father always seemed busy. Every morning he would rise early and ride six kilometers on horseback to the saw mill, which stood on the outskirts of town near the railway station. I watched my father build new businesses, one by one, and witnessed the rapid growth of our family's wealth.

We owned a large new house (built c. 1913) on the main street (*Bolshaya Ulitsa*) of town, and a summer cottage (*dacha*) in the mountains. My father's print shop was on the first floor of our house. The local daily newspaper was typeset and printed there, as were myriad other printed items, including theater programs and army regulation manuals. Commissioned by the treasury department, my father even printed stamps and paper money for the czarist regime. At the time of greatest productivity, my father employed over seventy workers at the print shop alone. Our immediate neighbors were also businessmen. To our right was a pharmacist. To our left lived a fur trader, and to his left a textile merchant.

Our family lived upstairs in a large, luxuriously appointed apartment, which faced the courtyard to the rear. The courtyard was used for practical rather than decorative purposes. Large quantities of logs were stacked and stored there to feed the voracious furnace in winter. One of our servants had the express job of regularly throwing wood from the courtyard through a hole in the wall, down a chute that led directly into the belly of the furnace. Two other smaller apartments on our floor faced the street. These my father rented out to other families or individuals. In the basement beneath the print shop was the furnace and storage space for all of our food for the entire winter. It was impossible to buy most foodstuffs from fall until late spring, so having ample storage was a necessity. To the rear of the courtyard there stood a second, smaller house. In it there were two additional apartments, one on the second and another on the third floor. Each apartment had five rooms. The first floor served as storage for the print shop and held paper, supplies, spare parts, and machinery. The furnace stood in the basement and there was an attic as well.

I was the youngest in the family. I had six brothers and a beautiful sister, all of whom I greatly admired. All were highly educated, having attended prestigious Russian and foreign universities. Our family was well-known, respected, and quite influential in our city. When I walked down the street, people would point at me and whisper to their companions. I knew they were talking about me and my family.

My oldest brother, Dmitri (*Mitya*), twenty-seven years my senior, was a medical doctor who had studied at the University of Tomsk. I grew to admire him deeply for his humanitarian compassion. He was short in stature and good natured, but unmarried. Unfortunately, he died of scarlet fever when I was only eight years old. Having caught the illness from a patient, he only noticed it when his friends pointed out the red spots on his hands as they were playing cards. He died five days later.

The next oldest brother, Simeon (*Syema*), had died before my birth, at around age seventeen. He had developed a tumor in his throat and my mother had taken him to Berlin in a desperate attempt to find a cure. Unfortunately, nothing could be done. Simeon died in Berlin. Later my father told us that of all his children, Simeon had been the most talented and intelligent.

Next eldest was my brother Matthew (*Motya*), seven years younger than Dmitri, who had studied printing in New York and then joined my father in the family business. Matthew was in charge of the printing office. He was tall and broad-shouldered with chestnut brown hair. A gifted artist, he helped decorate our home and also designed and manufactured playing cards decorated with pictures of the various indigenous peoples of Siberia. In 1913, the year he spent studying in New York, Matthew lived with an uncle, my father's brother, who was married and had five daughters.[3] Matthew traveled extensively while in the United States and took many photographs. I remember how intrigued I was when I saw these pictures, especially his photos of Yellowstone Park and of Native American people. They piqued my interest in America. From that time on, I began to think seriously about going there myself. After returning home from his year abroad, he married and had one son, but Matthew was generally not well. He suffered from a weak heart.

Next was my sister Berta (*Betya*), fifteen years older than I, who had graduated from the University of Kiev in philology. Subsequently she married a prominent Siberian treasury official Morris Kapushchevsky. Morris worked in Omsk, and Berta spent part of the year with him there. They had one son, Valentin. Berta was fairly short, extremely beautiful, and dark haired. In the summers, when my mother went to Karlsbad, Germany, to take the cure for her ailing liver and kidneys, Berta would take care of me at our dacha. I remember trying to spy on her through the keyhole while she was bathing.

Victor (*Vitya*), two years younger than Berta, was a lawyer and also worked for my father. He had studied law at the University of Tomsk. Victor was dark blond, tall, and extremely good looking.[4] All of my siblings were

---

[3] This uncle had changed his last name. Unfortunately, we eventually lost contact with this part of the family.

[4] In appearance, Victor resembled the French actor Charles Boyer.

serious-minded people who followed the strict moral code which prevailed in Russia at the time. Like my parents, they were also humble, modest, and avoided any obtrusive, flagrant show of extravagance. Victor was the exception. In a way, he was the "black sheep" of our family. He possessed a dazzlingly charming personality—free-spirited and mischievous. Fortunately, most of his offenses were harmless. In his last year of high school, Victor was almost expelled because he had appeared publicly in civilian clothes instead of the school uniform students were required to wear. He also visited off-limits locations, contrary to school regulations. A born show-off, Victor would make a point of arriving five minutes late every time he attended the theater, so that the audience would be forced to notice him. Victor was also very fond of wrestling. On occasion he would offer a cash reward equal to a day's wages to any of my father's workers who could beat him in an impromptu wrestling match. Few succeeded. While attending university, Victor managed to spend twice as much money as his brothers had. He also seemed to have a particular weakness for women and would lavish them with expensive gifts. In 1918, my father sent Victor to Harbin (in Manchuria—northeastern China, but then under Japanese influence) to oversee major business transactions. Most of the materials and equipment my father required for his printing business came from Japan via Harbin. Victor had to place the orders, make the payments, and then arrange for the materials to be transported to Krasnoyarsk by train.

Two years younger than Victor was Joseph (*Osya*). Joseph studied in Tomsk and in Heidelberg, Germany, and became a physician, following ably and admirably in the footsteps of our late brother Dmitri. Of all my brothers, Joseph was my favorite. Tall, dark, and slender, he looked like a Spaniard, and wore thin, wire-rimmed glasses. I remember his great kindness, and that he never asked to be paid for his services. He eventually married a woman who was also a doctor, and they had a son, Sasha. Long after the revolution, Joseph taught medicine at the University of Leningrad.

Five years my senior was my last brother, Jacob (*Jasha*). He was an excellent pianist who played Rachmaninoff particularly well. In 1918, during his first year at the University of Tomsk, the White Army (anti-communist) came through looking for recruits. Jacob, along with most of his friends, joined the White Army at that time and became embroiled in the massive struggle which would become the Russian Civil War.

My mother, Maria (Borovskaya), was short and had raven black hair. She spent much of her day busily directing the servants in the kitchen and elsewhere throughout the household. She had many friends and was a passionate patron of the performing arts. Our home was filled with music and steeped in culture. Opera singers were regularly invited to our home, and they would often favor us with a private performance. My mother relished attending the theater, the opera, and concerts. I remember having to help her dress by pulling the stays of her corset. It was no easy task. She had beautiful evening clothes and expensive jewelry. My father had given her a pair of exceptionally large diamond earrings which she particularly prized.

My mother loved all of her children deeply, but, as was the custom of the day, my parents engaged a nanny to tend to the daily needs of the younger children in the household. My first nanny was quite old and had taken care of all my other siblings before me. Although she died when I was small, I recall one incident in particular. Once, for some reason, I hit her. She started to cry bitterly and that startled me. I immediately felt very sorry for my actions. My nannies only cared for me during the school year. In the summers either my mother or my sister Berta would stay with me at our dacha. My other siblings rarely visited, and my father only came on weekends because he was occupied with his work in town during the week.

Meals were the only time the whole family gathered together. Friends of the family were often invited to dine with us. There was always much lively discussion and oftentimes I, too, wanted to participate. But being the youngest, whenever I tried to speak, I was invariably shushed. "Sha!" they would say. All I could do was to listen to the mature conversations of my parents and elder siblings and study their faces, moods, and mannerisms. Through this daily practice I learned the valuable skill of observation. On one rare occasion, I recall being allowed to speak during a dinner party. I announced to a duly impressed audience of family and guests that "a husband is happy when he sees a fire flickering in his fireplace and his smiling wife sitting beside him in the glow of it." On a similar occasion, I asked what I thought was a very sharp-minded question, "Why is it that only *married* women bear children?" This was met with a long silence and much consternation, since at that time this subject was not considered appropriate for polite conversation. Nevertheless, I was probably admired, at least silently, for my clear-minded observations. I did not know it then, but my ability to observe people would later save my life, more than once.

My parents and all of my siblings inspired me greatly. I wanted to be like my father, to follow in his footsteps and accomplish as much as he had. It impressed me that he was a self-made man, a truly dynamic individual. But of course, there was a problem: we were already wealthy. How could I, too, be a self-made man? I dreamed that I might someday enlarge my father's fortune. With this additional wealth, I hoped to create more new businesses and become a philanthropist who would make contributions to benefit the less fortunate, build schools and hospitals, establish fellowships for students, and more. I hoped to bring even more respect and recognition to my family in this way.

Although loved and protected by my family, I did on occasion encounter injustice and danger during my youth. One of my earliest memories is of a beating I received from my father when I was about three years of age. I was crawling under my father's work table while he and Victor were counting money. All of a sudden my father pulled me out from under the table, asked Victor for his belt, and proceeded to spank me with it. I felt both outraged and mystified as, in my opinion, I had done nothing to deserve this treatment. At the time I had no idea that I would have to face other unjustified beatings during my life.

When I was about four years old my parents took me for a ride in our open horse-drawn carriage. I was seated on the far left, closest to the middle of the street. My mother sat in the middle and my father on the far right. Riding down the main street of town, we encountered another carriage approaching from the opposite direction. Inside sat a general of the army. This carriage was drawn by a *troika*, a team of three horses abreast. In Russia, the troika was traditionally associated with persons of high social status. Typically, the center horse was a large, powerful specimen with a long, striding gait. The two outer horses were smaller and were trained to move at a light, quick gallop. The contrasting gaits of the horses, maintained at both high and low speeds, produced a distinctive rhythm unique to the troika.

As we approached, suddenly the troika coachman realized that our carriages were going to collide. He tried to halt the troika, but he reacted too slowly. The smaller horse nearest our carriage jumped directly into our carriage and came to a halt with one front hoof on the seat between my mother and me and the other foreleg waving frantically in the air, banging against the thin metal fender, trying to find a foothold. I found myself sitting between the legs of the horse, facing its breast, my head below its mouth and chin, and its leg waving and kicking up and down directly beside my ear. The coachman quickly came to my rescue and pulled me carefully out of the way while everyone around stood gaping in alarm. Not hurt at all, I could not see what all the fuss was about. Being but a small child, I did not understand how dangerous my predicament had been.

I had another close shave while swimming at Lake Shira, a vacation spot several hundred kilometers south of Krasnoyarsk. I was about four or five years old, and on holiday with my mother and Joseph. Because of the high salt content of the lake, it was very easy to float, ideal for a beginner like me. First I just crawled in the shallow water "walking" with my hands on the bottom of the lake, staying close to shore. When I kicked, my legs would float. Sometimes, however, I would encounter a deep hole and my hands would lose touch with the bottom. Out of fear, I moved my hands quickly and noticed that I could stay up on the surface without touching the bottom. Without realizing it, I was actually swimming. One day I decided to go into deeper water coming up to my chest. I noticed how other people would just lie on top of the water and then start to swim by moving their hands and feet. I tried imitating these motions, but my form was undoubtedly poor. Since I could not reach the bottom with my hands, I immediately lost confidence and went down like a rock. I was only in chest-deep water, so I could have easily "saved" myself just by standing up. But being in a state of panic, I didn't think of it. Instead I lay helplessly on the lake floor for quite some time. Finally, Joseph came and pulled me out. I remember it taking an appreciable amount of time to expel all the salty water from my lungs.

I was naturally curious. My inclination was to learn by observation and experimentation. Once, when I was six years old, I took a light bulb out of an electric lamp, put my finger in the hole, and turned on the switch. I wanted to know how the light worked and what came out of the hole. Of course, I got a terrible shock. I was frightened, but satisfied at the same time.

Once, Victor decided to play a nasty trick on me. Knowing how much I loved ice cream, he invited me to a small, dark ice cream shop run by a Mongolian. Mongolians were strange, frightening people to me. They wore distinctive clothing, spoke a foreign language, and had fierce black hair. The men usually wore sharp, pointy beards and moustaches. This particular Mongolian, however, made excellent ice cream, and I was happy to be eating it there in his shop. However, when I finished my bowl of ice cream, I looked up, and to my horror my brother was nowhere to be seen. There I was, alone in a small, dark room with the Mongolian, who now seemed especially frightening. I tried to run to the door, but the Mongolian blocked my way, demanding, "Where is my money?" I did not have any money. My brother had it all, and I did not know what to do. I imagined the Mongolian drawing out a long scimitar to slice off my head! In a total panic, I pushed him out of the way and ran all the way home. My brother was waiting for me in the living room. He, having paid the Mongolian himself beforehand, had sneaked out of the shop, leaving special instructions with the owner to scare me to death. From then on I kept a closer watch on Victor.

Although Siberia teemed with wildlife, few families actually kept wild animals as pets. We were an exception. When I was about thirteen years old, we acquired a bear and kept him for about a year. He came to us as a young cub when his mother was killed in the wild. We had him tied to a long chain in our courtyard, where he could walk on a fence and climb a pole. We fed him grain and played with him like a dog. My brothers would wrestle with him. As the cub grew older and heavier, this activity became more and more challenging. Finally, after catching and eating one of our chickens, the bear turned vicious. He had tasted blood and he was no longer playful, so we had to get rid of him. But it had been quite exciting for a young fellow like me to have a powerful wild animal in my backyard.

Probably due to my mother's influence, I was quite artistically inclined in my early years. An attractive youth, I had dark brown, curly hair which fell to my shoulders. On Sundays and on other special occasions my mother would dress me in a dark green velvet suit with a large lace-trimmed collar. My good looks may have attracted the interest of a local theater, which engaged me to play the part of William Tell's son. I remember having to stand with an apple on my head, but I am not clear how the effect of shooting it off my head was handled. The same theater also asked me to play the part of a young child in their presentation of *Uncle Tom's Cabin*. I was carried onto the stage by a woman playing the role of my mother. She pressed me tightly and continually to her firm breasts, an experience I recall liking very much. In kindergarten, I was selected to play the lead role in our production of the opera *Puss and Boots*. Also during that year, I had the opportunity to dance a Russian national dance on stage with my classmates.

I developed a special fondness for opera as a child. Since my family was prominent in town, on occasion we would entertain famous opera singers in our home, and sometimes they would offer to sing for us. Both of my parents were big opera fans, and as such, they gradually amassed a large collection of opera recordings. In time I began to learn some of the recorded arias by heart. At around age six I started to "perform" these arias for my family and their guests. My "professionalism" extended even to being dressed in proper costume and making a grand entrance from my parents' bedroom into the "proscenium" of our broad living room doorway. Soon I acquired a reputation for singing famous arias quite accurately, terribly loudly, and with vividly dramatic expression in my voice. Sometimes I was even invited to sing at the homes of our friends. Often they would give me candy or fruit to show their appreciation. Because the most famous Russian opera singer of that time, and perhaps of all time, was Feodor Chaliapin, my nickname became "Chalapa."

When I was about seven years old my mother took me to the opera house for the first time. I had begged long and hard for this opportunity and had insisted that my heart would break if she did not take me. Once in my seat I was spellbound and watched the performance with rapt attention. Then, all of a sudden, I began to hear an aria I recognized— it was part of my repertoire! I immediately began to sing along, very loudly, with my usual passion and enthusiasm. All the people around us were shocked and turned to look at me with amazement. My unexpected participation disrupted the performance of the singer, who might well have been Caruso or Chaliapin himself, I do not remember. My mother was very embarrassed and had great difficulty quieting me down. My early passion for music never diminished. Throughout my life I, like my mother, have been enthusiastic about music and all forms of artistic expression.

This last episode shows that at times I was reluctant to comply with my mother's commands. There were other times, however, when I followed my mother's instructions too literally. When I was eight years old, after a short and insufficient preparation, my mother sent me to take the entrance examination for elementary school. In those days, the Russian education system began schooling much later than we do today, and thus the pace of the early grades was much quicker. Even at eight years of age, I was about a year too young for this examination. However, my mother believed I could handle it. She told me that the most important thing was to be well-behaved.

"You must be very attentive to the teacher and *watch* him constantly," she warned.

After the recitation portion of the examination, which I passed with flying colors with my rendition of the fable, *The Raven and the Fox*, we all settled down in our seats. The teacher gave each child an examination notebook with problems to solve. Since my mother had told me that the main objective was to be attentive and to *watch* the teacher, I sat in my chair and stared continuously into the teacher's eyes, watching his mouth when he spoke. It was impossible for me to do two things at once, so I could not even glance at the exam booklet, let alone do any of the problems. Naturally, I flunked the exam. It was my mother's fault, of course.

This "failure" had a very positive outcome for me. Instead of beginning primary school, I was placed in a private kindergarten for six to eight-year-olds. It turned out to be an exceptional educational experience which afforded me many opportunities to develop my mind and talents. The teachers, and especially the director, were outstanding educators. From nine in the morning until noon we studied reading, math, and handicrafts, including cross-stitching. At noon we ate our lunch, which we had brought from home. Afterwards we sang songs and then played outside. Four times a year the entire class performed publicly in the town theater. As mentioned earlier, we staged the opera *Puss and Boots*, in which I sang the lead role. Another performance we presented was our rendition of an opera called *Strawberries* by the composer Ivanov in which we took on the roles of miniature creatures of the forest, including bugs, mushrooms, butterflies, and the like. Most memorable for me was a dance we had to learn for yet another public performance. The class was divided into couples (boy/girl) and each couple was dressed in the traditional costume of a particular country. I and Gala (Galina, the most beautiful girl in the class, who held my heart in her hands) were chosen to represent Russia. I wore a blue shirt and black pants, with high red boots. Gala wore a long dress and a crown on her head. The teachers had made all of our costumes, which were exquisitely beautiful. At the appropriate time I was to speak this line aloud: "There are many beautiful countries in the world, but the most beautiful of all is Russia."

In the afternoons the entire class went outside. There the class was divided into two groups. A leader had to be selected for each group. Among the requirements for leadership were a fighting spirit and a demonstration of physical prowess. I liked to accept a challenge, even at this early age, as I had a strong desire to be a leader. My given name fit me very well: Boris means "fighter." I had been born under the sign of Taurus, the Bull. I felt like a fighter, with a keen, unswerving desire to reach the goals I set for myself. In order to be the leader in this game, I had to fight hand to hand with another boy for the position. Having accepted the challenge, I defeated my opponent in front of all the other boys and girls who were gathered around us in a circle. This success was an especially proud moment for me. My fighting spirit would save me many times over in the years to come.

My natural curiosity led me to wonder about the physical differences between girls and boys. When I was quite young I caught a little neighbor girl about my age and tried to undress her. She did not know, of course, that my interest in her was only scientific. The girl began to scream. I got scared and let her go. About a year later I tried to kiss a girl of my age on the staircase leading to our front door. I wondered what effect the kiss would have on her. I soon found out. She too started screaming, and I let her go as well.

These scientific experiments aside, a vision of my future wife started forming in my mind early on. The woman I would someday meet and marry was beautiful, intelligent, graceful, gentle, and loving. I dreamed of this girl, the girl of my imagination, and became thoroughly devoted to her. Every girl I met I would compare to my ideal "dream girl." Few real, live girls could compare favorably, so I rarely showed much interest in any living, breathing females. There would be some notable exceptions, to be sure, but my early established attitudes toward women and romance would come to shape a large measure of my destiny.

The attitude that prevailed in my family, and in all of Krasnoyarsk society as far as I could tell, was that the love between a husband and wife was deep, invincible, and permanent. This is certainly what I saw between my mother and father, and between my siblings and their spouses. Adultery was considered the lowest, most shameful betrayal of that bond. To me such behavior was absolutely unthinkable. It gave me strength to grow up in a culture with such romantic ideals. It was that sort of marriage I wanted for myself, a marriage to one special girl I someday would find, and with whom I would have a life-long romance.

Strongly influenced by my successful and ambitious family, I had a deep desire to grow and develop, both physically and mentally. I wanted to make my family proud of me, to lead an interesting life, and to help people in need. I knew that to realize my goals I had to be courageous, cultivate my physical strength, and nurture my innate fighting spirit. Achieving success is a challenge for anyone. Fortunately, the conditions under which I lived were conducive to the development of those qualities I felt were necessary.

I saw the great Yenisei River as a source of inspiration, and as a mighty giant to conquer. Its terrific power could be heard in the springtime when the river would let out a tremendous noise, the thunderous crashing of breaking ice. These roars could be heard from miles away and continued for days on end. Huge chunks of ice were carried downstream.[5] When flowing, the mile-wide river looked deceptively smooth. It was very deep and traveled at a speed of ten miles an hour, or more. More water flows through the Yenisei (20,000 tons, or five million gallons per second) than all European rivers combined.

> *... we all drove up the left bank of the river to an old monastery about six versts [four miles] from the city, where*

---

[5] Some of them would be captured by people who would cart them home in their wagons to use in their ice cellars. Used like refrigerators, these cellars could hold enough ice to last the entire summer.

the people of Krasnoyarsk are accustomed to go in the summer for picnics. The road, which was a noteworthy triumph of monastic engineering, had been cut into the steep cliffs that border the Yenisei, or had been carried on the trestle-work along the faces of these cliffs high above the water, and at every salient angle it commanded a beautiful view of the majestic river, which, at this point, attains a width of more than a mile and glides swiftly past, between blue picturesque mountains, on its way from the wild vastnesses of Mongolia to the barren coast of the Arctic Ocean. [6]

Every summer I would spend three months at our family's dacha, not far from the monastery mentioned above. Not fifty yards from our door flowed the mighty Yenisei River. I spent most of my time lying on its shore, admiring the natural beauty all around and listening to the sound of huge masses of water rushing past me. The power and vigor of this river inspired me. Living next to it for so many weeks at a time, I soon came to feel its force flowing through my body as well, making me equally strong, powerful, and energetic. Contemplating the dream-like surrounding mountains made me a dreamer too, though a realistically-minded one. I grew to love this place and the river, which invigorated and challenged me at the same time. I wanted to accept its challenge and conquer it. If I could swim across the Yenisei, then I would be a true conqueror, like a fearless horseman taming a wild stallion.

The current was strong enough to throw a grown man down if he waded in up to his knees. I knew I had to devise a strategy in order to succeed against this formidable foe. Around age ten I began to train. Five to seven times each day I would swim for twenty or thirty minutes, a total of more than two hours a day. At first I would walk upstream for a mile or so and swim downstream with the current along the shore, ending up at my starting point.[7] Next I began to swim further away from shore and

---

[6] Kennan, *Siberia and the Exile System*, vol. 1, pp. 360-361.

[7] Because this was a remote area, swimming, especially for young children, was *au naturel*, so these walks and swims of mine were all in the nude. On occasions when young boys and girls went swimming together, the girls were given about a fifty-yard head start, and the boys (on the honor system) maintained that polite separation.

then head back to shore as I approached my point of origin. Gradually, my treks upstream grew longer, as I was able to swim further out into the river. Fortunately, there was an island in the middle of the river. If I got tired I could rest there if necessary.

One day, when I was about twelve years old, my mother came to the shore of the river looking for me. Until that time my mother had no idea I had been swimming so far out. She asked where I was, and someone told her that the little black dot in the water several hundred yards away was my head. Imagining that I was in danger of drowning, she screamed a long, loud descending glissando and dropped to the ground in a dead faint. Later on, fully recovered and completely outraged, she told me in a very serious and determined voice that would brook no objection that I was never again to swim so far out into the river. But it was not possible for her to restrain me. In general, I was an obedient boy, but this command went against my very soul, and I could not comply. Furthermore, I was fastidious about safety and never swam when conditions were hazardous, or when I was too tired. I was convinced that no disaster could befall me in the water.

In the summer of 1919, when I was fourteen years old, after training for several years, I finally swam across the entire Yenisei River. As usual, I swam alone. Other fourteen-year-old boys could have been trained to do the same thing, but I had had no coach and was entirely self-taught. In the course of my training, despite my cautious nature, I nearly drowned three times. Once I got a cramp in my leg and had to rest in the water before continuing. The other two times I became entangled in the ropes of ships. But I learned from my mistakes. I developed a distinct swimming style, swimming on my side most of the time, taking long strokes with my head under the water, taking and holding deep breaths and building endurance. This achievement gave me tremendous self-confidence. I learned that success was a matter of determination, will-power, careful planning, developing and using the proper methods and techniques, and above all possessing sufficient self-control. I knew I must be brave, but careful at the same time to be sure of success. I learned this bit of wisdom at an early age: Caution is not cowardice, and carelessness is not courage.

My victory over the Yenisei was a significant achievement, but there was another success in my youth that was of equal importance. When I was eight years old my mother sent me to a local piano teacher for lessons, despite my lack of interest in the instrument. My next oldest brother, Jacob, had also taken lessons and was an excellent pianist. After two weeks the teacher gave me a sealed envelope to bring home to my mother. His letter stated that it was no use for me to continue to study piano. I was unteachable. As a result, I did not return for any more lessons, which was fine with me. I was happy, my mother was happy, and my teacher was happy.

Four years later, at the age of twelve, purely by coincidence, I happened to hear a concert at the theater. The final piece was Mendelssohn's *Piano Concerto in G Minor* arranged for two pianos. Two high school boys, who were classmates of my brother Jacob, were performing. For some reason, at this particular moment, I was so impressed and excited by the performance that I ran home and told my mother that I wanted to study piano. Furthermore, I wanted to study with the teacher of the two students I had heard playing that day.

My mother said, "It's no use. Your piano teacher said you were hopeless."

But I kept after her, insisting that now I really wanted to study. I would let her have no peace until she finally gave in and contacted the teacher, a young man in his early twenties who had been the star pupil of a famous teacher at the St. Petersburg Conservatory. We had serious difficulties persuading him to accept me because he claimed to have no free time. But due to my persistence and insistence, he finally agreed to take me on. Three years later, at the age of fifteen, having practiced only twenty-seven months (in the summers at the dacha there was no piano), I played the same Mendelssohn concerto in the same theater. By then I was performing in student concerts in the city every month. I was usually selected to play last, a special honor. By the end of my four years of study at the conservatory I was judged to be the second best piano student in the school. Only three members of the faculty played better than I. The last piece I played in recital was *Etude de Concert No. 3* by Franz Liszt. The speed with which I had advanced was so remarkable that I became famous in our town. People referred to me as a new star rising on the horizon. Extremely self-confident, I considered my rapid progress merely evidence of my natural ability and innate drive. My practicing had been very methodical and consistent from the start. I practiced two and half hours a day each and every day. I also had the will, the desire, and the utmost faith in myself, qualities which I knew were necessary to succeed.

Likewise, I excelled academically, and held second place at school in all subjects. Although the youngest, I was physically the strongest in my class. I tried to be the best in everything I attempted. I idolized certain historical figures; among my favorites were Julius Caesar and Napoleon. In my room hung a large portrait of Napoleon, along with a large map of the world. I hoped to travel someday and wanted to learn all I could about the world to prepare myself. I was also a great admirer of Leonardo da Vinci because of his many wide-ranging accomplishments in art and science, and as an inventor.

My favorite composer was Beethoven. I felt most connected to his music because of the thrilling sense of power it often evokes. Being a Siberian, I was an advocate of freedom and was intolerant of injustice, oppression, and despotism. I could hear my own powerful feelings expressed in Beethoven's music. Even at that time I had established firm ideals concerning justice, honesty, peace, courage, kindness, beauty, and nobleness.

When I was fifteen, I fell deeply in love with a girl of my age. She was lovely, like a little princess. By this time, I had become a "famous" pianist in our town, and often after concerts I was surrounded by admiring girls. At times they asked me to play pieces just for them. Although I liked some of them quite a lot, and appreciated their attentions, I was too shy to pursue any friendships beyond a platonic level. I was keenly aware of my emerging sexual drive, but being reared in a family and community with such strict moral rules, I remained very conservative and disciplined. My idealism and sense of honesty also held me in check, and prevented me from having any early sexual adventures. I had respect for these girls and did not want to take advantage of them. But because of my timidity, the girl with whom I had been so in love eventually became impatient and grew tired of waiting for me to make a move. In the end she broke off our friendship. I was heartbroken for several months.

My discomfort with organized religion started early in my youth when I was taken to church on Sundays by my nannies, who were, variously, Orthodox, Catholic, or Protestant. In attending all these churches, I could not understand why so many different creeds were necessary, and why those who called themselves Christians could not live in peace, and worship together under the same roof. As I grew older, I noticed what a strong influence the Russian clergy had over people. As a result of their preaching, nearly everyone I knew, regardless of social station, had personally "seen" a witch or a devil. In Krasnoyarsk there were many empty houses where no one would consent to live because ghosts had been sighted inside at night. In such a superstitious climate, it is no wonder that the mystic monk Rasputin had such success in the high ranks of society and with the family of the Czar.

In my own home, in the kitchen after dinner, I would listen to our five servants tell the most fascinating stories. Every one of them had seen a witch or a devil at one time or another. They told me that one could see devils (of which there were several different varieties) in certain special places at midnight during the full moon. After listening to these stories it was a most dangerous undertaking for me to go to my bedroom, undress quickly, and slip into the safety of my bed. Even then, I could hear a devil breathing under my bed, and so I would quickly throw the covers over my head. Underneath them I felt somewhat more protected, though still frightened. As a result of these experiences, I actually found myself believing in the Devil, whom I had "experienced," but not in God. I grew to resent the clergy, because rather than appealing to the good side of human nature, priests would instead attempt to scare people into submission. Others, more militant than I, also came to resent the clergy and their hypocrisy. Instead of protesting openly against the injustices inflicted on the poor during the reign of the Czars, the priests would tell the populace that their misfortunes were "the will of God" and that they must obey "Father Czar." During the communist revolution, many priests were killed despite the fact that most of them had come from the lower classes. On the other hand, doctors, who were mostly from the upper classes, were typically spared because of their unselfish service to humanity.

Many Siberians, because of their independent spirit—for which they had been banished to Siberia in the first place—were freethinkers. So, too, were all the members of my family, including me. Rather than call myself an agnostic, I have always preferred to say that I am a "deeply religious non-believer." Although I have never held with any organized sect or established canon, I have always been idealistic and spiritual. I believe that

God, in some form, created the universe, but that people have created the many "one" Gods they worship from their own imaginations. Since people throughout the world are different, then the God in people's minds must be different too.

Above all, it was my two physician brothers, Dmitri and Joseph, who influenced me the most in my youth in matters of religion and everything else. Russian physicians were greatly esteemed at this time for their high ideals, and for their devoted sense of responsibility to mankind. They generally came from wealthy families, because only the wealthy could afford the schooling. Thus they had chosen their extremely challenging profession not to make money, which they already possessed, but to help people. Often doctors would give their poor patients money so that they could purchase medicine and food. It did not matter how poor, dirty, or uncivilized the patient was; because he was a human being, he obtained the attention he required from these physicians. The selfless attitude of my brothers made a lasting impression on me. Whenever one of them would receive an emergency call, even in the middle of the night, he would scramble quickly into action and run, not walk, out the door to reach his patient, as if that patient were his own son.

Because of their devotion to humanity, Russian physicians were highly admired and respected among the populace. Therefore, doctors were not generally persecuted during the reign of terror following the communist takeover, in spite of their aristocratic roots. Sometimes even when entire families were executed, the physician in the family was spared. After the revolution, everyone was addressed as "Tovarisch" (Comrade), but a physician was addressed, as a special honor, as "Tovarisch Doctor," or even as "Your Excellency" or "Your Honor."

Most Russian physicians were atheists, largely in reaction to the anti-medical theology of the Russian clergy. If a priest were attending a gravely ill patient, he would encourage him to confess his sins, and then to give up—to accept death in a state of grace and thus gain admission to heaven. My brothers told me that they always tried to reach their patients as rapidly as possible, not so much to arrive before the illness had advanced, but to arrive before the priest, to be able to treat the patient before the priest could persuade him to die. Priests regularly got angry, even furious, at my brothers for saving patients' lives after the last rites had been administered.

Thus the typical Russian physician was not religious, but was nevertheless an extremely ethical, moral person, with a strong sense of duty to humanity. Influenced by Joseph and Dmitri, I developed a deep respect and reverence for life itself. Their ideals of justice, peace, honesty, and compassion for humanity became my lifelong ideals as well. Their influence made me feel that it was only right for people to help other people in need. It was expected; it was a duty. I felt, too, that if ever I was in need, others would certainly come to my aid as well.

Although I would never abandon these ideals, I was soon to learn of a very different kind of reality. All too quickly, my magical youth would come to an abrupt end.

BORIS AT AGE FOUR

Железноводск 19⁵⁄₁₂ 24.

MARIA AND JULIUS KOCHANOWSKY, BORIS' PARENTS.
THE COUPLE IS SEEN HERE ON VACATION IN THE CAUCASUS.

DIMITRI (*MITYA*)

MATTHEW (*MOTYA*)

BERTA (*BETYA*)

VICTOR (*VITYA*)

JOSEPH (*OSYA*)

JACOB (*JASHA*)

FORMER KOCHANOWSKY HOME AND PRINT SHOP IN KRASNOYARSK (MODERN DAY)

KRASNOYARSK, CITY MARKET WITH THE KAPHEDRALNY CATHEDRAL (1861-1937) IN THE BACKGROUND

KRASNOYARSK, BLAGOVESHENSKAY STREET, CA. 1900

Красноярскъ. № 2.
Общій видъ.

PANORAMA OF **Krasnoyarsk** WITH VIEW OF THE **Yenisei River**, CA. 1900

Chapter 2

OF DREAMS AND NIGHTMARES

Her skin was white as leprosy,
The nightmare Life-in-Death was she,
Who thicks man's blood with cold.

—Samuel Taylor Coleridge, *The Ancient Mariner*

In Krasnoyarsk we were quite removed from the mechanics of Russian politics. Situated in the middle of Siberia, our community was like a distant planet which paid homage from afar to our sun, the Czar and his regime. In 1913 the whole town celebrated the 300-year jubilee of the Romanov dynasty with great fanfare. Flags and banners flew everywhere. Patriotic pictures of Czar Nicholas II were on display in many shop windows. I shall never forget the magnificence of this celebration.

Even World War I (1914-1917) scarcely touched our day-to-day existence. Russia was allied with Britain and France against Germany and Austria-Hungary. However, all of the fighting took place in Europe and West Russia. The only signs of the war in our city were the German and Austrian prisoners who were frequently herded through the streets. They were held in great numbers in prison camps not far from town. Many of them died during the winters because they did not have sufficient protection from the Siberian cold.

If the First World War did not affect my remote Siberian life, the Russian Revolution of 1917 eventually did. On March 15, 1917, Czar

Nicholas II was forced to abdicate. The new more liberal, but still non-communist government, first under Prince Lvov and then under Kerensky, could maintain control only for a short period of time. Soon it, too, was overthrown by the more radical Bolshevik or "majority" faction led by Lenin and Trotsky. In response, an anti-Bolshevik "White" army was formed, beginning a horrible civil war that would last for three years. It has been estimated that during the first year of the Russian civil war about five million men were killed. This figure includes combat casualties and executions. Thousands were massacred. The purges instigated by the Red Army alone resulted in the executions of 25 bishops, 1,200 priests, 4,000 monks, 40,000 army officers, 45,000 police officers, 320,000 intellectuals (students, authors, etc.), and 400,000 peasants.[8] On July 16, 1918, the whole imperial family was executed at Ekaterinburg.

When Lenin and Trotsky took power, local Bolshevik outposts were set up all over Russia, including in Krasnoyarsk. Resistance was strongest in the provinces furthest from St. Petersburg. Each division of the White Army fought in a separate region and was commanded by a different general. General Denikin, and later General Wrangel, commanded the forces in the Ukraine. General Judenitsch fought in West Russia and Admiral Kolchak in Siberia. Admiral Kolchak, who became the temporary head of the Siberian government, had achieved great fame as an arctic explorer and was highly respected by Russians and foreigners alike.

Around this time, my nineteen-year-old brother Jacob, then a student of natural sciences at the University of Tomsk, volunteered, along with most of his classmates, to fight in the White Army against the Bolsheviks. The commander of the White garrison at Krasnoyarsk, a close friend of our family, invited Jacob to take a desk job in Krasnoyarsk instead. However, my idealistically minded brother turned down the offer. Jacob was eventually sent to the western front along the Volga River.

The United States, England, France, Italy, and several other countries assisted the White Army by supplying weapons and stationing troops in various strategic locations throughout Russia. Krasnoyarsk was one of these important military sites where many foreign soldiers and large quantities of munitions were housed. However, these troops took no active part in the

---

[8] Edwin Erich Dwinger, *Zwischen Weiss und Rot*, Freiburg I. Br. [Germany]: Dikreiter Verlagsgesellschaft m.b.H., 1950, p. 261.

fighting. The only foreign troops to get involved were the Czechs. These Czechs were not sent from Czechoslovakia, but were former prisoners of war who had been released from Siberian camps and had regrouped under the command of General Gajda. The main objective of the Czech Legion was to open a path homeward by securing the Trans-Siberian railway line. By May of 1918 the Czech troops under General Gajda had succeeded in defeating the Bolshevik forces in Siberia at many points along the railway, including at Krasnoyarsk. As a result, with the city captured by the Whites, the Bolshevik leaders in Krasnoyarsk tried to flee. They attempted to reach a ship on the Yenisei and escape to the Arctic Ocean. However, the White Army volunteer corps mobilized quickly to stop them.

By coincidence, my mother, who had traveled that day from our dacha to Krasnoyarsk to shop, suddenly found herself caught between the communists, who were trying to reach the river, and the White Army volunteers, who were chasing them. My mother, tossed in the frenzy from one street to another, finally succeeded in entering the house of a friend on the shore of the Yenisei. From the protection of this house she was able to witness the skirmish between the Reds and the Whites.

The Bolshevik leaders were caught and brought back to town. The people, having heard of their capture, flooded the streets, waiting eagerly to catch a glimpse of the Bolsheviks being marched off to prison. The authorities, however, decided not to transport them through the city during the day, fearing that the people might try to lynch them. At night, when the streets were empty, an elite Cossack guard escorted them to the prison. However, even at night they met resistance, and not all of the prisoners made it to the prison alive.

After the liberation of Siberia from the communists, fighting with the partisans began in earnest on the western front and in other areas. I remember the funeral of thirty-four White Army officers massacred by Red partisans near our town. They were carried in open coffins, followed by a military guard, the townspeople, and assembled pupils from the city's schools. The faces of the dead could readily be seen, horribly disfigured. Noses and ears had been amputated, leaving gaping holes. Such atrocities were commonly committed by both the Red and White armies during the revolution.

After a few months, it became clear to the Czech troops that their goal of reaching Czechoslovakia by a western route was more difficult than they had at first imagined. It now seemed that Red control of European Russia was not soon to be broken. As more areas fell to the communists, the Czech fighters became increasingly impatient with the situation. One day, unexpectedly, they left the front and started heading east, back through Siberia to the Pacific. Their new plan was to get home by ship from the Far East.[9] The Czech troops had often disobeyed the orders of Admiral Kolchak before, but their sudden unauthorized retreat truly outraged the White Russians who were now at a clear disadvantage. Their weakened state allowed the Red Army to break through. This incident initiated the White Army's long retreat from the banks of the Volga eastward through Siberia, one of the costliest retreats in military history.

The first 2,000 miles of the retreat, from the Volga to Krasnoyarsk, were disastrous. Along with Genghis Khan's barbaric rampage through central Asia, this retreat might be considered among the worst disasters in the history of mankind. Much of the retreat took place during the treacherous Siberian winter, when temperatures commonly fall to 70 degrees below zero Fahrenheit. Just pausing to rest in the snow too long could mean death. In just a few months over a million soldiers were killed or frozen. Among the dead were 200,000 men killed in the streets of Novonikolayevsk (now Novosibirsk), a city of 70,000 residents at the time. Only 10,000 troops survived this battle. Over 70,000 men were killed in Atchinsk. In one steppe encampment, due to a sudden overnight drop in temperature, 40,000 horses lay dead on the ground the following morning.[10] Napoleon's retreat from Moscow in 1812 may be more famous, but it was not nearly as long, in time or distance, nor one quarter as deadly, with the loss of fewer than 200,000 men.

On November 2, 1919, during the early stages of the White Army's retreat, my brother Jacob met my oldest surviving brother Matthew in Omsk, the seat of the Kolchak government. Matthew asked the young soldier to return home to Krasnoyarsk with him on a train which was evacuating the treasury department of the Siberian government. My father was a good friend of Mr. Skorochodov, the director of the treasury

---

[9] St. George, p. 37.

[10] Dwinger, pp. 295, 306, 416.

department, so it would have been easy to get a seat for Jacob on the train. Not wanting to desert the army, Jacob refused to join Matthew.

Siberia had only one highway. It ran parallel to the railway line and connected the west with the east. Both armies had to follow this route or risk getting lost in the snow. The route passed directly through Krasnoyarsk. As the fleeing White Army and the pursuing Red Army were nearing us, a revolt broke out in the Krasnoyarsk garrison. Many White officers were killed trying unsuccessfully to suppress it. It was December 18, 1919. Overnight the garrison of the White Army suddenly became a Red Army stronghold. A few days later, several thousand Bolshevik partisans, mostly former convicts who had escaped from prison camps, came from their hiding places in the taiga (Siberian virgin evergreen forest) and entered Krasnoyarsk to join the Reds. The townspeople, and even the members of the Red Army themselves, were frightened by the appearance of these partisans from the forest, who had, as fugitives, reverted to something like wild men. Many of the taiga partisans, wearing heavy furs, were so huge that only the head and the tail of the small Siberian horses they were riding could be seen.

The retreating White Army was pushing before it an enormous stream of refugees trying to escape the Reds.[11] Many of them were on foot; others traveled by horse-drawn sledge. Over 100,000 exhausted refugees poured into Krasnoyarsk a day or two ahead of the armies. The broad, straight streets of the town filled up with sledges and with dying, or already dead horses. These unfortunate animals became the food supply of the refugees. Many of the refugees found shelter in the warm houses of the residents. Most of them were in horrible condition and were in need of medical attention. Many had frozen fingers, ears, and noses, as brittle as glass, which they eventually lost. I felt tremendous pity for these suffering people, especially the children. Pregnant women on this journey had to give birth in empty freight cars or on sleds. Many of the newborns, and doubtless a fair number of the mothers, had already died in the cold.

The Reds in the garrison made use of the large stores of foreign weapons and ammunition that had been kept there. A large machine gun or other heavy piece of artillery was placed at every street corner in town. A

---

[11] The total number of refugees may have numbered more than 750,000 according to Dwinger, p. 416.

battle was expected imminently in the city. It would prove to be the White Army's last major stand against the Reds.

My home was located right in the center of town. When the battle finally broke out on the outskirts of town, out of curiosity, and without telling anyone, I set out alone toward the battle line to watch the fighting. As I walked, I saw wounded soldiers being carried back toward the hospital. Before I had gotten very far, I was hailed by Red soldiers standing ready by their guns. They shouted at me, "Idi domoi!" (Go home!) I was fourteen years old.

During the two-day battle of Krasnoyarsk, 80,000 men were killed, frozen, wounded, or taken prisoner.[12] The Fourth Army of General Kolchak and the Third Army of General Kappel fought the insurgent garrison at Krasnoyarsk on the outlying hills less than two miles from my home. After my foolhardy attempt to witness the battle from the ground, I returned home and was able to see some of it from the upper floor windows of our house. The snow made it easier to make out what was going on. It was also possible to hear the sound of artillery, cannon, and machine gun fire from there.

My brother Jacob served in the Third Army under General Kappel and had retreated with the army 2,000 miles, all the way from the Volga to the hills outside of Krasnoyarsk. Jacob was killed on those hills, less than two miles from his home. He may even have been able to see his home from his position there. It was Christmas Day (by the Russian Orthodox calendar), January 6, 1920.

The White Army had lost the battle of Krasnoyarsk. This meant the end of any serious resistance against the communists throughout Russia, a complete victory for the Reds. Jacob and thousands of his fellow soldiers had met their end in this battle. No better fate awaited the Supreme Ruler, Admiral Kolchak, for whom I had great admiration. An anti-Kolchak revolt had taken place in Irkutsk on December 24. On January 4, Kolchak was forced to abdicate as Supreme Ruler of Siberia. After the battle of Krasnoyarsk, Kolchak had tried to escape to the Far East. But he was captured and arrested en route on January 15. About three weeks later,

---

[12] Dwinger, p. 337.

on February 7, the Reds executed him in Irkutsk. Dwinger describes his execution:

> *When Kolchak was put against the wall to be shot, as he finished smoking a last cigarette, he gave his cigarette case to the Red soldier who had escorted him to the wall. His face looked as if it were cut out of stone and was completely calm. The Red soldiers aimed their rifles at him. The officer gave the order to fire. But not one [man] fired. The calmness in the face and the noble attitude of the Supreme Regent overpowered and stunned the soldiers. They were not able to pull the trigger. Suddenly Kolchak threw away his cigarette, raised his right hand, and gave the command "Fire." This was his last word.*[13]

Quite soon after their victory, the Reds decided to pull down the crosses of the Orthodox cathedral. Thousands of women from the town and from the surrounding area, having somehow gotten wind of their intention, encircled the church. They created a massive human barrier which the Reds, even on horseback, could not breach. Whenever the soldiers tried to ride into the crowd they would be pulled down off their horses by the screaming, infuriated women. Perhaps if they had fired shots into the crowd the soldiers might have had more success. However, they did not fire. They merely retreated for the moment and waited until the women went home. Then the soldiers returned and took down the crosses.

Most of the hundred thousand refugees who had flooded the town before the Reds gained control of the city were now considered enemies of the state. Many of them were able to hide, at least for a time, in the homes of the townspeople. Over the next few years thousands of them, as well as some of the residents, were executed. A few people, not many, were able to escape to the east.

There were several places of execution in the city that the Bolsheviks attempted to hide from the public. Yet it was not so difficult to guess where they were. One was inside the building used by the Cheka, the Bolshevik secret police, near the city park. Late in the evening, truck engines could

---

[13] Dwinger, p. 397.

be heard from inside its courtyard, revving their engines unusually high for no apparent reason. Everyone knew that the truck noise was masking the sound of gunshots within the building, and that executions were taking place.

In most revolutions, killing becomes a routine practice. The actions of men are motivated by a terrible and obsessive hate. When thousands of people are executed, mistakes are often made. A story circulated about a man who was released by the Cheka and who had returned a few days later to collect his identification papers. Apparently, he had originally been released by mistake, instead of someone else. No doubt that another person had been executed in his place. When the man returned to the Cheka building, he too must have been executed, for he was never seen again.

We had taken several refugees into our home. A few of them were Jacob's school friends who had served with him in the White Army. Some were sick with typhoid and my brother Joseph did his best to cure them. One refugee, who stayed with us for several months, happened to be an excellent violinist. He fell in love with the daughter of our neighbor, the pharmacist.[14] Another one of our refugees was a fellow I grew to admire very much. He was Boris Skorochodov, a tall, handsome naval officer, about twenty-four years of age. He was an excellent singer and spoke many different languages. His father, a good friend of our family, had been the director of the treasury in Omsk under the Kolchak government. Because we were housing so many refugees, space in our apartment became tight. We had to share beds. I shared mine with Boris Skorochodov and thus got to know him and learn a little about his past. As a teenager he had traveled all over the world with his father. His father considered these trips an important part of his son's education. But what shocked me was that in all of these foreign countries his father would routinely push Boris out onto the street and tell him to find his own way home. He was given no money or assistance of any kind, so that he had to make it back by hook or by crook. These experiences no doubt taught him how to be very resourceful.

---

[14] Sonya, the pharmacist's daughter, who studied with the same piano teacher as I, married the famous big game hunter, J.J. Fenykovi, who bagged the giant elephant now standing in the Smithsonian Museum of National History in Washington DC. They eventually moved to Madrid, where I was able to visit her occasionally in later years.

Boris was planning an escape to the east. However, a few days before he intended to leave, he was arrested on the street and executed. I would eventually have to deliver this sad news to his father.

At this time, our family was very close to the family of the sister of Dr. Ferdinand Ossendowski, the former vice-director of the treasury assisting Mr. Skorochodov. Mr. Ossendowski had come from Omsk to Krasnoyarsk to live with his sister under an assumed name, trying to hide from the Bolsheviks. One day his seven-year-old niece was playing in the kitchen. Talking to herself, she said: "How strange that my uncle was once called Ossendowski and now his name is Nikolajev."

When the servants in the kitchen heard this they informed the Cheka. Soon the house was surrounded. Ossendowski, however, was already gone. The neighbors had warned him in time and he was able to flee. An exceptionally dynamic individual, Ossendowski would later chronicle his escape and his subsequent adventures in Tibet and Manchuria in his book *Beasts, Men and Gods*, which was published in 1923. Although Ossendowski escaped, his relatives in Krasnoyarsk were not so fortunate. They were arrested and thrown into prison. Among them was a mother with twin babies, only six months old. Both babies died in the Cheka prison.

In addition to the executions, thousands of people around Krasnoyarsk died from a terrible typhoid epidemic. My brother Joseph had contracted the disease himself shortly before our town was occupied by the Bolsheviks. Our whole family had been given an opportunity to flee by train to Manchuria, where Victor was living. But because of Joseph's illness my mother refused to leave. She wanted to stay and care for him. Berta made the journey to Harbin alone at this time. The rest of us, my parents, Matthew, Joseph, and I, stayed behind. By the time Joseph's illness had subsided it was too late to escape. Although we very much wished to leave the country, it now seemed impossible to do so.

Although life had changed so much for us after the Reds took control, I continued to play piano concerts. I had a sobering experience in connection with one particular performance. I was leaving home to go to the concert hall early, although it was already dark. Joseph took me aside and explained that the streets in that area were no longer safe after dark. He instructed me to walk down the middle of the street and avoid the shadows and alleys on either side. Then he handed me a Browning handgun and told me to carry it and to use it if I was attacked. I walked to the concert hall, down the middle of the street as instructed, and played the concert with the pistol in my pocket. When I returned home, I gave the Browning back to my brother. It was the only time I ever carried a gun.

My father had been one of the wealthiest men in Siberia, and therefore under the new communist order, he was liable at any time to be labeled an enemy of the people. We lived in continuous terror. Each time the doorbell rang, everyone in the family would turn white in the face thinking that it was a Cheka officer coming to arrest us and put us in prison. Perhaps they would execute us all on the spot. When we went out on the street, we never knew if we would return home. When we went to sleep, we didn't know if we would find ourselves in our own beds the next morning.

In 1918 a British company had offered my father the equivalent of one million dollars for all of his businesses and associated property. But my father's businesses were thriving at the time and no one thought then that the communists would win the Civil War or remain in power for long. So my father had refused to sell. Once the communists were firmly established in Krasnoyarsk, my father received a short letter stating that all his property—his industrial plants, his shops, his bank accounts, his several houses, worth millions of dollars—were confiscated. The next morning, we were given twenty-four hours to vacate our luxurious home. In fact, we were not even given that much time. Just two or three hours later, immediately after lunch, Red soldiers came and forced us out. The authorities allowed us to take several beds, a few chairs, a table, and our clothing. Everything else, furniture and even house plants, which were of no use to the government, were simply thrown out of the windows onto the street, to be scavenged eventually for firewood. Our beautiful black grand piano was taken from us. The soldiers forced the lock with an ax and rolled it down the rough cobblestone street.

We were able to move into one of the small apartments in the house to the rear of our courtyard. A White Army general had been the last tenant there. He had lived in the apartment on the second floor, but had vacated the premises some time ago. We moved into the apartment on the third floor, directly above the one that had been his.

A few days later, a Cheka officer came with several soldiers armed with heavy Mausers. After a quick search through our apartment, they went up to the attic and found a number of rifles and several sacks of ammunition buried in the sand which served as insulation. The officer wanted to arrest my father, who was then sixty-seven years old, accusing him of hiding munitions in preparation for a counter-revolution. The whole family knew this was an absurd accusation. My father was a businessman, not a vigilante. We also knew there would be no fair trial. There was no doubt that this accusation would automatically lead to execution. My two brothers, Matthew and Joseph, together begged the Cheka officer to leave our father in peace and to arrest them instead. Since I loved my father and both of my brothers deeply, I feared greatly for their fate. The situation was heartbreaking, one which I shall never forget. Someone in my family, either my father or one of my brothers, someone I loved, was going to be executed.

What a source of strength it was to me to know that I belonged to a family where such love prevailed. To sacrifice one's life for someone else is an unmistakable sign of true love. As tragic as the situation was, I felt that it was only natural for my brothers to offer to die in my father's place. Their courage in standing up to the Cheka officer to save my father was of the highest possible order.

Another act of courage, from an unexpected source, would save the day. The Cheka officer complied with my brothers' request and arrested Matthew. Later that day our former coachman testified before the Cheka on behalf of my family. He told them that before we had moved into the apartment, he had seen several White Army officers, each carrying two rifles, enter the building. After staying overnight in the apartment of the White Army general, who was the father of one of the officers, they left, each carrying a single rifle. That explained where the rifles had come from and why they were in the attic of the building where we were living. Since the coachman was a commoner, his word was believed and my brother was released. Our former coachman had saved my brother's life. It had required a lot of courage and moral strength, even for a commoner, to face the dreaded Cheka, who were famous for only seeing one side of a story, and to explain to them that they had made a mistake. It was a great tribute to my brother that the coachman had admired him enough to take such a risk on his behalf.

Later we were able to find a small apartment elsewhere in the city. But life in our new accommodations was far from comfortable. All of our servants had left us by this time. My mother's health had deteriorated considerably, yet she insisted on doing the family shopping, cooking, and cleaning. The ice box was outside on the staircase where it was quite cold. Going up and down the stairs continually, she soon began to suffer terribly from swelling in her legs and feet due to her untreatable kidney ailment. I would frequently assist her and learned to cook under her tutelage.

Eventually, one of the rooms of our small apartment was assigned to a Red commissar and his wife. The commissar had formerly been a colonel in a special regiment to the Czar in St. Petersburg. His beautiful twenty-four-year-old wife was a writer. Very inquisitive, she was always trying to find new material for her articles. One evening as we were all coming home from one of my concerts, we met her in the stairway leading up to our apartment. Suddenly she took my head and pressed it lovingly to her breast. I felt flattered and overwhelmed by this unexpected show of affection. For a time, she continued to show signs of her willingness to become my lover. Although I was tempted, my strict moral upbringing won out and I gave her no encouragement. Finally, she gave up.

The communists reorganized the school system in Krasnoyarsk and introduced an accelerated program. At the time of the Red victory, I was halfway through my fifth year of high school (*gymnasium*). Under the old system there were nine grades. Now the number of grades was reduced to eight, and a twelve-month school year was introduced. During the next academic year (from the fall of 1920 to the fall of 1921) I was to complete three grades (6-8) in one year. Because of this intensified learning pace and the lack of certain textbooks, I felt that the education I was receiving was inadequate. I was able to pass all the tests that were administered, but just barely. Even today, I still notice major gaps in my early education. I tried to compensate for this lack of learning by reading books—any books I could get my hands on. Of lasting importance to me was a book on psychology that belonged to Joseph, with whom I was now sharing a bedroom. Because of my intense interest in the subject,

I became quite familiar with the contents of this book. There was a chapter on physiognomy, the science of reading character and temperament from the features of the face. According to this book, the human face accurately reflects will, intellect, and feeling. Of these three attributes a person may exhibit one, two, or even all three well-developed traits. The degree to which they are manifested is revealed in the countenance because certain muscles in the face become strongly developed by these inner forces. Excellent illustrations were included showing people with different types of facial features, accompanied by descriptions of their different personalities. This seems like a simplistic study nowadays, undoubtedly lacking in any significant scientific rigor. However, I took it to heart and put the information to good use later when the occasion arose.

In addition to turning to books to bolster my education, I also petitioned the school administration for permission to repeat a year of school because I felt I had not mastered the material well enough to satisfy my own standards. I had to make my case before a panel of school officials. By chance, afterwards I happened to pass by a room in the same building and overheard these same officials discussing my case. I paused at the open doorway to listen. Their consensus was that I was arrogant and presumptuous to place my own standards of learning above those of the Soviet school system. Shortly thereafter I received a letter stating that my request had been denied.

The communist school system devoted much of its energies to educating adult peasants. A strong effort was made to rid them of their religious beliefs and superstitions, indoctrinating them instead to favor the anti-religious beliefs of Marx and Lenin. I remember overhearing one peasant man commenting on a class he had attended on Darwin's theory of evolution. "It's crazy," he said. "It's like this: Here comes a frog: 'croak, croak, croak,' and then he turns into an elephant!" With educational challenges such as this among the adult population, it was no wonder that the quality of schooling for the youth declined under the communist regime.

I could not accept being denied a good education. I wanted to continue to enjoy the exhilaration of growing physically, mentally, and spiritually, and to create a happy life for myself and my family, as well as to be useful to mankind. I was motivated to seek out a better life than what was offered by the new order in Russia. Because I belonged to the now-hated and persecuted capitalistic class, I sensed I would have no opportunity to fulfill my goals under these conditions. I felt trapped. I wanted to be free to live without continuous discrimination, humiliation, and suppression. I wanted to get an excellent education, like my siblings had received. At this time, immediately after the revolution, only the sons of peasants and workers were permitted to go to college. That opportunity was denied me as the son of a capitalist.[15]

My family and my surroundings had imparted to me the strength, the courage, and the faith I needed. I felt I could move mountains. That was why I believed that I *could* and *must* leave the Russia I loved so much, and to go to a place where I could convert my dreams into reality. The only way to achieve this goal was to escape to the east.

---

[15] This policy was changed in 1927 with Lenin's Five-Year Plan.

KRASNOYARSK NEIGHBOR'S DAUGHTER, SONYA WITH HER
HUSBAND J. J. FENYKOVI (WEDDING PHOTO 1920)

BORIS SKOROCHODOV, WHO SHARED BORIS' BED
AFTER THE FALL OF THE WHITE ARMY

BORIS' PASSPORT PICTURE (1922)

Chapter 3

DREAMS OF HOPE

I know how men in exile feed on dreams of hope.

—Aeschylus, *Agamemnon*

O ne day in November 1921 my brother Joseph, by then conscripted
   as a Red Army physician, received an order to go to Kiakhta, a
town near the border of Mongolia. Not far from Kiakhta, the last military
operations against the remnants of Baron Ungern-Sternberg's White troops
were underway. Since all private property and all merchandise in stores
had been confiscated by the communists, nothing could be purchased
anywhere. Food, clothes, and daily necessities were distributed to the
population by means of issued ration stamps honored only at state stores.
Because Joseph was in the army, he was among those who received the
largest quantity of these rations. He was, therefore, our family's main
source of food. The problem of finding sufficient food at the time was so
great, that to avoid the very real possibility of starvation, my family decided
to accompany Joseph to Kiakhta.

My mother was now sixty-one years old and my father sixty-eight.
My mother's kidney ailment was worsening. I had taken over her duties as
chief cook and housekeeper, as my mother's legs would swell up painfully
after only a few minutes on her feet. She spent most of her time in bed.
Unfortunately, there was no adequate medicine or proper food for her in
Krasnoyarsk.

Each day one train would pass through town traveling in an eastbound direction, toward Manchuria, but the schedule was erratic and unpredictable. Passengers had to remain at the railway station all day and night to wait for the train. (Such a scene is well depicted in the 1965 film *Dr. Zhivago*.) My family tried to catch the train on two separate occasions, without success. Because it was winter, people crowded inside the station. Real cigarettes were no longer available, so smokers had resorted to using dried cabbage leaves cut into small pieces and rolled in strips of newspaper. These makeshift cigarettes created a disgusting odor and thick, dense smoke. Each time we arrived at the railway station and attempted to endure the wait, my mother would faint, overcome by the heavy, acrid smoke that permeated the entire station.

On our third attempt, however, we were lucky enough to get there just as the train was arriving. Consisting entirely of freight cars, the train was already over-filled with passengers. When it stopped, the people waiting to board the train violently attacked the door of each car. A veritable battle ensued among the people trying to get out of the car, the people trying to board it, and the people who wished to remain in the car but did not want additional passengers exacerbating the already unbearably overcrowded conditions. The law of the jungle prevailed and only those with the strongest muscles were able to get on the train. We quickly realized that it would be impossible for us to get my invalid mother on board under these conditions.

Fortune smiled on us a few days later when Joseph learned of a train coming through Krasnoyarsk sponsored by the Swiss Red Cross. It was evacuating children from the Volga region where famine was claiming millions of lives. The director of the Red Cross evacuation was pleased to have an additional doctor for the children, so it was a simple matter for my brother to obtain permission to travel on this train, and to take us along. There would have been no other way for my mother to leave the city. It is doubtful that any of us, except Joseph, who was under orders, would have left Krasnoyarsk without her. For this reason, as well as others which shall be detailed later, I owe the Swiss a large debt of gratitude.

Joseph, my parents, and I boarded the Red Cross train on December 25, 1921, having secured permission to travel in a fourth-class coach reserved for the soldiers guarding the train. Matthew stayed behind in

Krasnoyarsk with his wife and son. As the train finally lurched forward and pulled away from the railway station, I sensed something breaking within my heart. Watching Krasnoyarsk gradually disappear into the distance, I felt as if my heart were being torn out of my chest. I was sixteen years old when I bade this sad farewell to my birthplace. I had no idea whether I would ever return.

The train was so long that when it traveled uphill it was necessary to divide it into two sections. The locomotive would take the first half of the train to the next station, leaving the rear cars standing in place for many hours. Our seats were toward the back of the train. One night when we were left behind waiting for the locomotive, I looked out into the darkness and saw the eyes of a thousand Siberian wolves staring back at me.

The 850-mile trip from Krasnoyarsk to the next major city to the east, Irkutsk, normally lasted thirty-six hours. It took us eight days. Joseph was expected in Irkutsk before our scheduled arrival, so after a few days he arranged to board a regular, faster train. When we arrived at the railway station in Irkutsk, my parents asked me to go into the city and ask our friends, Mr. and Mrs. Itsikson, former residents of Krasnoyarsk, if we might stay with them for a few days.

Before the revolution, the Itsiksons had owned a jewelry shop in Krasnoyarsk and were quite wealthy. Unbeknownst to all, their eldest child, an eighteen-year-old daughter, had become a communist. No one knew of her affiliation with the communist party until the arrival of the Red Army. After the revolution she was appointed to a high position within the communist government. Hers was not an isolated case. There were several other secret communist supporters in Krasnoyarsk, some of whom held high positions in society, such as the president of a local bank and the president of a prominent gold mining company.

Between the railway station and the city of Irkutsk flows the remarkably beautiful Angara River. It originates from Lake Baikal, which is 395 miles wide, over a mile deep and covers an area of 11,780 square miles. Baikal is the largest lake in Europe and Asia, and the deepest in the world. Containing about eighteen percent of the fresh water (15,500 cubic miles) on the earth's surface, Lake Baikal has as much water as all five of the American Great Lakes combined. Due to its low salt and mineral content, the water is extremely clear. Objects far below the surface of the water could, at least at that time, easily be seen. Lake Baikal is surrounded by mountains many thousands of feet high. In a popular Russian poem, the Angara River, which almost completely surrounds the city, is compared with a beautiful blue-eyed blonde who embraces Irkutsk in her arms.

As I left the railway station and walked across the bridge over the frozen Angara toward Irkutsk, I saw an open car with two men approaching from the opposite direction. The men were dressed in the Cherkess uniform[16] with short fur hats topped with red cloth on which was sewn a shining cross of silver. The uniforms looked so elegant and unusual that without thinking I stopped and stared at the men until their car disappeared behind me. I did not know then that these men—one of them, Mr. Bergman, the head of the Irkutsk Cheka, and the other, his assistant—were on their way to the railway station to arrest my parents. Believing my parents were trying to escape Russia, they assumed that they were trying to smuggle jewels and gold out of the country.

Once at the railway station, the Cheka personnel entered my parents' coach and made a thorough search of my father and my ailing mother, their luggage, the coach itself, and of all the other people traveling in it. They had come expecting a fine catch, but since they could find nothing of value, and seeing how elderly and broken my parents were, and how sick my mother was, they left my parents in peace.

At first we all stayed with Mr. and Mrs. Itsikson in their home. Later we were able to find a room in a single-story wooden house located on the corner of an intersection. The walls of this house were riddled with bullet holes, remnants of the recent battles between the White and Red Armies. To spare my mother, I continued to handle all the cooking and cleaning chores. Our life in Irkutsk was every bit as dismal as it had been in Krasnoyarsk. It seemed we had reaped very little reward for our long, arduous journey.

Within weeks Joseph received a new assignment far to the north, in an area much less hospitable than Kiakhta would have been. My parents decided that they could not follow him there and that they would try to

---

[16] The Cherkess, also known as the *Circassians* or the *Adyghe* people, were an ethnic group that lived in the north Caucasus. The traditional garment for men was the *cherkesska*, a knee-length caftan with an opening down the front and no collar. It was usually gathered at the waist and wide at the bottom.

return to Krasnoyarsk, where my elder brother Matthew remained with his wife and son. I, on the other hand, did not want to return. I had set my mind and heart on continuing eastward to China. When I told them of my plans, my parents just stared at me in disbelief. With conditions as they were, I might as well have said I was going to the moon. To reach China I would have to travel more than 2,000 miles, over rough terrain, in bitterly cold weather, through a wilderness populated mostly by bears and wolves. Although the territory was sparsely populated, the border was heavily guarded. Such an escape had been possible between 1917 and 1919, during the Civil War. Then the situation was much more chaotic and the border was not yet secure. Over a million White Russians had been able to escape during those early years. Now everything was different. The new regime had become organized, as well as ruthless and merciless. Exit from Russia was strictly regulated.

Joseph also felt my plan was lunacy. He called me a dreamer. Such a trip was madness and absolutely impossible, he claimed. I replied with a Russian saying "Whoever has the will, can do it," the Russian equivalent of "Where there's a will, there's a way."

Joseph had been a surgeon in the Russian army (Czarist, White, and Red) for eight years, since the beginning of World War I. He certainly possessed steely nerves and tremendous courage, yet I had shocked him. What I had in mind must truly have seemed like madness, especially considering my youth. However, as he was explaining the folly of my plan, my brother stopped suddenly and looked at me with an expression I shall never forget. It radiated astonishment, admiration, and pride in a younger brother's courage, enterprising spirit, and indomitable will. Knowing me well, and my former accomplishments, it suddenly occurred to him that maybe I could actually succeed with this incredible scheme. I knew I was strong and powerful as a bear, and I was convinced that I could do anything I set out to do. It was an added boost to my confidence and pride that my honored brother gave me his blessing. Joseph soon had to depart for the north. I bid him farewell with great sadness, quite certain that I would never see him again. It was late January, 1922.

My feeling of strength and courage was, of course, largely imagination. However, such an imagination can be useful, especially in dangerous situations. I suspect that it was because of my imaginative powers that I was able to survive the dangers I had to face. I was fit and well prepared physically and spiritually for the enterprise I had in mind. I was determined to go to China. No one could sway my resolve. My plan was to go first to Harbin in Manchuria, where my brother Victor and my sister Berta were now living. I felt that I could succeed if I applied the same kind of strategies I had used to cross the Yenisei, or to become a renowned pianist in my town. Although I had great faith in myself, I did not know yet how I was going to accomplish my goal. My parents did not know either, but they gave in to my determination, and decided to stay in Irkutsk with me until we could all find a way to make the trip to Manchuria together.

Soon there arose an opportunity for me to join a group of young men planning to escape to China from Irkutsk. Because my parents and I had already made plans to travel together, I decided not to join this group. It turned out to be a fortunate decision. The group was caught before they could reach the border. Although two of the youths managed to escape and return to Irkutsk, one of the two was later found and executed.

Sometimes I would go to the railway station and look with great longing at the trains traveling east. Once I met a girl there who struck me with her beauty. She was so lovely I could not take my eyes off of her. Through a strange set of coincidences, I would meet her again later on three separate occasions: on the train which I would eventually take to Harbin, on the shore of the Sungari River in Harbin, and finally, once more in Berlin. She was from Odessa.

One day, five months after my arrival in Irkutsk, I happened to meet a fellow on the street whom I had known in Krasnoyarsk. He was just a little older than I, perhaps around twenty. He invited me to come home with him. His "home" was just a small room, but inside it, to my great surprise, there stood a grand piano! At once I sat down and started to play with great feeling and the same joy that I had experienced in earlier days when I played regularly in concerts. After a few minutes a door opened, and a lady about twenty-five years of age entered. She told me that she was impressed with my playing and quite surprised to see a boy so young playing with such feeling and command. She started to ask me many questions, including questions about my parents, my life, and my future plans. I frankly told her everything: that I had a sick mother, older parents who had been wealthy but had lost everything, and that I wanted to go to the United States to study. I naively trusted her. I did not know that the lady questioning me was the mistress of Mr. Bergman, the head of the Cheka, who had driven past me the day I arrived in Irkutsk. He was certainly the most powerful man, and the most dangerous, in all of eastern Siberia.

Soon after I met her, Bergman's mistress arranged for a doctor to visit and examine my mother. This doctor, who was also a member of the communist party, confirmed that my mother was seriously ill. He told us that if she stayed in Russia without adequate food and medicine she would soon die. Even under the best of circumstances, her life expectancy would be short. The doctor reported his findings to my benefactress, and as a result, she offered to help us leave Russia. I am inclined to think that her real objective was to help me and not to aid my mother. I sensed she was quite fond of me and admired my pianistic skills. She had openly expressed her concern about my future, knowing that as the son of a capitalist I would have no future if I remained in communist Russia.

One day she instructed me to go to the Cheka building to meet with Bergman himself. Just as had been the case in Krasnoyarsk, the Cheka building in Irkutsk was a place greatly feared by the populace. People even avoided going down the street where it was located. Many executions took place there, including that of Admiral Kolchak. Those who entered often never came out. Being still quite young, I did not fully comprehend the danger I was facing. I had always been excited by danger and had been curious, even eager, to encounter dangerous situations. Thus I found within myself the courage, or perhaps foolhardiness, to go. Besides, this was my only hope of escaping Russia.

When I entered the Cheka building, the heavy front door closed and locked behind me automatically. The wide corridor I found myself in was filled with cigarette smoke. Many soldiers were lounging around, with their rifles and Mausers lying on the floor nearby. These were the same soldiers who had executed hundreds, if not thousands, of people. It was frightening just to look at the stony faces and into the cold eyes of these executioners. I told the officer at the reception desk that I was there to see Mr. Bergman. He made a phone call, and then another soldier guided me up a staircase to a large corner room where Bergman, who was in his twenties, had his office. Bergman spoke with me for a few minutes and then asked me to come back a few days later. On my return I had to pass through the same corridor of horror. This time Bergman gave me a piece of paper, a written authorization, permitting my mother and me to travel to Harbin, in the Far East Republic. My father was not listed on the permit; he was to remain in Irkutsk. The Far East Republic was a buffer state artificially created at this time, which separated Japanese Manchuria and Soviet Russia.

I came home with the travel permit. It saddened my father to learn that he would have to stay behind, but because he loved my mother so deeply, he was glad that she could go and live under better conditions in Harbin. After our departure, my father returned to Krasnoyarsk to live with my oldest brother, Matthew.[17] I never saw him or Matthew again. I later learned that Bergman, the man who had ordered the executions of so many people in Irkutsk, was eventually executed himself.

It was July when my mother and I boarded the train in Irkutsk, the same train which I had so often and so sadly watched disappear to the east. This time I was sitting inside it. I spent the first few hours of the trip standing in front of an open corridor window, admiring the scenery, especially the beauty of Lake Baikal. At one point the train slowed down to cross a bridge. Suddenly, a soldier appeared outside the window. He shouted at me to close the window, probably enforcing some rule. I tried to close the window, but I found that it was jammed and would not budge. The soldier soon lost his patience and took aim at me with his rifle. I did not know what to do, whether to continue my efforts to close the window or to throw myself down onto the floor. Fortunately, the train was advancing. In a couple of seconds the soldier was out of sight and the terrifying incident ended abruptly.

The border between Soviet Russia and the Far East Republic was near Verkhneudinsk, a few hundred miles east of Irkutsk. Before we crossed the border we had to stop at the railway station in Verkhneudinsk. There I learned that all passengers were required to purchase an additional ticket in order to continue the journey. I was not expecting this and did not have enough money. We were still over a thousand miles from our destination, and my mother, feeling unwell, was lying on the berth of our

---

[17] Matthew died of typhoid in the late 1920's.

coach. I had to figure out a way to handle this crisis myself. I remained calm, not realizing how precarious the situation really was. Most of the passengers had already disembarked from the train and were standing on the platform outside the station. I exited the train and began to make a careful study of all the faces around me. Finally, I selected a man whose features seemed the most welcoming. In making my decision I relied on what I had learned from Joseph's book on physiognomy and psychology, as well as my youthful experiences as an observer of people at the dinner table. I approached the man I had so carefully selected. He was an elderly gentleman, tall and slender, and had a kind look on his face. I told him my situation, about my sick mother on the train and our lack of money to buy the necessary tickets. He looked at me very attentively. Suddenly his face turned sad and without saying a word, he put his hand into his pocket and he gave me a ten ruble gold coin. He did not even ask my name or address. I asked for his, so that I could return the money later on. I was able to buy our tickets and we could continue our trip to Chita, the capital of the Far East Republic. In Chita, I picked up money my brother Victor had sent us, and we then continued our trip to Harbin, Manchuria.

At this point in my life I had achieved three great successes: swimming across the Yenisei River, mastering the piano, and escaping from Russia. I owed this last success mainly to my coincidental meeting with Bergman's mistress. Without her help I would have never been able to leave Russia. But my self-confidence, determination, and patience—I had waited five months in Irkutsk before this opportunity arose—played an important part as well. Whether justified or not, I had always had the feeling that I could and must succeed in my escape from Russia, and that now I was, in fact, already a "success" despite my tender age and inexperience. I had become a free man, free from fear and oppression.

In Harbin we were met by my brother Victor and my sister Berta. Berta's husband, Morris Kapushchevsky, a former treasury official, had left Omsk and had managed to reach Harbin a few months after Berta's arrival there from Krasnoyarsk. Morris had taken a dangerous route through an area of Siberia controlled by bandits, the most famous of whom was Ataman Semyonov. Morris and Berta's young son, Valentin (*Vala*), born around 1917, was an energetic youngster who liked to ride on my back at every opportunity.

The exotic atmosphere in Harbin intrigued me. I was particularly struck by the strange songs and cries the street vendors used to attract customers. Chickens and other delicacies were available on every street corner. This scene of plenty contrasted greatly with what we had experienced over the past year and a half.

Victor, who by this time had been living in Harbin for several years managing our father's business affairs, had also been attracted by the exotic elements of life in this city. For some time, he had been living with an operetta prima donna, Zagorskaya. Our father had left Victor over $100,000 in various bank accounts, a very large sum of money in those days, to manage transactions with the Japanese industrial company Kuhara. What happened to all of the money was something of a mystery.

When Victor had first fallen in love with the operetta singer, he began to spend exorbitant amounts of money on her. At first they lived together in the best hotels in Vladivostok and Harbin using the money in our father's bank accounts. One day all of the operetta singer's jewels and clothes were stolen. Victor chivalrously offered to replace everything, again using our father's money. I suspect that the singer may have faked the theft to defraud Victor, but there was no way to prove it. By the time we arrived in Harbin, Victor was nearly bankrupt, yet his mistress was still living with him in a small two-bedroom apartment in the center of the city. My mother and I joined them there. Victor and his mistress had one of the bedrooms; my mother took the other. I slept on the couch in the small living room which also served as the dining room. Everyone had to walk across the living room and pass right next to my couch to get to the bathroom. The situation was awkward as there was very little privacy.

Every evening the operetta singer would take a bath. Wearing her robe, she would pass directly beside my bed. I had not found Victor's mistress particularly attractive. Although she had a lovely voice, she was quite short and inelegantly built, or so I thought, but once on her way back to the bedroom after her bath, she stopped by my bed and opened her robe. Only then did I realize that she actually had a very beautiful body, despite her short stature. She had beautiful breasts and the curves of her waist, thighs, and legs were very pleasing. I was seventeen years old and physically mature by now. Being a good swimmer and having trained physically as much as possible, I had become a strong fellow and had a sex drive to match. When the singer opened her robe, blood shot up into my head and to all of my extremities. I was eager to take hold of this woman and caress her whole body. But at the same time I reminded myself that she was intimately involved with my brother, for whom I cared very much. I soon regained control of my senses and let her pass. It was even more difficult for me to control my urges when she exposed herself to me a second time, but somehow my loyalty to my brother prevailed.

Later the operetta singer and I went on an outing together to the Sungari River. We rowed out to an island and swam along its shore. The situation was even more seductive than in our apartment because we were far from home, surrounded by the wildness of nature itself. Not a soul was around, and we were wearing only our bathing suits. Again, although I knew she would have been willing, I made sure nothing happened between us. Had I permitted my natural desire to overcome my will and self-discipline, I think it would have proved a turning point in my life, a turn for the worse. Thereafter, I probably would have been less principled and more inclined to take advantage of other women who came into my life.

I was glad that I had overcome temptation and kept my brother's trust. The experience prepared me for even more important personal challenges I was yet to face. Later on, when Victor finally lost everything, his mistress left him. But he loved her still, despite her fickleness.

Prior to the revolution, Siberia, like America, had become a haven for independent thinkers and those in search of freedom. Many people in conflict with the despotism of the Czarist government had been banished, or had come voluntarily, to Siberia. People from Poland and the Baltic States were sent to Siberia as political prisoners because they had fought for independence. During the frequent wars Russia had waged against other nations, prisoners of war were shipped to camps in Siberia. Many of those prisoners chose to remain there after being released, rather than return to their native lands. In addition, there were the gold seekers, the adventurers, and the outlaws, who made Siberia analogous to the American Old West in many ways. These Siberian "immigrants" had a natural affinity for the native Siberians, a rugged and resourceful people, and for the vast, challenging country itself. Like America, Siberia became a melting pot of many nationalities. Like Americans, Siberians were also a dynamic, adventurous, and freedom-loving people. At one point there had even been a political party advocating the unification of Siberia and the United States. European Russians preferred the French, or other European nationalities, but Siberians had a strong affection for Americans. When the statesman and author George Kennan came to Russia in 1885, he visited Mr. Kusnezoff and his sister in Krasnoyarsk. Kennan was amazed to discover that both of his hosts spoke English fluently, and that they knew more about America than he did. Mr. Kusnezoff had visited the United States several times, traveling from coast to coast. He had met several distinguished Americans, including General Sheridan and Buffalo Bill. When Vice-president Richard Nixon visited Russia in 1959, he was more cordially received in Novosibirsk, the capital of Siberia, than in the cities of European Russia.

As a boy, I had developed a great affection for America and Americans. On my bedroom wall I had hung pictures of America given to me by my brother Matthew, who had studied there. I loved reading stories about American Indians and American history. As I grew older I learned that America was a place where anyone, through his own efforts, could rise to a position of recognition and wealth, and where possibilities were limitless. Surely someone like me, blessed with ambition, initiative, drive, and courage, could hope for a bright future there. The fact that America was also a huge and powerful country like Russia made it even more attractive to me. Since I had lost my home and my country, which I loved deeply, there was no doubt in my mind when I arrived in Harbin that I was bound for the United States. Scholarships were available. It should have been easy for me to realize my goal. However, at this point, fate turned my life in a completely different direction.

While in Harbin I paid a visit to Mr. Skorochodov, the father of Boris Skorochodov who had shared my room in Krasnoyarsk after the victory of the Red Army. I sadly told him of his son's execution. By this time, Boris' brother, Alexander, had also been killed. Mr. Skorochodov was heartbroken to learn that he had lost both of his fine, handsome sons. He still had one daughter, but he said, "In my sons was my strength. It is bitter to lose them."

After discovering my intention to go to the United States, he said to me, "Go first to Freiberg, Germany. There in Freiberg is the oldest, largest, and most famous mining school in the world. The great Lomonosov and other famous Russians studied there. That is where Mendeleyev invented the periodic table, and where the German poet Goethe, Alexander von Humboldt, and many famous American engineers and scientists received their education. Many mining schools throughout the world are patterned after the Freiberg School of Mines.[18] It is the foremost school in the world."

At first I resisted his suggestion. I had never before considered mining engineering as a career. In the back of my mind I still hoped to pursue music. Yet I knew it would be a risky field to enter, especially since I no longer had any family wealth to fall back on. I was a dreamer and an idealist, but I was naturally cautious too. I realized that I needed to find a steady, reliable profession. But I had also dreamed of going to America, and this dream I did not wish to relinquish.

Mr. Skorochodov continued, "Go first to Freiberg. Then, after graduation, go to the United States and build your fortune. When the counterrevolution comes, you can return to Russia. Russia will be in need of mining engineers."

Mr. Skorochodov had been a high official in St. Petersburg during the Czar's reign and the Director of the Treasury Department while Kolchak was in power. I had tremendous respect for him. He had been a close friend of my father and my brothers for many years. Coming from him, and certainly seeming very logical and well-considered, the plan won my reluctant acceptance. If the plan had not included eventual immigration to the United States, I probably would have rejected it. Based on this single conversation, my life's direction was now determined, for better or for worse. So as not to be lured back into the field of music, I did not touch the piano and avoided attending concerts for the next seventeen years. I was afraid that my deep love of music would draw me back into an uncertain future.

---

[18] Before the First World War the letterhead of the Montana School of Mines read: "Montana School of Mines, the Freiberg of America." Freiberg, in what became East Germany, should not be confused with the city of Freiburg, which also has a renowned university, but is located near the Rhine in western Germany.

Again, I was confronted with difficult challenges. I was seventeen years old and had no money. Although fellowships were available to foreign students in the United States, none were offered by Germany. In 1923 Germans were still very hostile toward their former war-time enemies. My Soviet Russian school certificate was not recognized by German universities, so I had to pass a proficiency examination at the high school in Harbin, which was still operating under the old Czarist system, and therefore was recognized in Germany. Much of the school year had already passed, so there was not much time remaining for me to prepare if I wanted to begin my studies in Freiberg the next fall. I was uneasy about losing an entire school year. So I enrolled in a special private preparatory school for several months prior to the exams. Being a hard-working, methodical student, I was able to earn the certificate in time.

My main regret was leaving my family, particularly my mother, behind. My mother was very worried about me, thinking that I was still too young and inexperienced to face a world filled with danger, fraud, and seduction. We both knew, of course, that it was necessary for me to go and find a life worth living. So that I might have some pocket money, she sold her treasured diamond earrings which she had somehow managed to hide from the Cheka inspectors at the Irkutsk railway station. This money, about $50, was her last gift to me. Saying farewell to my old and sick mother, when we both knew we would never see each other again, was a horrible, heartbreaking experience. I felt bitterness, an overwhelming sadness, as well as deep pity for her. I admired her sacrifice in letting me go. She fainted at my departure. Eventually she returned to Krasnoyarsk to be with my father, but her illness soon overtook her. I never saw her again. Nor did I ever see Victor again. In 1928 he was killed in a train wreck in Japan.

Each week a group of twenty students left for the United States, but only one group per month went to Europe. There were seventeen in my group. I cannot recall how I got my ticket. It may have been purchased by the Y.M.C.A., which frequently sponsored student refugees. To get to Germany one could no longer take the most direct route through Soviet Russia. The only way was to travel two months by boat, by way of Singapore, India, Africa, and the Suez Canal.

Even this was not daunting to me. I was intrigued by the challenges of travel, learning a new language, and making my way in a foreign country.

I believed I was about to begin a most interesting and exciting adventure. Thoughts of possible dangers and difficulties did not shake my confidence. I had been given the opportunity that I, the son of a wealthy father, never expected to get: the chance to become a self-made man, like my father whom I so admired. I had already survived a life of danger and horrors. I did not imagine that I should have to face greater difficulties or more dangerous situations than I had already encountered. How wrong I was.

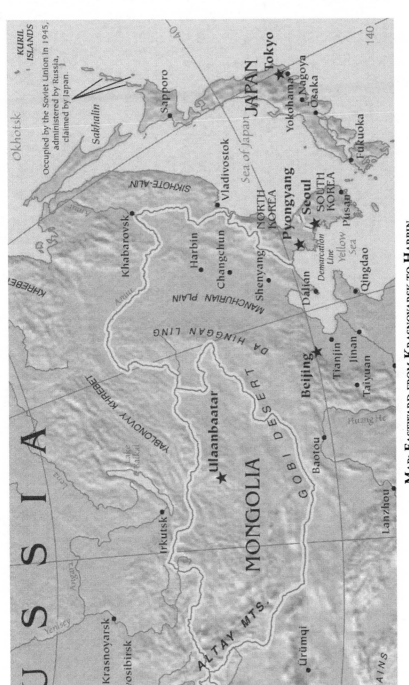

MAP: EASTWARD FROM KRASNOYARSK TO HARBIN

SOURCE: 2004 EDITION OF THE CENTRAL INTELLIGENCE AGENCY WORLD FACTBOOK

Chapter 4

GAUDEAMUS IGITUR

Gaudeamus, igitur	Let us be glad, then,
Iuvenes dum sumus.	While we are young men.

—Medieval student song

I left Harbin on Christmas day 1922, exactly one year after my departure from Krasnoyarsk. First I traveled by train through Mukden (now Shenyang) to Dairen (Luda), near Port Arthur (Lüshun) in northeastern China. There I boarded a Japanese ship, the *Nagasaki Maru*, and went to Shanghai by way of Qingdao. In Shanghai I took a French ship owned by the Messageries Maritimes Company called the *André Lebon*. My two-month journey continued with additional stops in Hong Kong, Haiphong, Saigon, Singapore, Penang, Colombo, Djibouti, Suez, Port Said, and Marseille. We remained in each port for several hours, staying just long enough to permit some sightseeing. From Marseille I continued my journey by train, traveling through France, Italy, Austria, and Czechoslovakia to Freiberg, Germany, my final destination.

For a youth of seventeen, this trip certainly was an unforgettable adventure. On the *Nagasaki Maru* I became acquainted with a Czech officer. Although I never saw him in uniform, he routinely carried a large pistol. When we arrived in Shanghai the evening of December 31, 1922, we were initially told that we could not disembark until the next morning. However, there were many citizens of Shanghai on board who wished to go home that evening to celebrate the New Year. Perhaps the ship's personnel grew weary of hearing so many complaints, or maybe they were eager to begin a celebration of their own. In any case, the captain finally ordered all passengers to leave the ship immediately and declared that there would be no customs inspections.

The Czech officer and I decided to travel together into Shanghai. Both of us planned to board the *André Lebon* in a few days and we had made arrangements to stay at the Savoy Hotel during the layover. We hailed a taxi at the dock and learned from the driver that it would take an hour to reach the Savoy. After a brief discussion with the driver, we agreed on a price. The driver, after traveling about a mile, suddenly stopped and demanded additional money from us. It was dark and we could see no sign of civilization around us. Being completely at the driver's mercy, we agreed. After another mile he stopped the car again and asked for more money. We hesitated briefly, but agreed to his new, higher price. Within a few minutes, the driver stopped for the third time, turned around and asked for even more money. I do not know what I would have done had I been alone. To my amazement and relief, my companion suddenly took out his enormous pistol and, without saying a word, aimed it at the taxi driver's head. The driver, visibly shocked and frightened, stopped talking and took us directly to the Savoy Hotel. He accepted the original fare we had agreed upon without complaint.

After this experience my friend, the officer, became my hero. I was grateful to him and admired his courage exceedingly. Later on, upon our arrival in Marseille, everyone had to be vaccinated against smallpox. How disillusioned I felt when my Czech hero, who was standing right in front of me in line, fainted at the sight of the needle when his turn came up.

My voyage on the *André Lebon* also rewarded me with new experiences. For example, while in Saigon I bought a bunch of green bananas. It was far too heavy for me to carry back to the ship, so I hired a rickshaw. I hung the bananas up on deck, so that they could be ripened by the sun. Unfortunately, for the first two days I did not get any ripe bananas. As they ripened, someone else would always get to them first. I discovered that the only way I could enjoy any of the bananas myself was to stand watch over them and wait for them to ripen before my very eyes.

In each port there were many people who would attempt to cheat the passengers. Taxi drivers would promise to show famous sites within an impossibly short amount of time. Fruit salesmen and other sellers of wares would overcharge us. I eventually learned to ask the price of an item first and then to tell the salesman how much I was willing to pay for it. Otherwise, I would end up paying twice as much. We were also cheated by so-called magicians who showed us different card tricks and lured us into guessing and gambling on the results.

In Singapore, my Czech friend invited me to go with him to a bordello. The girls laughed and giggled when we entered. It was an entirely new experience for me. I was both curious and scared at the same time. However, in the end, nothing contrary to my ideals occurred there, to my friend or to me. My strict upbringing and my dearly-held dream of my future wife held me in check. She would truly be a fair lady, a gentle and charming girl, a good comrade, whom I could love more than anyone else in the world, and to whose happiness I would devote my entire life. I imagined sex to be the most tender expression of love, too holy for occasional, casual fun. I wanted to save this wonderful experience for my life-long partner. This attitude, deeply ingrained from my youth, kept me away from romantic adventures for a long time.

Upon our arrival in Marseille, all the passengers had to go through an immigration inspection process. Because I was a Russian refugee, I was temporarily asked to step to the side. After everyone else had been checked through, the inspectors began asking me many questions: When was I born? Where was I born? Why was I born? Where was I going? Why was I going there? How long was I staying? How long did I plan to continue living? The questions seemed to go on forever and many of them seemed nonsensical to me. Apparently the authorities were afraid of all Russians. They thought that the communists might be trying to send spies to Europe to stir up a revolution. After all the persecutions and suffering I and my family had gone through at the hands of the communists, it seemed ridiculous that these people could believe such a thing of me, a youth of only seventeen.

On my way to Freiberg I stopped in Italy and in Prague, Czechoslovakia. In both places I was offered fellowships. In Prague I was even guaranteed a job after graduation. Even though I knew I would eventually need money and that I had no hope of receiving any more from my family, I did not accept any of the fellowships offered to me. I knew I wanted to go to Freiberg. I wanted no assistance. My dream was to become a self-made man just as my father had been.

Shortly before arriving in Freiberg, I started talking with one of the other passengers on the train. I hoped to get some preliminary information about Germany, particularly about Freiberg. We spoke for almost an hour, but because of my poor command of German, I had great difficulty understanding what the fellow was saying. Although I sensed he was not a native speaker, I could tell that his German was much better than mine and I admired his fluency. Finally, I asked him his nationality. He said he was a Russian refugee! From that moment on our conversation flowed much more smoothly.

I arrived in Freiberg in March of 1923. Of the $50 my mother had given me from the sale of her earrings, I still had $35. Inflation was so severe in Germany then that this amount of money, when converted to German marks, was enough to cover my living expenses for five months. I had no difficulty gaining admission to the School of Mines (in German: *Bergakademie*). One thousand students were enrolled. Because of a quota set by the school, thirty-three percent of them were foreign students. Of these foreign students, about sixty were Russians. Most of them had come from Siberia or the Caucasus.

One requirement I had yet to fulfill before I could begin my studies in October was a six-month stint as a laborer in a mine. An additional six-month period of labor was required before graduation. Getting a job in a German mine was not easy for a Russian refugee. Only five years had passed since the end of the war, and many Germans still felt a great deal of animosity toward Russians. However, after a long search, I finally found a job with the Concordia coal mine in Oelsnitz, Saxony. A sign posted at the entrance to this mine caught my attention. I was amazed to see my own philosophy, the creed by which I had succeeded in crossing the Yenisei, displayed for all to see: "Caution is not cowardice. Carelessness is not courage." Good advice for both swimmers and miners alike.

The mine was very old and over 3,000 feet deep. The working conditions were far from favorable. With so much rock above and all around, ventilation was poor and the heat nearly unbearable. Most of the miners wore no clothes or shoes. The only thing worn, for safety reasons, was a hard hat. Each worker drank at least a gallon of liquid, usually water or coffee, during an eight-hour shift. All fluid consumed was quickly lost through perspiration. A worker's body was perpetually covered with sweat from head to toe. In the dim light of the mine the glistening physique of a young muscular laborer resembled a beautiful piece of sculpture.

On my first day of work, I was lowered by a hoist down to the mining level where I was to meet with my supervisor. The coal miners passing by looked at me with curiosity. Some of them were surprised to see my long, white, thin fingers, which had served me well as a pianist but which were not conditioned for the work of a coal miner. Some of the workers even touched my hands in amazement.

Unfortunately, I was placed under a foreman who disliked foreigners, especially Russians. During the First World War many Russian prisoners of war were assigned to work in this mine. Some of them had even committed suicide because of their dismal situation. This foreman, as I found out later, had placed me in an area with the worst working conditions. It was so hot, and the air so bad, that men could only work for fifteen minutes at a time. They would then retreat back to the tunnel, where they could breathe more easily. This "breathing period" was necessary even for workers who had grown accustomed to the environment over the years. For a beginner like me the conditions were truly hell. However, I knew that I had no option. If I gave up now, I would be done for.

My job was to carry about twenty pounds of coal in an iron trough from the coal face to the rail car, a distance of approximately twenty-five feet. The height at the coal face was less than five feet and it gradually decreased to less than four feet where the waiting rail car stood in the tunnel. The floor of the tunnel was three feet lower than the floor of our working space. It took fifty loads to fill the car and I had to fill it four times during each shift. Each day I made over two hundred trips with a bent-over, nearly doubled-over, body posture, carrying twenty pounds of coal. Such work would have been somewhat easier for a shorter man. I was five feet, nine inches tall. After every few agonizing trips I had to lie down on the floor and stretch out. Exhausted, I experienced terrible pain throughout my body. In my mind I compared my life to that of a Roman slave 2,000 years ago. But even Roman slaves probably had better air to breathe. I quickly grew to resent the conditions, especially the heat and the poor ventilation. To cool myself a little, I would often wrap my naked body around a newly arrived steel coal car, cooled by the temperatures closer to the surface.

After six weeks of this grueling work, I arrived late for my shift one evening, having forgotten that the night shift started two hours earlier on Saturdays. Consequently, someone else had been assigned to my job. I was then transferred to another foreman, whose treatment of me was kinder. I rejoiced. The worst was over. The previous six weeks had prepared me for anything. I found that although mining was never easy, it was never again as difficult as it had been during those first weeks.

As I struggled to survive in my new homeland, one of the most important tasks I faced was learning the German language, and along the way I made my share of bizarre language mistakes. For example, one day in the Concordia coal mine, I was working alone with just one other man, an experienced older worker. He was testing the roof supports, when one of them started to give way. He grabbed the wooden pillar with one arm and held it in place. With the other arm he gestured to me and ordered me, with some urgency, to bring him a particular tool. Unfortunately, I could not understand what tool he wanted. I had learned the German words for all of our mining tools—hammer, saw, chisel, and so forth—but this older fellow spoke in an old-fashioned dialect of the region, so his words were unintelligible to me. I reasoned that he wanted the hammer to knock the support into position, but as I approached him with the hammer he screamed: "Nein! Nein!" So I went back and tried bringing the saw. Maybe he wanted to cut off part of the pillar. Again, he responded: "Nein! Nein! Nein!!" He was starting to weaken under the weight of the beam. Finally, I figured out that he wanted the rope to tie the loose pillar to a solid support. The crisis was ultimately averted.

Afterwards the elder miner said to me, "Look young fellow, you are not at the university now. Here in the mines you have to use your brain."

After working in the mines for the required six months, I continued to work as a miner during all my school vacations: Christmas, Easter, Pentecost, and during the summers. I depended on the income to pay my living and school expenses. Usually my money would start running low by the time the next vacation started. I found this periodic alternation of academic and physical work beneficial for both the spirit and the body. In spite of working in the mines about five months out of each year, I still managed to graduate on schedule.

As a mine worker I faced dangerous situations and a variety of other difficulties. Once I had a written invitation to work in an ore mine in the Harz region along with my classmate Gerhard Grassmück, who was also a refugee. When we arrived at the mine, the manager, when he realized we were foreigners, refused to honor our contracts. He did not even feel obliged to pay for our travel expenses. Since we had spent the last of our savings traveling there, we were faced with real hardship. Of course we were outraged, but as foreign refugees we had little recourse.

One time I went to Beuthen (now Bytom, Poland) in Upper Silesia without having secured a job in advance. I hoped to find employment in one of the mines there, but upon my arrival I found that there were no openings. Having spent all my money to get there, I went to the local police station and asked if I might spend a few nights in their jail. That is where I slept until I was finally able to secure a job several days later.

Mining is very hazardous work. Still a relatively inexperienced miner during my student years, I escaped several potentially fatal accidents. Once the roof, which consisted of a single block of rock twenty-seven feet wide by thirty feet long and ten feet thick, weighing about 700 tons, came crashing down during our fifteen-minute lunch break. Because all the men were outside eating their lunch, every member of the eleven-man crew escaped injury. We would all have been killed had the roof collapsed at any other time. Earlier in the day we had set off two blasts of explosives to break up some big boulders in the area. The roof collapse was a delayed reaction to those blasts.

In a different mine I experienced another cave-in. This time I was buried under rocks, but was able to escape with relatively minor injuries. I still have several blue-tinted scars because of the coal dust which filled my open wounds. Another time a rock fell on my hand and it bled quite profusely. I took another hit on my face, close to my right eye. Yet I never took the dangers of the job very seriously. In my youth, I felt only the rush of excitement when faced with perilous situations.

In October of 1923 I began my studies in Freiberg. One Saturday shortly after my arrival I saw about two hundred people on the plaza near the post office. Out of curiosity I came closer to investigate. I learned that some communists were attempting to surround a truck carrying armed soldiers. The truck was slowly backing down one of the side streets. When I reached a spot about fifty feet away, I suddenly heard the sound of rifle and machine gun fire. A few people standing in front of me fell to the ground. Most of the onlookers, including myself, started running in all directions. I learned later that day that thirty-six men had been killed in the incident. Hearing this made me very sad. I had just escaped the communists in Russia and now they were surrounding me again.

I accosted one of the townspeople on the street that evening and asked him how long he thought the uprising would last. He replied with an air of confidence, "Until Monday."

It was self-evident to him that on Monday everyone would have to go back to work. Only on weekends was there time for revolution. When I heard this practical analysis, my fears began to ease. To conduct a revolution, one needs time, I reasoned. The Germans are hard workers, far too busy to sustain a revolt.

The School of Mines in Freiberg was world-renowned, and the professors there were all distinguished experts in the field. Many of them were famous for their arrogance and iron discipline, but I managed to get them to crack an occasional smile, mostly because of my imperfect German.

In chemistry lab one day we were mixing chemicals and noting the reactions that were taking place. The professor was making the rounds among the students, quizzing them on their knowledge and observations. The professor came up to me, pointed to my test tube and said, "What do you observe in this reaction?"

Misusing the noun, I pointed to the test tube and replied, "There are some *girlies*."[19]

The professor's eyes widened and he perked up. "Oh, really?" he said, "And what are the *girlies* doing?"

---

[19] *Die Kleinen* (pl. noun: the little girls or little ones)

In the most scientifically authoritative manner I could muster, this time making an error in my choice of verb, I responded, "They are *swearing*."[20]

My professor could hardly contain himself. He turned quickly and walked away. I did not realize my mistakes until much later.

On another occasion, when the same professor asked me to describe my procedure, I answered, "I am *arresting*[21] calcium carbonate with sulfuric acid."

He replied, "OK, keep on *arresting*."

Another incident that compromised the extreme dignity of a professor caused such a stir that it was reported in the local newspaper. This time, fortunately, I was not the hapless perpetrator, but only a witness. Our mining professor was reviewing material in class for an upcoming examination. The professor asked one student, "Tell me, is it dangerous to be in a mine where the air contains carbon dioxide?"

"Yes," responded the student, "it is very dangerous."

This was the wrong answer. It is carbon *monoxide* that is dangerous. So, the professor tried to give the student a hint.

"But look at me," he said, "look how strong and vigorous I am, and I have been in mines with carbon dioxide many times."

Now the student knew he was in a bind and he needed to find a way out. "Yes," he stated hesitantly, "but carbon dioxide only affects the brain."

To say such a thing to a distinguished professor was unheard of. The whole class nearly died of laughter. I believe even the professor laughed openly at this response.

I was strong, friendly, yet often clumsy—qualities which resembled those of a bear. For this reason, wherever I went, my nickname was always "bear" (Russia: *Mischka*; Germany: *Teddy*; France: *Michou*; Spain: *Oso*). I was proud of my physical strength and stamina, yet sometimes when I tried out new sports I fell short in embarrassing ways.

During my student days in Freiberg I tried to maintain my physical fitness by practicing various sports. I had more success with some of them than others. I joined a rowing club in Dresden and spent every

---

[20] *fluchen* (verb: to swear) instead of *verflüchtigen* (verb: to evaporate)

[21] *verhaften* (verb: to arrest), instead of *verhalten sich* (reflexive verb: to react with each other)

summer weekend rowing on the Elba River through the beautiful "Switzerland of Saxony." In addition, every day I would either swim or team up with my friends to work out with a ten-pound medicine ball. We became real acrobats, perfecting throws and catches from all sorts of challenging positions. In the winter I swam daily in the natatorium, and on the weekends I went skiing. One thing about swimming in Germany surprised me: When it rained, even if it was only a brief shower, and not a thunderstorm, the Germans would leave the pool and go inside. This seemed silly to me. Were they afraid of getting wet? When swimming in Russia, we had never stopped swimming just because of rain. Anyway, when it rained at the pool, I would continue swimming, all alone. I felt others should join me, so to call attention to myself, and maybe to show off a little, I got an umbrella and swam one-armed, holding the umbrella over me with my other hand as I swam.

My friend Gerhard Grassmück was an excellent athlete and a sports fanatic. One day he took me along when he went to practice field events, a branch of athletics completely unfamiliar to me. First Gerhard threw a big steel ball at me. I had never seen such a ball before, and I did not know how heavy it was (15 lbs.), so I attempted to catch it in the air with my hands. Of course, I could not hold on to the ball and it knocked me down, landing squarely on my left thigh. Fortunately, no bones were broken, but I was in pain for a week. I tried to put the shot several times, imitating my friend, but whether from a straight standing position or with a wind-up, my longest put was a measly five yards.

Then I tried the long jump. I could manage no more than five yards. The coach told me to raise my feet higher to get a longer jump. I tried several times without success. Then, the coach started shouting: "Higher, higher!" That made me angry. The next time I ran I raised my legs up as high as I could. They went up too high and I landed in the sandpit, directly on my tailbone. The jump was longer, but when I hit the sand it felt as if my head, now lodged in my stomach, had been rammed right through my neck.

After taking a few minutes to recover, I decided to try the javelin. I had been watching how my friend was throwing it. He was a strong fellow and known to be an excellent javelin thrower. Once he threw the javelin so hard it broke in two in flight due to aerodynamic vibrations. By this time, I was seething and miserable because of my many failures that day. Determined to do something right, I grabbed the javelin, ran and pulled my arm back as far as possible with all my might, intending to hurl it forcefully into the air. Suddenly I felt a searing pain in my back and realized that I had lanced myself with the javelin. I was certain I had broken my spine. I hadn't, but for a month I carried around a colorful stripe on my back which continually changed shades of red, purple, blue, and green.

I had had enough of field sports. But my friend Gerhard insisted that I have one more try, this time with the discus. This sport looked so graceful, that in spite of the pains in my thigh, back, and neck, I agreed. My first throw was twenty-four yards. Gerhard said that for a beginner that was an excellent throw.

"This is your sport," he said. "You must train yourself in discus throwing."

I was proud of myself at last. In the coming weeks I trained diligently. But strangely, the more I trained, the shorter my throws became. When my throw finally got down to nineteen yards, I gave up. It was unusual for me to admit defeat. Normally I would persevere until I attained my goal, or mastered a skill. Perhaps in this case, I realized it was hopeless.

While at Freiberg I also tried gymnastics. I started with the parallel bars and attempted to imitate other gymnasts I saw. After the first swing on the bars, I fell backwards and almost dislocated my shoulder. For a long time I could not raise my arm. I never tried gymnastics again.

I was disappointed with my failures in field athletics and gymnastics. However, later on I enjoyed taking a course in boxing. I chose boxing because I thought it might be useful to know how to defend myself and learn how to take punches. One surprising thing I learned right away was that taking punches is not the most demanding part of the sport. The hardest thing is keeping your balance. One must keep the body light and float over the floor while sparring. The feet must be kept in constant motion; otherwise a boxer can easily be knocked to the ground. This takes tremendous stamina, even for someone in good physical condition. Strangely enough, even though boxing is one of the most violent sports, I was never injured while boxing. Although I did not study boxing for long, I was able to use the skills I learned to good advantage later on.

I also ran into some bad luck when first learning how to ski. On the first day, within the first few minutes, I fell and injured the big toe of my left foot. I felt immediate, intense pain. At the time I did not know, or even think, that my toe had been broken. I assumed the tight new ski boots I was wearing would have lent me some protection. As it turned out, I had actually fractured my toe, but I did not know it until five years later when it was finally x-rayed by a physician.[22] The whole day was a disaster. The slope was icy, with just a thin layer of snow over the ice, conditions much too dangerous for a beginner. I spent the entire day sliding down the ice on my back or on my face. I was foolish not to quit. But because I happened to be with a beautiful young lady who had volunteered to teach me to ski, I did not wish to show my discomfort, or appear to be a failure. So, I skied all day long, or tried to, compounding the pain in my toe with countless additional injuries. I'm not sure I succeeded in fooling my instructor. Perhaps she thought I was crazy, or maybe she admired me for my effort and resiliency.

On another occasion during a sporting activity, I made a sudden move that strained the small of my back. Thereafter I could not bend my back at all without severe pain. I went to see my doctor. His nurse brought me into the examination room and had me lie down on the table face down. A heat lamp attached to the table was used to give some relief to my strained muscles. In order to get the full benefit of the heat treatment, the nurse instructed me to lower my trousers. After ten or fifteen minutes of treatment, the nurse came back and turned off the light. I rolled onto my back and tried to sit up. But it was impossible; I could not raise myself an inch. The pain was so excruciating. Then the nurse tried to pull me up, but I weighed 180 pounds and she could not do it. Finally, she said, "Put your arms around my neck tightly and I will pull you up." I embraced her, as she had directed, very tightly. To get a good hold on me, she put her arms around me, too. At that moment the door opened and the doctor

---

[22] After a day or two the pain subsided, and I thought nothing more of it until five years later, when for no apparent reason the pain returned. This time I had my toe x-rayed and found that it indeed had been fractured in the skiing accident. Surgery was recommended. Distrustful of German doctors, I refused to submit to surgery, thinking the pain would subside on its own, as it had before. In fact, for many years I felt no discomfort at all, unless I walked more than a mile. Things remained this way for many years until 1967 when the pain suddenly became so severe that I resolved to have the operation. (See Chapter 12, pp. 227-228)

entered the room. He saw me with my trousers down around my knees, embracing his nurse.

Seemingly shocked, he exclaimed loudly, "What is going on in here?" Quickly I responded, "Too bad, you caught us!" We all laughed.

The Russian students whom I saw daily at meals and on frequent other occasions were much older than I, some as old as thirty-five. One of them began his studies the same year I was born. He and I eventually sat for our masters diploma examinations on the same day. Many of these students had served in the First World War and in the Russian Civil War, when rape was a common pastime for soldiers. In 1923, a time of strong devaluation of the German currency, many things could be obtained easily for cash, including young girls.

For the past two centuries one-third of Freiberg's student population had consisted of foreigners. It was a common belief amongst the townspeople that foreign students led an immoral lifestyle. In general, these students had little concern for the girls they used for sex, as most of them had no intention of staying in Germany after completing their studies. Every Saturday night local girls and girls from neighboring towns who had arrived by train would go to Tivoli Hall. This was the usual meeting place for young people, where dances were held on the weekends. Here students and girls paired up to make love in the city park, in the forest, or in the students' rooms. These girls were mostly of the working class: waitresses, salesgirls, chambermaids, etc. The lower and middle classes were less opposed to foreigners, perhaps seeing in their contact with students the possibility of upward social mobility. The attitude was different, however, in well-to-do families. They hated foreigners who practiced free love with their daughters. It was extremely rare for a girl of the upper class to be engaged in an affair with a student. Mingling daily with other Russian students, I was continually ridiculed for my lack of experience with women. The older fellows would often try to persuade me to seduce a girl. I was certainly intrigued with the idea; however, my idealistic upbringing would not permit it. I deliberately fought against my strong sexual drives. This self-inflicted repression would sometimes result in nightly "wet" dreams. I always felt embarrassed when the daughter of my landlady came into my room to make the bed the next morning.

Several times, charming girls were attracted to me. I liked them too, but since I knew I was not interested in marriage, I did not want to take advantage of them. I knew it would be better for both of us to "save" ourselves for our future partners. In the 1920's a woman's virginity was taken much more seriously than it is today.

Since I worked in the mines three to four times a year, each time in a different location, I had many opportunities to meet girls wherever I went. Often I would rent a room in the home of a family with young daughters. In Freiberg, too, there were many opportunities to make the acquaintance of young women. In spite of all these temptations, I resisted, with one exception. My friend, Grassmück, who was somewhat older than I, had already had numerous affairs with women. Because I had recently turned twenty-one, he felt that it was time for me to "become a man" and have an affair of my own. On our way to a mining job in Silesia, we met a girl on the train. She was pleasant and pretty, and willingly accepted our invitation to join us that evening. I was reluctant to encourage her and felt like Goethe's Faust being tempted by Mephistopheles. Nevertheless, my friend finally persuaded me to take this girl to a hotel, threatening that he would otherwise seduce her himself. After an expensive dinner she and I went to the bedroom.

When we were alone, she asked me not to make love to her that night, but to wait another day. I was afraid she would desert me, and at this point I was committed to going through with it. I insisted. The next morning when we rose, I saw several large stains on the bed linens. I understood then why she had wanted to wait. She was having her period. Quickly we left the hotel. I was already very embarrassed over the incident. To make matters worse, later that day I was summoned to the local police station. After asking several rude, intimate, cynical questions, the officers forced me to pay the hotel for the bed linens. They obviously had great fun humiliating me. Not surprisingly, my interest in amorous adventures was soundly squelched. The Siberian bear had tried to get the honey, but was caught and stung by the bees. This was my first and last sexual experience for many years.

The lesson I took from this was that my original lofty ideals were valid, and that I should rededicate myself to upholding them. If I had continued to indulge in sexual adventures, my reputation and character would have eventually been damaged. Of this I was certain. My future survival and success might be at stake as a result.

Although I abstained from sex for the rest of my time in Freiberg, I did cultivate an unusual friendship with one young German woman. She was an attractive blond, with blue eyes and a lovely figure. We made a handsome couple and even kissed at times. She was known among the students as a free lover, but our relationship was completely sex-free. Knowing that I was very principled, she soon came to realize that I was trustworthy. We were good friends, so she felt comfortable confiding in me. I learned that all of her former lovers ignored her in public. They would never walk down the street with her, or dance with her at parties because of the reputation she had among the students and townspeople. I, however, was never ashamed to be with her. I danced with her and walked on crowded streets with her. Her parents were grateful to me for this. I felt that since she had not hurt anyone by her actions, then she should not be treated like a second class citizen. She was not a bad person, nor was she guilty of any crime. Among her lovers were a Mexican Vice Consul and, later on, a wealthy shoe manufacturer. Both became engaged to her, but she broke these engagements off for reasons of her own. She never said anything, but I like to think she chose not to marry them because she did not wish to give up her relationship with me. She enjoyed our friendship, and recognized and respected my idealism.

Two years later, in 1928, I was in Poland and met a girl who was very attracted to me. We spent many wonderful days rowing, playing tennis, kissing, and even petting, but nothing more. She had wealthy parents. When I returned to Freiberg, she convinced her parents to allow her to study painting at the Arts Academy in Dresden, only twenty miles from Freiberg. I know she had her heart set on marrying me. She made several physical advances toward me. But since I knew I did not want to marry her, I did not want to take advantage of her. She finally left Dresden, disappointed.

Then in early 1929 I met Annaliese Scholz and we became good friends. She was just as enthusiastic about sports as I was. It was she who had given me my first skiing lesson. We also enjoyed swimming and rowing together. We had a lot of fun and were excellent companions. However, there was never any sex in this relationship either. I was still holding back, still searching and waiting for the girl in those youthful dreams—someone I could love with deep devotion for my entire life.

My success with women probably was not only due to my character and looks, but it may have also had something to do with the clothes I wore. I always liked to be well dressed, even though money was often tight as I worked my way through school. The first suit I purchased in Germany was made by the best and most expensive tailor in Dresden. Movie stars and other wealthy people, some of them coming from abroad, were customers of this tailor. I paid 210 German marks for my suit, a month's salary for a coal miner. As it turned out, it was the cheapest suit I ever owned. I wore it for ten years, and in spite of wearing it every day, it always looked new. My fellow students admired it too, and it actually became "famous." It was dark blue and so handsome that sometimes my friends would borrow it when they were going to be photographed. I had to stay at home in my underwear until they returned. I had an old Russian suit too, but it was worn out and my vanity kept me from wearing it anywhere in public.

Because I was a foreigner, student life in Germany posed for me its own kind of challenges. The usual hardships of youth were perhaps magnified, but all in all, student life agreed with me quite well. It was like a breath of fresh air in contrast to the stifling existence I had endured in communist Russia. I had started a new life in Germany. It would prove to be a very good life, at least for a few short years.

BORIS STANDING ON FAR LEFT WITH COLLEAGUES AT THE CONCORDIA COAL MINE IN SAXONY, GERMANY (1923)

BORIS SITTING IN A COAL CAR (LEFT) AT THE CONCORDIA MINE IN SAXONY (1923)

BORIS USING THE TRANSIT IN A SURVEYING CLASS AT FREIBERG

SPORTS IN FREIBERG: BORIS FAR LEFT

BORIS WEARING HIS "FAMOUS" SUIT

ANNALIESE SCHOLZ

Chapter 5

ARISE TO FALL

He that strives to touch the stars,
Oft stumbles at a straw.

—Edmund Spenser, *The Shepheardes Calender*

In 1927 I received a diploma in mine surveying from the Freiberg School
of Mines. Two years later, in the summer of 1929, I earned another
diploma in mining engineering. Shortly after my second graduation, I
received a letter from the local German government in Dresden stating
that I could stay in Germany if I wished, but without the right to work.
This rigid restriction was imposed on all foreigners because of high
unemployment among German workers. The adverse economic conditions
since the end of World War I had exacted a heavy toll, imposing much
hardship on the German people. This unfavorable economic climate may
well have aided Hitler's quick rise to power.

My situation seemed hopeless. I could not go back to Russia, and with
the depression in full swing in the United States as well, immigration
quotas there were severely restricted, especially for Russians. In fact,
economic conditions worldwide were so bad that no other country would
grant me a visa. I was stuck in Germany, and as a foreigner, I now had
no right to earn a living. Because I was agnostic, I did not belong to a
church, nor was I affiliated with any fraternal organization. These kinds of
establishments often helped struggling young people. My professors at the

School of Mines were very sympathetic to my plight and tried everything they could to assist me, but to no avail.

Just a few years earlier, a new organization called the Bergbauverein (Mining Association) had been established in Essen, Germany. Its purpose was to study the coal mining operations of the Ruhr district in western Germany in order to find ways to reduce costs and increase productivity. The organization was like a combination of the American Bureau of Mines and the Coal Mine Owners Association. It provided an important service in this region, where 300 coal mines were producing 130 million tons of coal per year. The Bergbauverein engaged a large, expert staff, had the latest tabulating equipment, an ample budget, and it was doing an excellent job.

I sent a letter of introduction to the director of the Bergbauverein, a man named Wedding. I explained that I had just received my diploma in mining engineering, was in search of employment, and would be visiting him personally in the near future. He replied immediately, recommending that I not come to see him since he had no job for me. I wrote back saying that I still would like to pay him a visit at my own expense and risk. He wrote again telling me emphatically that there was absolutely no possibility of employment, especially for me, since I was a foreigner. He told me the trip would be a waste of my time. I sent him another letter indicating that my departure for Essen was imminent. Wedding responded with a telegram commanding me not to come under any circumstances. I went.

On the day of my trip I took some time in the morning to buy an expensive, fashionable hat so that I would look more respectable for my interview. Until that time I had rarely worn hats. After purchasing the hat, I stopped by the Dean's office at school briefly. After concluding my business with the Dean's secretary, I took a hat lying on a nearby table and started to walk toward the door. A man sitting in the waiting room spoke up and told me that I had taken his hat. I insisted that it was my hat and we argued heatedly about it for some time. Suddenly, it dawned on me that the man might be right after all. I checked the corridor outside and saw my hat hanging on a hook. I had hung it there earlier, but had then forgotten all about it.

A short time later I arrived at the Freiberg railway station with my hat and a small suitcase in hand. There I came upon a coin-operated scale. As part of my athletic regimen, I was in the habit of checking my weight daily, so I paused to use the scale, laying my hat on top of it. I then proceeded to board the train. When I took my seat, I noticed that my hat was missing. I had left it on top of the scale. I jumped off the train, dashed back to the scale, rescued the hat, and ran madly back to the coach. I regained my seat, quite exhausted, just as the train began to move. I had almost missed the train because of that hat, but I was happy to have it back. When I got off the train in Essen, however, I forgot my hat again and left it lying on the rack in the coach. I never saw it again. I had owned the expensive hat for only a few short hours and had hardly worn it more than a few minutes. I had to go hatless to the interview with my unwilling host.

After arriving in Essen, I went immediately to Mr. Wedding's office. He was from Westphalia, where, as was well known, the people are hardworking, but brusque and stubborn at times. Perhaps this is why many excellent engineers come from this area. They have the necessary qualities of persistence, forcefulness, and fearlessness. Mr. Wedding, as head of the prestigious Bergbauverein, could have refused to see me, but he did not. Why did he grant me an interview? Perhaps it was out of a combination of curiosity and anger—he was curious to know who this arrogant new graduate was, and, because I had so defiantly disobeyed him, he may have been eager to express his anger toward me in person.

When he first saw me, his face turned beet red and he shouted, "I told you not to come here! Why did you come?"

"Herr Director," I replied, "I have brought you something you need."

Hearing this overconfident statement coming from the mouth of a young, newly graduated engineer, Mr. Wedding became even more furious and seemed ready to throw me out of the room. But my unusual air of self-confidence may have dissuaded him. He decided to find out what I was talking about.

Wasting no time, I showed him a book called *The Analytical Course of Mining Operations*, written in 1905 by a Russian, Boris Boky. Boky was an internationally known professor at the Mining Institute in St. Petersburg. This book, written in Russian, was of great value for any mining research. There was nothing else written in such depth, in any language, on the subject of mining. Director Wedding realized at once that I was right. He asked me to translate the table of contents, which I did. Within a few minutes he offered me a job as research assistant at 300 marks a month ($75). This was an excellent salary for that time. Since Mr. Wedding could not find a more qualified German engineer than me, as I had the advantage of knowing both German and Russian, it was easy for him to justify hiring me, and the German government granted him permission to do so.

Each of the Bergbauverein's many departments was headed by an expert in that particular field. When a problem had to be investigated within the industry, the head of the appropriate department in Essen would contact the head of the industrial engineering department of each local mine in question. In simple cases, communication went by mail. In more complex cases, the problem was handled on-site by young engineers.

To know which portion of the book I should concentrate on first, I had to begin by gaining a better insight into the problems the Bergbauverein handled. To do this, I requested permission to visit several mines, acting as one of these young liaison officers. Over a period of about three months I was able to gather a wealth of information on efficiency and cost, vital to the mining industry. Without the insights I gained from these early assignments, I would not have been able to advance in my profession or become nearly as successful. Only much later did I realize that I had followed the only possible path to success open to me. My future had hung by a thin thread. Perhaps it was by instinct and luck, rather than vision that I ended up taking the right road. Had I not done so, I might have become a coal miner, and eventually, if I were lucky, at best, a foreman in a mine. More likely, I would have been lost in poverty and obscurity.

I compared my success in obtaining my first job under such unfavorable conditions with my previous successes: swimming across the Yenisei River, becoming a notable pianist, escaping from Russia, traveling to Europe with very little money, and putting myself through college by working as a coal miner. I did not know then that more difficult and dangerous challenges were still awaiting me. Very few people, if any, anticipated the horrors of the Second World War.

After working at the Bergbauverein for three months, I received a letter from one of my former professors in Freiberg, Dr. Alfred Ohnesorge, offering me a position as his assistant. A manufacturing company had hired him to write a textbook on open-pit mining. At the same time, he had been invited by the Soviet Russian government to act as an expert consultant for its open-pit mining operations for the next two years. Because he wished to pursue the work in Russia, he wanted to find someone to do field research in Germany for the book while he was away. He also felt it would be an advantage to engage someone fluent in both German and Russian.

Since I had not yet finished my work at the Bergbauverein, Director Wedding, who had been so eager to eject me from his office at our initial meeting, was now unwilling to let me go. However, realizing that the job at the School of Mines was a wonderful opportunity for me, and after a short verbal struggle by telephone with my former professor, he finally accepted my resignation. Again the German government allowed Dr. Ohnesorge to hire me because no one else had my qualifications.

I was put in charge of researching and writing the book on open-pit mining. Dr. Ohnesorge funded my travel to various mines and manufacturing companies so that I could collect all the necessary data. I was permitted to write and sign all business correspondence in his name. He trusted me completely. My salary remained 300 marks, half of which I spent on living expenses. I saved the rest and bought a second-hand car, an Opel, and with it made several trips through Europe.

One of these trips was particularly memorable. I had sent letters to two mining schools in search of students interested in joining me on a three-month tour of mining operations all over Europe. Two young men responded immediately; we became a team of three, sharing expenses along the way. At every mine we visited we were given free food and lodging, and sometimes gasoline and oil for the car. The equipment repair facilities in the mines would even make small repairs on my car at no charge. In order to keep expenses even lower, we regularly slept in a tent. We also bought very inexpensive food, mostly bread, sardines, and tomatoes. In addition, we "borrowed" grapes from countryside vineyards, sampling the finest fruits of France, Spain, and Italy. When I think back on our antics, I am amazed that we three "thieves" later went on to very illustrious careers. One of the students became the president of a German university; the other became a department head at the Krupp Company, a giant in the mining industry.

At the beginning of my assistantship in Freiberg, for recreation, I studied social dancing at the top local dancing school and joined a social club in Dresden. I very much enjoyed dancing and soon became quite accomplished. Because of my ability, I was sometimes invited into the homes of prominent local families. One evening the wife of one of my former professors invited me to their home, explaining that she wanted me to teach her how to dance. While we were dancing, our bodies naturally came into close contact several times. But during those moments my partner would begin to tremble with excitement and take in loud, long breaths. I was confused and embarrassed. I did not know if this reaction was some kind of sexual advance, or if it was just an involuntary response which she could not hide. Because she was a married woman, and the wife of a former professor who had tried to help me on several occasions, I did not want to take advantage of the situation.

Once back in Freiberg, I also reestablished contact with my good friend Miss Scholz. Lately she had become interested in learning Spanish, and so as to have more opportunity to practice the language, she arranged to take a job in Spain. Around the same time, I was planning a two-month road trip through Europe, partly for business, partly for pleasure. With the permission of her parents, I escorted her to Spain. We traveled together for several days, but our relationship remained platonic, just as it had always been. I left her in Spain, continued my trip, and then returned to Freiberg without incident. Some weeks later, Miss Scholz returned home. It came out that her Spanish hosts had inferred from our behavior that we were having an affair and had passed that allegation on to the girl's parents. Consequently, her parents, especially her mother, were furious with her. Finally, when she could stand their anger no longer, she came to me and asked if I would resolve the matter by marrying her. This was an awkward moment for me. We had been good companions for so long, and yet I had never had any intention of marrying her. She was not the girl of my dreams, the one I was still waiting for. Yet I did not want Miss Scholz to be left out on the street in disgrace. Fortunately, my landlady, Mrs. Wunderwald, kindly gave her a small room where she could stay for the time being.

I had been lucky to find as kind and sympathetic a landlady as Mrs. Wunderwald. I rented two rooms in her home and felt welcome and at ease with her family. She had a daughter my age and two sons. Soon she came to be like a mother to me, too. I even called her "Mutti" (German for "Mom"). She had generously given Miss Scholz a room, yet I knew this could only be a temporary solution. I stewed over this problem for a long time. Finally, I decided to contact Annaliese's family minister to ask his advice. He too was furious with both of us, and he accused me of behaving immorally.

In return I became furious with him and replied, "Do you think I would have come to you for advice if our relationship had been dishonorable? Should I have called the fire brigade instead?"

But that did not impress him. He asked me if I was not ashamed to have a "girlfriend."

I said, "What about Goethe? He had several 'girlfriends!'" Mutti, who was in the room at the time, stifled a laugh. She obviously enjoyed listening to our argument. Although the minister was of no help, the furor over Annaliese and me eventually subsided.

My job with Professor Ohnesorge lasted two and half years. By the time he returned from Russia, I had finished writing two volumes on open-pit mining. My name was listed on the title page as co-author. This achievement was to be of great importance to me later on. Of even greater importance was the invaluable knowledge I obtained while visiting manufacturing and mining companies throughout Europe.

Since I had completed my assignment, I was once more unemployed. A few weeks later I received another letter from the German government stating that while I had permission to remain in Germany, I still had no right to seek employment. The political and economic climate in Germany had remained highly unstable. Unemployment continued to hover around thirty percent. The German people were desperately searching for some glimmer of hope. Solutions, such as those of Hitler, as insane as they were, eventually became acceptable to the struggling populace.

During my earlier trips through Europe I had become acquainted with a number of important people in the mining field. These contacts ended up being my salvation. Although I was barred from holding a paying job, I could at least begin working on my doctoral thesis. The Flottmann Company in Herne, Westphalia, allowed me to conduct research on drilling at their facility. I was at liberty to study and make use of whatever equipment or materials I wanted, but was to receive no payment for my work. For the first five months I subsisted entirely on unemployment insurance, only about 75 marks (about $18) per month. I was on an extremely tight budget, but I had enough to live on.

I regretted having to leave my kindly landlady in Freiberg. I had had to sell my car to make ends meet, so Mutti lent me her bicycle so I could get to my new residence in Herne, a journey of three days.

Once in Herne, I discovered that I needed to obtain a number of large rock samples for my research. Such samples were expensive because of the difficulties of loading and transporting them to the laboratory. The chief engineer at the Flottmann Company suggested that I contact the Rheinische Kalksteinwerke Company in Wülfrath. He told me that the president there, Mr. Ludowigs, was a kind person who would likely be sympathetic to my needs.

I arrived in Wülfrath one morning a few days later, and was told by Mr. Ludowig's secretary, Fräulein Homan, that he was out of the office, but that he would return again in the afternoon. She suggested I spend the morning visiting the quarries. The Rheinische Kalksteinwerke Company was the world's largest producer of lime and Europe's biggest dolomite producer. It belonged to the German United Steel Corporation which was controlled by the Krupp and Thyssen companies. The quarries I visited that morning were the largest in Europe. Only one quarry in the United States boasted a greater annual production. I was astonished to see how well mechanized the operation was. Having seen mines, quarries, open pits, and machine manufacturing plants all over Europe, and having spent two and a half years writing on open-pit mining, I was up on the latest technology and research in the mining industry. This background enabled me to uncover, in just a few hours of touring the quarries, two mistakes in their operating procedures, both of which could be easily remedied.

In the afternoon I met with Mr. Ludowigs. As I entered his office, I saw a man six feet in height and about forty-five years of age. His blue eyes expressed so much kindness and warmth that right away I felt as if he were embracing me like my best friend or a kind father. He was both personable and highly charismatic. After talking with him for a few minutes, I had the feeling that he knew me better than I knew myself. He agreed at once to send free rock samples to Flottmann for my experiments. Out of gratitude,

I told him what he could do to improve the operation of his quarries. One improvement concerned blasting, the other, the deployment of the equipment. I also told him that he could save money on blasting if the quarry faces were turned ninety degrees. President Ludowigs was surprised to hear these suggestions from a young newcomer who had spent only two hours at his plant.

Intrigued, he said, "Look, I have many engineers here with many years of experience and service, and none of them have told me about these problems. Are you sure a large cost reduction could be realized with these changes?"

With confidence, I said, "There is no doubt in my mind."

"How much time would you need to prove your theory?"

"Three months," I replied promptly.

"Look," he said, "I can pay you the salary of a regular worker, 150 marks ($37) per month for three months. Will you accept the job?"

Indeed, I did accept. It was a tremendous opportunity, a special assignment from the president of the largest quarry in Europe. President Ludowigs had no difficulty getting the necessary permission from the German government to hire me.

In three months I proved to him that the number of explosives being used could be reduced by over twenty percent. Because of the large amount of rock production, this represented a considerable savings. As I worked on the project, I found other areas where costs could be cut, and Mr. Ludowigs was obviously pleased with the results of my advice. In today's values (in 1972), I saved the company over $100,000. When the three months were almost over, I asked the manager of operations if I would really have to leave. He replied, "Don't you *dare* go. We shall keep you here for sure. You *must* stay."

When my appointment was officially at an end, Mr. Ludowigs promoted me. I became his special assistant for operations, planning, development, and research. My focus was to be cost efficiency. My salary doubled to 300 marks per month, and I received an immediate bonus of 750 marks. A bonus of 300 marks followed at Christmas. Within the year my salary increased to 400 marks per month, with thirteen payments per year. This was really big money, considering that the plant manager's salary, even after his many years of service, was only 800 marks per month.

Again I budgeted my expenses so that I could afford to buy a car. This time I bought a beautiful blue Mercedes-Benz. I was really living high! I had a fantastic, interesting job and was proud to be working for such a large and reputable company. I had access to any office, plant, or quarry in the company. I could travel to any mining operation in Germany, or abroad, to do research. In less than a year, I had risen from desperation to influence, a remarkably quick change of fortune.

Several times per week, usually around six o'clock in the evening, Mr. Ludowigs would call me into his office to discuss planning, development, or operational problems. He seemed very fond of me and appreciative of my abilities. Some of my German colleagues, engineers with many years of experience, were furious with jealousy at times. But I was protected by the top man himself, so they had no recourse. Also, the president's secretary, Miss Homan, a kind and clever person herself, treated me with great courtesy and respect. As secretary to the president, she held a powerful position in her own right, although she herself was quite small in physical stature.

I am not certain if it was a deliberate psychological trick on the part of Mr. Ludowigs or not, but I always had the feeling that he overestimated my capabilities and overpaid me. Because I was afraid to lose his high esteem, I worked extremely hard, often into the evenings and a few hours every Sunday, to prove myself worthy of his commendation. He knew how to motivate a man. Later on, when I was working as the manager of a mine in Argentina, I used the same method with great success. Of course, I had to have good insight when I first evaluated an employee. Once I was satisfied, I showed him my "over-esteem" and paid him more than he expected. The result was fantastic. Each employee was afraid to lose the esteem of his superior, just as I had been. They worked industriously and enthusiastically. Most of the other workers were envious of the few I had selected and frequently tried to compete with them. In this way, the efficiency of all the workers was very high. They were motivated by the hope of future reward and were appreciative and cooperative.

In one quarry, over one hundred blasts were being detonated each year. This gave me an excellent opportunity to do some research on blasting. I soon was put in charge of planning, calculating, and executing these blasts, in addition to the other work I was doing. These blasts were the biggest ever made in civil industry in Europe. My research was always scientifically planned and executed. Through my observations and calculations, I soon made discoveries which led me to the creation of a new theory of blasting and to the improvement of existing blasting techniques. I learned how to take hundreds of thousands of tons of rock and skillfully throw the entire mass in any direction I chose. I had already started to use the "directional blast" in 1934, a method which became widely known only around 1960. Without hesitation I set off huge blasts charged with several tons of explosives only a hundred yards away from factories worth millions of dollars, because I knew how to use the explosives and how to make them perform the way I wanted. Consequently, I soon became an esteemed authority in blasting throughout Germany.

One day in 1936 I received a visit from the Oberberghauptman (the Chief Minister of Mines), the highest mining official in Germany. He invited me to become his advisor. With the permission of President Ludowigs, I accepted this position and became the number one man in blasting and in open-pit operations in Germany. The first assignment I received from the Minister, which lasted until 1938, was to improve mining operations at the iron mine at Eisenerz-Erzberg in Austria. This mine was, with the exception of the Kiruna iron mine in Sweden, the largest open-pit iron ore operation in Europe.

In three years I had advanced from the bottom to the top. I was extremely proud, not only because of the speed of my success, but because I, a foreigner, had succeeded in Germany. Hitler's "Superman" theory held that only Germans were capable of making important innovations. If a successful man were not himself a German, then at least one of his parents or grandparents must have had a few drops of German blood in their veins. I certainly did not have any German blood in me, and this made me doubly proud of my achievements. I was a living example of the fallacy of Hitler's claims. Although I personally despised Hitler and his racism, I was as yet unaware of the terrible implications of his persuasive propaganda. Soon they would become all too clear.

In German restaurants, beer was (and still is) drunk in amazing quantities, as was wine. One could not order water or milk. I was never a drinker, so I usually ordered soft drinks. This practice frequently irritated my German hosts and acquaintances. Some of them would say to me with an expression of deep sadness, "It is truly a great pity to satisfy your thirst with soft drinks instead of beer, a great pity for your thirst." Sometimes their tone would turn sarcastic, and they would say that it was perhaps normal for a girl or a woman, but not for a man. Of course, such insinuations were embarrassing. Finally, I made a secret agreement with all the waitresses in the restaurants I frequented to serve me grape juice when I ordered "wine." The appearance was the same as wine, so my friends thought I was joining them in their drinking habits, and they felt more comfortable.

At social events organized by our company, where I had to be present because of my position, drinking during the meal, and for hours afterwards, was the norm. Many of the people became drunk; some would even literally slide under the table. The others who were still upright were very much surprised to see me sober. They had great respect for such resistance to alcohol. The only explanation they could think of was that I had come from Siberia, where people routinely drink vodka in great quantities.

Because of my professional position in Wülfrath, I soon became a popular figure in the community. At one point an 18x18 inch photograph of me was exhibited in the window of a photographer's shop in the main shopping district (*Königsallee*) of Düsseldorf, the closest large city. I maintained friendly relations with everyone I knew in town and within the company. Often I would entertain people in my home, sharing with them the famous Russian hospitality my own family had offered to many when I was a young boy.[23] I would frequently invite people to ride with me in my handsome blue Mercedes-Benz, even local policemen, Nazi party militiamen (called SA, Brownshirts, or Stormtroopers), and other influential men of the region. All my acquaintances were very friendly and seemed to have a high regard for me. I could not imagine that I would ever have any trouble with these amiable people. Several girls, who were either employees of the company or who resided in town, indicated by

---

[23] In 1965 I met a gentleman in Wülfrath who said he remembered being a guest at my home when he was eight years old. I had offered him a banana as I greeted him at the door.

their attentions that they wished to become romantically involved with me. However, I had not yet found the right girl to marry.

Several times in my life I have been pursued by married women. Frequently they were unhappy with their husbands, and were looking for sympathy and understanding. Other times they were simply in search of adventure. A man can easily take advantage of a woman under these circumstances. He need only show understanding for her difficulties, and she will fall readily into his arms, with little thought of future consequences.

One such instance arose with my first landlady in Wülfrath. When I first arrived I rented a room in the home of a man who worked in one of the company offices. He was honest and hard-working, about forty years of age. His wife was a good-looking woman in her mid-thirties. They had a school-age daughter. After only a few weeks in their home, I had the embarrassing experience of having to ward off the wife's affectionate advances. Perhaps the attraction was only physical, or maybe she was interested in me because of my position in the company. As encouragement, she would say to me, "Was man nicht weiss, macht nicht heiss." (What he doesn't know, won't burn him.) Because of my idealistic nature, I could not allow myself to give in to her advances. Also, I would not have been able to face her husband, whom I saw at home and in the office daily. I considered her selfish and shameful. It seemed to me that she had everything she needed to be happy, yet she was looking for adventure and excitement at the expense of the man who had placed his trust in her. If discovered, she would certainly hurt those closest to her.

I was still convinced that sex should be the fulfillment of genuine love—the most gentle and tender expression between two people. Marriage was a sacred human relationship, and lovemaking without loving affection could not possibly bring complete enjoyment and happiness. I knew that I was extremely idealistically minded and something of a dreamer, but I liked this ideal and wanted to hold on to my dream. I believed that idealistic dreams made life richer and more meaningful. Because of my strong ethics, I became known to my friends as a "Moral Athlete." Being honest and moral, and disciplining myself not to harm anyone—especially for any selfish reasons—made me feel strong. Somehow I felt these ideals would protect me. Nothing evil could happen, as long as I believed in and upheld my moral code. Perhaps it was a naive philosophy, but I upheld it, almost like a religion. My ideals, like a belief in God, helped to strengthen my resolve.

After a few months of ignoring and resisting the advances of my landlady, I decided to move out. My second living situation in Wülfrath proved to be far superior. I found a room in the home of the foreman of one of our quarries. His wife was kind, and they had two boys. I liked this family, and we had an agreeable relationship. I stayed with them for several years, until 1939, when I was forced to leave Wülfrath.

My job at the Rheinische Kalksteinwerke interested me a great deal and provided me with many opportunities to be creative. I invented new types of machinery and successful new mining methods. In spite of this exciting job, and the fact that my salary had risen very quickly, my goal and dream, which I had had since 1922, was still to immigrate to the United States. I never relinquished that hope. However, I first wanted to finish my doctoral thesis under Professor Kegel at the School of Mines in Freiberg. I also hoped to amass an appreciable amount of money so that I could go to the United States fairly well financed. I was continuously making discoveries in the field of blasting—discoveries I wanted to include in my thesis. However, because of my job, only part of my time could be devoted to thesis work. Consequently, my progress was slow. I could have stopped further research and finished the thesis using the material I already had, but I chose instead to continue the research before writing. This postponement proved to be a nearly fatal mistake.

Being involved with so many fascinating and urgent projects, I became quite preoccupied and paid little attention to political events taking place in Germany and abroad. In a sense my intense concentration blocked my awareness of the world outside my immediate sphere of occupation. However, one evening in November of 1938 everything changed. I had come to Düsseldorf to have my car repaired. Suddenly, I saw a large gang of Hitler Youth in uniform approaching. They were breaking the windows of the business establishments and private homes of Jews. Some of them went inside the buildings and threw furniture from the windows of every floor. On the street the police and fire brigade were assembled in order to maintain "law and order" and to insure the "safety" of the pedestrians, meaning they were trying to keep the falling property from hitting the people standing in the street.

Goebbels, Hitler's propaganda minister, described the event as a "spontaneous outburst" of the German people, caused by indignation over the Paris assassination of German diplomat Ernst vom Rath by Herschel Grynszpan, a German-born Polish Jew. However, since the same thing occurred simultaneously all over Germany, it was obviously a well-planned maneuver, organized by the government. This event was the famous *Kristallnacht*, or "Night of Broken Glass," named for the broken glass of Jewish homes and businesses all over Germany.

It is still unbelievable to me that Hitler's barbaric persecution of the Jews could take place in the twentieth century. Hitler maintained that not only Jews, but all so-called non-Aryans, as well as certain Aryans like Russians and other Slavic peoples, were inferior and should therefore be exterminated. Not only were millions of Jews killed, but millions of Russians were also put to death during the war, either as victims of the Nazi occupation, or in Germany as prisoners of war.

I shudder to think what might have happened if Hitler had started the war earlier. The world was still asleep, just as I had been, and Hitler would have had a better chance of subduing it to his will. Think of how many more millions might have been killed all because the world was too self-absorbed, too complacent, too uninterested, and too fearful of becoming involved to recognize how dangerous Hitler and Nazism really were. Everyone hoped that catastrophe would pass him by. Because of this complacent attitude and a general reluctance to make a stand, Hitler was able to destroy his opponents one by one. First he attacked the communists, then the Democrats, then the Jews, then his enemies in the right-wing parties, and then the Church. Soon he occupied the Ruhr Valley, Austria, and Czechoslovakia. Even when Hitler resorted to warfare, the world merely looked on while he crushed Poland into submission. Nobody moved against him. Consequently, Hitler was able to concentrate his entire army at a single target each time. Each successive country attacked could not defend itself against the combined German forces. Hitler won the early battles easily, making some clever strategic decisions. He knew when and how quickly to strike. Had all the countries of Europe combined their defensive forces and attacked Hitler early and simultaneously, he would have been defeated, and much, much suffering could have been averted.

Just as the whole world was in danger, I, too, was in personal danger. The governments of the countries surrounding Germany had waited too long, hoping that nothing devastating would happen. I had made the same mistake. Witnessing the treatment of the Jews during *Kristallnacht* in Düsseldorf, I was shocked and disgusted. I did not want to live in a country where such things could happen. At that moment, I realized I had made a terrible mistake by staying in Germany so long. I knew I should try to leave at once, but I did not know how to do so. I might travel as a tourist, but with a tourist visa alone, my stay could only be temporary. I would eventually have to return to Germany. As a stateless citizen, I was not protected by any government. I had no affiliation with a church or any other organization. I suddenly started to feel insecure, as if there were no ground under my feet. I was uncertain where to go or to whom to turn.

Shortly after the incident in Düsseldorf, I traveled to Sweden. My official purpose was to visit mines, but my real purpose was to find a way to immigrate. I made the trip from Emden, Germany to Narvik in Norway on a Krupp company freighter. From Narvik I traveled to the vast Swedish iron ore mines in Kiruna, then to a gold mine in Boliden, and then to Stockholm. I tried to get permission to stay in Sweden, but was unsuccessful, perhaps because I was not experienced enough in diplomacy. I did not fully realize it at the time, but to the Swedish I was a German. They did not trust me, perhaps suspecting I might be a spy. I was only seventeen years old when I arrived in Germany, and I had lived there for fifteen years, effectively my whole adult life. The influence of German culture was therefore quite evident. I behaved like a German, and I even looked like a German. My movements and my manner of talking had strong German characteristics. I walked with slow, long, energetic, self-confident steps, and having taken care to build a good physique, I probably appeared to be a typical German "Führer-type."

After encountering the suspicions of the Swedish, I came to feel that I would be suspected of being a German spy no matter where I went. I needed to have a sponsor who would guarantee that I was a politically reliable person and provide me with financial support. But I knew of no one abroad who could assume that role. I felt trapped. I realized that I was in serious trouble, that at any time something disastrous could happen to me. By waiting too long, by not leaving Germany much earlier, I had made the biggest mistake of my life. Soon I would face the consequences. My worst fears would become reality.

THE THREE TRAVELING "THIEVES"
(BORIS IN CENTER)

Frau Wunderwald (*Mutti*)

BORIS WITH MUTTI'S BICYCLE ON HIS WAY TO WESTPHALIA

PAUL LUDOWIGS, DIRECTOR OF THE RHEINISCHE KALKSTEINWERKE

RHEINISCHE KALKSTEINWERKE, ADMINISTRATION BUILDING

RHEINISCHE KALKSTEINWERKE MINING OPERATION SITE

Chapter 6

AND MEN HAVE LOST
THEIR REASON

O judgment! Thou art fled to brutish beasts,
And men have lost their reason.

—William Shakespeare, *Julius Caesar*

B y now the Gestapo was seriously intent on eliminating all of the
Führer's enemies, including anyone merely suspected of being
anti-Nazi. I was a foreigner, and as a blasting expert, I had easy access
to explosives. Because of my important position in one of Germany's
largest mining companies, I had been associating regularly with people
of distinction all over the country, including high ranking Nazi officials.
After witnessing *Kristallnacht*, I became increasingly incensed over the
hateful attitude of the Nazis towards the Jewish people. In time, the Nazis
also began actively condemning Russians as an inferior people, a political
stance that of course particularly offended me. At social gatherings, I
found myself forced to hide my indignation over the unjust treatment of
those who expressed opposition to the Third Reich. It was easy for a keen
Nazi observer (and they were everywhere) to sense my disapproval of Nazi
injustice. When engaged in conversations with Nazis, I struggled to keep
my disgust from showing in my face and in my tone of voice.

The evening of the annual Rheinische Kalksteinwerke banquet I was
seated, as usual, at the head table with the president, vice presidents, their

wives, and other prominent guests. Seated next to me that night was the Obersturmführer, the head of the local Nazi party and leader of their local militia, known as the SA (or Stormtroopers, German: *Sturmabteilung*). The situation made it impossible for me to avoid his conversation. He talked, of course, about Hitler and about the Jews, whom he hated and whom he "could smell fifty yards away." At first he seemed to like me. Maybe my appearance and self-confident manner suggested to him that I might be a "Führer type," a good candidate for the party. He even asked me if I would like to become a Stormtrooper or join the elite SS (Shield Squadron). I politely declined his invitation saying I was too busy doing extremely important work for Germany's mining industry.

He also asked me how I liked German girls. I answered impulsively, "German girls are like German apples. From the outside they may not look so beautiful, but if you bite them, they taste good." It was a slightly improper answer, given from off the top of my head, but everyone laughed and seemed to take it in good humor. The evening continued in that vein and remained polite for a time.

Suddenly, the Obersturmführer declared that the Baltic States and the Ukraine, all Russian states at the time, should be annexed to Germany. Shocked, I bluntly asked why.

"Because many Germans are living there," he answered.

"How many Germans live there?" I inquired.

"At least two percent," he replied. "And they are all of the Führer's race."

His chauvinistic responses angered me a great deal, as they were directed at my Mother Country. I tried to restrain my disgust, because I was aware of the possible consequences. However, he must have seen the keen indignation in my facial expression. It is quite possible that he was trying to provoke me on purpose, to test my loyalty to the Third Reich. Thus he had, no doubt, discovered that I could not be trusted. He knew I was an explosives expert who had easy access to top Nazi leaders. If I were a Russian spy I might be planning some spectacular assassination. So in his view, he had a duty to protect the Fatherland. Almost at once, I realized that I had fallen into his trap, and from then on I knew that I was in grave danger.

If he had not already made up his mind, then certainly as a result of this conversation, the Obersturmführer decided to have me eliminated as a bad risk. Shortly, I came to learn that the Gestapo was conducting extensive investigations in all the locales I had lived since my arrival in Germany in 1923.

The favored means of elimination among the Nazis was to declare their target a communist or a Jew. Because I had held a high position in German industry for many years, it would be difficult to contend that I was a communist. It was much easier to declare that my parents or grandparents had been Jewish. When the Nazis declared you a Jew, it was difficult to prove that you were not. As Hermann Goering once said, "It is I who decides who is a Jew or not a Jew." Goering valued the talent and loyalty of his Field Marshal Milch so highly that he arranged to have Milch's Jewish ancestry officially denied. Next to Goering, Marshal Milch was the most important man in the air force. Under Hitler, the Chinese people were considered non-Aryan, belonging to the Yellow Race. However, the Japanese were considered Aryan, because Hitler needed their cooperation. I knew if the Gestapo decided I was Jewish there could be no possible defense.

My friend Annaliese from Freiberg, who knew nothing of my perilous situation, visited me during her vacation in late February. I finally confided in her after a few days. She took it calmly, quite to my surprise. To help me take my mind off my worries, she suggested that we take a skiing trip together in the mountains. The break and the exercise did me good. But late one evening we decided to stop for the night at a large, beautiful spa hotel (*Kurhaus*) near Winterberg, in the Sauerland. When we entered the lobby, we found ourselves in the midst of a huge, frightening throng of hundreds of Stormtroopers. The whole hotel was swarming with them. Instantly, we turned and tried to leave. But when some of the men noticed us, a beautiful blond girl with her handsome, strong escort, whom they assumed was German, they called to us to join them. By closing ranks around us, they forced us to stay.

I went to the desk clerk and asked for two rooms. A clutch of Stormtroopers, laughing and joking in the vicinity of the front desk, overheard my request and began to protest, "What? *Two* bedrooms? This handsome couple surely would prefer *one* bedroom!" It was impossible for me, or for the hotel clerk, to argue with the mob, so in the end I was compelled to register for one room. For the first time, I spent the night in the same room with Miss Scholz, thanks to a gang of Nazi Stormtroopers. They probably felt they were doing a service to their Fatherland and to Hitler, who encouraged healthy German couples to produce as many "genetically superior" children as possible. Only with the strictest discipline did I manage to keep my friendship with Miss Scholz platonic that night. I wonder what would have happened had the Stormtroopers known I was not a German and that I was already on the Gestapo's "undesirable" list.

As the weeks passed, international politics heated up. Tension was high, and it looked like war might break out at any time. On March 23, 1939, I received an "invitation" to appear at the local police station. There two Gestapo men questioned me about my place of birth, the name and age of my parents, and other details about my past. At the end of their interrogation, they told me that I was a Jew, and therefore, from that point on, I would be treated accordingly. They then called my landlady and asked her to come to the police station, since her husband was not available at that hour. When she arrived, the Gestapo told her to throw me out of her home because I was a Jew and therefore undesirable. My landlady told them, with a steely courage that astonished me, that she had never met a more decent fellow than I, and she saw no reason to throw me out of her home. Furthermore, she said, since she had known me for six years, and they did not know me at all, she must be right and they must be wrong. Both men looked at her furiously, but they let us go. I was extremely grateful to my landlady for standing up to the intimidation of the Gestapo. I had enjoyed living in her pleasant home for years, but had never realized she possessed such fortitude of character.

When the Gestapo declared me a Jew, I was suddenly in a most perilous situation. I was shocked, suddenly realizing that I was powerless to defend myself. However, as I left the police station, I felt curiously stimulated and began to wonder what I would do in response to this injustice. Moreover, I actually rejoiced, thinking that now, finally, I would be compelled to leave Germany. I might somehow be able to fulfill my old dream of immigrating to the United States. I was in terrible danger, but it was actually exciting to me at the time. Now, in hindsight, I can only attribute this attitude to the foolhardiness of youth. For many years in Russia I had lived under the continuous threat of persecution, so in some ways I was accustomed to this feeling. Now, as then, I felt invincible, thinking that death could not possibly overtake me yet. I was simply young and naive.

I was also profoundly offended, just as I had been in Russia. No one can choose one's parents. In Russia, I faced peril because my father had been a capitalist. The communists assumed all capitalists were bloodthirsty exploiters of the working class and therefore a lower form of life. Now the Nazis were persecuting me because of the supposed origin of my parents. According to their view, everyone of Jewish origin was a parasite, a coward, and a cheat. In Russia, and now once more in Germany, I felt deeply humiliated and degraded. Being persecuted, not for what I really was, but because of false assumptions and prejudice, added a disgusting irony to my predicament.

Although I knew that I had a few drops of Jewish blood in my veins, I had attended only Christian churches as a child, and had never considered myself Jewish. First and foremost, I was a proud Siberian, and as an agnostic I was not associated with any religion. In Siberia only a tiny percentage of the population was Jewish. Many of them were freethinkers, rather than practicing Jews. Most were completely assimilated into the culture of the Russian majority. One could not notice any difference in their speech or behavior from that of the rest of the population, and I never perceived any antagonistic feelings against them, at least until the Revolution. Then things started to change, when European Russian refugees, including some that were Jewish, began arriving in Siberia. These Jews were not as fully assimilated as the Siberian Jews, and as a result anti-Semitism soon began to boil up.

One day when I was twelve, my class was outside playing on the playground, when one student began to shout, "Beat the Jews to death! Save Russia!" All the other students joined in and began to march around chanting this childish slogan. I joined in too and didn't think anything of it. It was an incident not unlike other senseless childish outbursts. I couldn't imagine then that such anti-Jewish sentiment existed in the adult world and had no idea that many adults actually took such ignorant hatred seriously.

Later that same year, I was sitting on the bench in front of my house when three senior high school boys walked by. They were refugees from

Europe, all Russian aristocrats, as I could tell from their French accents. As they passed I could hear one of them say, "How can you call me a citizen, when each damn Jew and every bastard calls himself a citizen now?" I was shocked to hear him speak such hateful words. Only then did I begin to understand what anti-Semitism meant, and how ugly and demeaning it was.

My condemnation by the Gestapo resulted in an immediate and total destruction of my position in the mining industry and in society. Needless to say, my government position was also eliminated. Up until that moment I had been a well-regarded member of the community. People liked me, and were proud to be seen with me. Many had enjoyed my hospitality on a regular basis. But now, suddenly, I became an outcast. People were afraid to associate with me, fearing that they might jeopardize their safety and the safety of their families. The safest strategy for them would be to denounce me publicly, or even to attack me physically.

Now I was truly at the bottom. I had lost nearly everything—my job and my status in society. By this time, I had also lost all contact with my family. From 1922 until 1933 I had been able to correspond with Joseph and Berta. During that period, my parents and my other brothers had died. Suddenly in 1933 the letters stopped arriving, and because the last letters had contained indirect references to some serious misfortunes, I assumed that Joseph and Berta had also perished.[24]

Singled out as a victim of Nazi persecution, I was certainly down, but not yet defeated. The powerful Yenisei River was still running through my heart and soul. I still felt powerful, like a fearsome Siberian bear. My deep belief in justice, honesty, freedom, and goodness kept me spiritually strong. I was convinced that Hitler was a lunatic and a criminal, who could not possibly succeed in the end. He had used fear and hate as weapons, and had turned the desperate economic situation in Germany to his advantage. So far, he had had success in mobilizing Germany and steering it toward his twisted vision for mankind. But I was still, as always, idealistic and optimistic, and continued to have faith in the basic goodness of people. I could not accept a world in which hate could triumph.

I hoped that the United States, as the most powerful country in the world, and the Americans, a people who loved freedom, would stop Hitler

---

[24] See chapter 12, p. 230.

from conquering the world. Although I worried about Russia's fate, I also had faith in her ability to resist Hitler's advances. History had shown that the size of the country and the rough, cold winters were excellent defensive deterrents working in Russia's favor.

Although deeply shaken by the Gestapo interrogation, I kept myself under control. After leaving the police station, I stopped at a grocery store before returning to my rooms. The house stood in a relatively isolated location, near the edge of town. I parked my car in front on the street, just as I usually did. Once inside, I ate my lunch and afterwards settled down on the sofa to rest. Surprisingly, I soon fell asleep. It is interesting how differently people react to horrific circumstances. Some attempt to run away, some turn to alcohol, some take drugs, some indulge in sex, some consider suicide. I sought refuge in sleep.

At 8 p.m. my landlord and landlady awoke me. The room was dark, but an unusual brightness could be seen outside on the street. With frightened faces, the couple told me that Nazi Stormtroopers were surrounding the house. I peeked through the curtains and saw about forty SA men, in their characteristic brown uniforms with the swastika on the left sleeve. They were indeed surrounding the house. The bright light streaming in through the window came from the headlights of their cars, which were all pointed directly at the house. I noticed that all the tires of my own car were flat.

Tension filled the air. My landlord naturally feared that the Stormtroopers might damage his home by breaking the windows or battering in the door. I did not know what to do, but I tried to remain calm. That was my nature. Because of my experience as an explosives engineer, I had developed the ability to keep my nerves under control under all circumstances. In admiration of this trait, some of my colleagues had called me "Der Mann mit der eisernen Ruhe" (The man with the calmness of steel). I had been responsible for the planning and execution of hundreds of the largest multi-chambered blasts in civil industry in Europe. This is not a business for excitable individuals. Sometimes detonation would not occur when expected, and I would have to go, with an assistant, and determine the cause of failure. Entering a dark tunnel, moving in, and standing right next to an explosive charge that was supposed to have already gone off, is a nerve-testing duty. I was constantly telling myself that, logically, nothing could go wrong. But another voice within me was more doubtful, cautioning that you never know what might happen, the explosive could unexpectedly detonate and kill you. Courage and calmness were required to do such a job. Courage I had already developed as a boy. It now would serve me well.

I had a strong, almost fanatic faith in my future. I was thirty-four years old, too young to die. My dreams had not yet been fulfilled. I had not yet had a deep, loving relationship with a woman. I was still waiting for my future wife, whom I had adored since my youth, visualizing her in my dreams. I still had much to look forward to. I just could not imagine that this was the moment I would have to give up my life. Of course, I was aware of the possibility, but I could not believe that it would actually happen. Everything within me revolted against the thought. It was simply impossible. Evidently the SA men had been ordered to beat me to death, following the latest custom throughout Germany. A few weeks earlier, another man, a communist, had been beaten on the street in Wülfrath by Stormtroopers. As a result of this attack, he suffered two ruptured kidneys and died soon afterward in prison. Another couple chose to commit suicide because they were marked for a similar fate.

Many of the men standing outside of the house had been among my "friends" just a few hours earlier. It must have been strange, even difficult, for some of them to change their attitude toward me so rapidly. Something must have had a profound and powerful effect on them to compel them to ignore the normal loyalties of an honored friendship. I longed to know what they were thinking and feeling. Some had just recently eaten dinner at my home or had ridden in my car. Theoretically, I suppose they could have felt indignant that I had "pretended" not to be a Jew, but could they really believe that this was the truth of the situation? The question haunted me: what was the source of this injustice? Although I did not picture myself as a Christ figure, I suddenly understood very deeply the meaning of the words Jesus spoke on the cross: "They know not what they do."

I knew that at any moment the SA men might break into the house and the beating would start. There was no way to escape. If I tried to run away like a scared rabbit, they would quickly track me down and, aroused by the chase, kill me with even greater passion. No, I would not run. If I was to die, I preferred to do so looking directly into the eyes of the Stormtroopers, remaining as calm as possible. I resolved to approach the situation with dignity, knowing that this attitude would impress at least some of the men. Even if they killed me, they would someday recall with shame their hasty, irrational, unjust act. I knew their hatred had been artificially incited against me. Among them surely were some good people who had never committed any violence before, but now felt forced to participate. There was no other alternative for them in this age of mob hysteria, when the word *justice* no longer had a place in the language or understanding of men. If they refused to take part, they would face the same situation that I now did. Their jobs, their families, and their lives would be in danger. On the other hand, a few of them might be deriving some sort of deranged pleasure or excitement from an opportunity like this. These would be the "born killers," the sadists, those who enjoyed torturing and killing. Certainly the operation of concentration camps and gas chambers would not have been possible without people with these kinds of tendencies.

People are sometimes like sheep, running in the direction they are pushed. They are not willing to criticize, or call attention to themselves by opposing the prevailing order, even when it is unjust. They prefer to avoid anything that might endanger themselves or their loved ones. They hesitate in the face of deep personal sacrifice or seemingly impossible effort. Although in times of peace they may be quite civilized, when a difficult or dangerous situation arises, not much can be expected of them. Under duress, they fail in their obligations to others. Because of complacency and fear, Hitler was able to advance in power and perpetrate his horror. But of course, listening to your conscience is extremely difficult in the face of such a powerful opposition. An unshakable commitment to justice, based on deeply instilled ideals, a belief in the goodness of mankind, and tremendous courage in the face of retribution are required. Such qualities are rare.

There in my landlord's living room, each minute seemed to pass more slowly than the one before it. As the tension mounted, it was as if the air were filled with an explosive about to be detonated. Only a single spark was needed. I felt sure the moment would come as soon as the attackers got a glimpse of me. For now, I was still out of their sight, inside the house of my unfortunate hosts. My landlord had worked hard all his life to build this house and acquire his household property. Now everything could be lost in the wake of a crazed Nazi militia. Of course, he and his wife were also frightened for me, especially my landlady, who had always shown admiration and affection for me.

Someone had to take responsibility for giving the order to attack the house. There were always those who were looking for self-advancement at any cost. The situation presented an opportunity for a leader to distinguish himself and gain recognition. No doubt these men felt self-assured and unhurried, knowing that I could not escape nor defend myself against forty men. Nobody had actually seen me, so there might have been some doubt as to whether I was actually inside. Perhaps this doubt deterred the SA from starting the attack right away.

Trying to remain calm, I began to picture myself and my surroundings as if from above, looking down. I wanted to stop time, to prevent the event about to happen, or to go back to a time when nothing so terrible could possibly happen. I kept thinking that this was all imagined. It was just a terrible nightmare from which I would soon awaken. But the reality of the situation was beginning to solidify in my mind. I was condemned to die in the ugliest way I could imagine—dragged out and beaten to death on the street by forty hysterical men who had been my friends and neighbors. Why? How could such a thing be possible? Did I commit a crime, or harm any one of these attackers standing just outside the door? That mob, hypnotized by Hitler's doctrine and Goebbels' propaganda, now believed that beating others to death was normal, justified, and a duty. It *must* happen. My fate seemed unavoidable, as if I were falling from a mountaintop under the force of gravity. I was like a housefly in a hurricane or a chunk of driftwood in a tidal wave. There was no way I could resist. The only honorable alternative I had was to die with courage and dignity.

Suddenly we heard voices close to the house, as if in discussion. Then came the sound of heavy boots on the steps leading to the front door. The bell rang once, then a second time. The moment had arrived. Any second the angry Stormtroopers would burst into the room and drag me out to the street, beat me, and probably kill me. There was no point in delaying them and arousing their anger further. They might break down the door and start needlessly destroying the house and its contents. I could visualize them breaking the furniture and throwing it out of the windows, just as I had seen in Düsseldorf during *Kristallnacht* and in my own home in

Krasnoyarsk when the communists threw us out. My landlord, having no choice, opened the door. Several heavily armed local policemen—not the Stormtroopers—stood there. They had kind and polite, yet sad expressions on their faces. One of them said, "Mr. Ko,[25] please come with us. We will give you protection and take you to the police station. You can sleep there safely tonight. Tomorrow the Gestapo will probably take you, but tonight, at least, you can sleep quietly."

They positioned me between them as we calmly walked out through the crowd of Stormtroopers, who stared at us in stunned silence. It took only a few seconds for the officers to escort me to their car. We drove off immediately. The Stormtroopers had not expected the local police to intervene, and they were uncertain how to react. Because of their confusion, I had somehow been saved, at least for the moment.

At the police station, I was given food and a clean bed. The policemen told me again that I could sleep without fear; nothing would happen to me during the night. Once in bed, I began to wonder why the policemen had arrived at such an opportune time. Someone must have called them and asked them (or ordered them) to save me. I was mystified. After pondering the matter for a long while, I could think of no one but Mr. Ludowigs. He was like a father to me. But such boldness would have been too dangerous, even for him, during this time of intense Nazi aggressiveness, and with war so close at hand. By opposing the Nazis, he could lose his position as president of the world's largest lime operation, and jeopardize the welfare of his wife and three children. In the end, I decided that he could not have been responsible for my rescue. I remained puzzled.

If Mr. Ludowigs had not been involved, then he would surely be greatly disappointed when he learned that I had fallen out of favor. I became concerned about what he might think. Would he be dismayed or angry at me? If so, I knew I would be crushed. His disappointment in me would hurt much more than a beating by Stormtroopers. If someone of such superior character could not believe in me, then I felt I would rather die. But, I told myself, surely Mr. Ludowigs, of all people, would stand by me. I have always been an optimist at heart. Even if an executioner were

---

[25] Because of my long last name which many had difficulty pronouncing, people, especially those who liked me, would often call me Mr. Ko.

to place a rope around my neck, I would expect the rope to break at the crucial moment.

So there in the Wülfrath jail I was safe, at least for the moment. I was still alive, and the logical thing for me to do was to figure out how to stay that way. Life, in spite of its dangers, was beautiful. I was still looking forward to an exciting and interesting future. I wanted to use my natural drive, creative power, and talents to achieve great things for myself, my future family, and mankind. I knew that I had many more obstacles to face. I had not actually been saved, except for this one night. However, I felt I would survive. I *must* survive.

The next morning, two Gestapo men arrived to escort me to a prison in Elberfeld, a few miles away. They looked like ordinary men except for their eyes. They were dull, cold, and lifeless, without any sign of feeling. If a man's eyes reflect his inner emotions, then these men could cut a man into pieces without pity or compassion. It did not seem so long ago, when I was in Russia, in Irkutsk, that I saw a similar coldness in the eyes of the men at the Cheka headquarters.

Because I had left Russia voluntarily in 1922, I had lost my citizenship, and as a refugee, I was carrying a Nansen passport, a special passport for refugees established by the League of Nations. On the way to Elberfeld, my Gestapo escorts took away my Nansen passport, saying that I would not need it any more. They asked me how much money I had been earning, perhaps to learn of my importance within the company. My salary at the time was comparatively high.

At the Elberfeld prison I was asked to empty my pockets and to give the officials my tie. I had spent the previous night in jail, but had felt more like a guest under protection, rather than under arrest. Now things were different—I really felt like a prisoner. Lunch was only soup and bread. The guard who brought my meal was very disdainful and uncouth. He tried to humiliate me by using arrogant, insulting language, and by being rude and antagonistic. As I sat meditating afterwards alone in my cell I again thought of Mr. Ludowigs. I wondered what he was thinking and whether he was disappointed in me. I also thought of Mrs. Wunderwald ("Mutti"), my former landlady in Freiberg. I thought about my current landlady and her courage. I felt that surely these friends were on my side.

These feelings gave me new strength and courage. I also thought of my friend Miss Scholz. Of course, she could not help me. Perhaps no one could, but it was reassuring to remember I still had friends in the world. I felt no intense fear. In my heart, I was convinced that nobody could harm me, because I had never deliberately hurt anyone in my life. Since some people still had faith in me, they would try to help me, I felt sure. It was a naive philosophy, but it helped sustain my optimism.

At 4 p.m. I was guided to a room where I was greeted by Mr. Ludowigs and Dr. Ohnesorge, the professor for whom I had worked for over two years in Freiberg. It was an overwhelming moment for me, one which I shall never forget. I almost fainted from stress and emotion. I could hardly see the two gentlemen in front of me because my eyes were filling with tears. I was deeply humbled as Mr. Ludowigs looked at me the way a father would look at his beloved son. A deep admiration, almost adoration, welled up within me. Throughout my entire life, among the thousands of people I met, from all walks of life, I never again met a man like President Ludowigs, who, in addition to being a recognized expert in his field, possessed tremendous courage and deep compassion for his fellow human beings.

I looked directly at Mr. Ludowigs, searching for some sign of acknowledgement that I had indeed endured a terrible injustice. Both men knew my life's story. They knew I had left Siberia at age sixteen with nothing and that I had worked as a coal miner under the worst of conditions to pay for my education. They knew too of my honesty, my ideals, and my fierce independence. They must have realized how hard it was for me to understand why, again, as in Soviet Russia, I should be labeled a parasite, an outcast, and an inferior, undesirable human being.

Mr. Ludowigs took my hand in his and pressed it strongly. I understood at once that he was on my side and that he had empathy for my situation. I knew he would try to help me. I was happy and deeply grateful, and I admired him more than ever. I began to feel more hopeful, but at the same time I found it necessary to press my lips together tightly to hold back my tears—tears of appreciation for this man who was placing himself and his family in jeopardy for the sake of a foreigner. I knew Mr. Ludowigs was gambling with his position because of me, and I wondered if I were worthy of such a sacrifice. It was now clear to me that Mr. Ludowigs had indeed been behind my rescue the evening before. Dr. Ohnesorge, my former professor, had been in Wülfrath by coincidence, and Mr. Ludowigs had asked him to come along. Dr. Ohnesorge also gave me his hand, but I noticed that it was trembling. No wonder. How dangerous it was for both of these men to be associating with me.

Mr. Ludowigs then stepped out and spoke with the clerk at the front desk, a big, strapping fellow. Then he and Mr. Ohnesorge left the prison. Shortly thereafter, the clerk called me out and started asking me questions. I soon realized that he was neither a member of the Gestapo, nor a Nazi, and that he seemed to be commiserating with me, probably because of some explanation given to him by Mr. Ludowigs. The Gestapo agent who had been sitting there earlier was now absent.

The clerk asked me, "If you could leave Elberfeld, where would you go?"

"Back to Wülfrath," I replied.

"Are you not afraid to return there?"

"No, I would hope the tension is over by now," I answered naively.

Then he said sternly, "No, you cannot go back there. It would put you and your close associates, such as your landlords, for example, in great danger. You must try to flee from Germany, get to France, or Switzerland, or to some other country."

I muttered, "I wouldn't know how to do that. None of those countries will grant me a visa. I have no relatives or close friends abroad that could help me. I do not belong to a church or any kind of international organization. If I try to flee, I could be caught at the border and be sent to prison."

"It is quite possible that could happen," he replied, "but there is no alternative." He suggested I try to reach Cologne and see what help might be found for me there. Then the Gestapo agent returned to the room, and the conversation was over. The clerk offered no further advice, but with curt efficiency he returned my Nansen passport, and released me from prison. He had given me some valuable advice, but I did not know yet how I was going to implement it.

Before departing for Cologne, as the clerk had advised, I first went to bid farewell to Paul Flachsenberg, a friend who lived in Elberfeld and who had a position in the company similar to mine. We both were in charge of special assignments and had been assistants to President Ludowigs.

126

Flachsenberg had married a few years earlier and his wife had just borne their first child. I was kindly received by him and his wife, in spite of my now diminished status. After spending a few hours in their apartment, I left for Cologne, where I rented a room in a hotel near the railway station, in sight of the great Cologne cathedral, world famous for its lofty spires.

There the optimist in me revived. Gazing up at the breathtaking architecture, I thought that if only I could succeed in escaping from Germany, I might finally realize my long-held dream of going to the United States and starting a new life there. That country was famous throughout the world for its open-armed welcome to those seeking freedom. I now had a renewed dream and a goal for which to fight. I had always been ready to accept a challenge when the objective was genuine and worthy. Thoughts of possible future American citizenship made me feel joyful. My life seemed worth living again, despite the desperate days I knew lay ahead.

Nazis march in Wülfrath, Germany

PAUL FLACHSENBERG

Chapter 7

ESCAPE

And as he, who with laboring breath has
escaped from the deep to the shore,
Turns to the perilous waters and gazes.

—Dante, *Inferno*

My only hope now was to flee to another country. Even though the Gestapo had released me, they still knew my name and my whereabouts, and might at any time arrest me again or send me to a concentration camp. Attempting to find a way out, I contacted an old school colleague now living in Paris. I hoped he might be able to obtain permission for me to enter France legally. When I telephoned him, I was told he had left Paris on an extended trip, and could not be reached. Then I remembered that before the First World War my parents had financially supported one of our relatives in Switzerland so that she could attend medical school. She and her husband were now both physicians. I hoped they might help me find a way to leave Germany.

I traveled to Oberstdorf, Bavaria to visit Mrs. Wunderwald (Mutti), my landlady during my student days in Freiberg. Since my departure, she had retired and moved to Oberstdorf. Shocked to learn what had happened to me, she became frightened because she realized that it would be difficult for her to hide me in the small village where she lived. Some of her neighbors already knew me from previous visits, and there was a chance someone would find out I was "undesirable." Mutti made a genuine effort to overcome her fears for my sake, and tried to help me as much as she could. At my request, Mutti traveled to Switzerland, located my relative, and talked to her. As a result of Mutti's visit, I learned that the couple, particularly the husband, was unwilling to do anything for me, possibly because of my becoming a financial burden to them. This was a bitter disappointment in light of my family's earlier generosity, especially considering that in all likelihood I would have been able to find work easily and repay them quickly. In any case, I lost hope of entering Switzerland legally.

After considering the situation, Mutti and I came up with a more creative plan for my escape across the Swiss border. We studied maps carefully and selected a remote area where I would attempt to cross over the mountains on skis. We decided the area near Bludenz, Austria would be best. I bought furs to attach to the undersides of my skis for traction on the steep slopes. Mutti sewed white coveralls for me out of her bed sheets, so that I would not be seen against the snow by border patrols. The evening before my departure we played a piano duet together, the third movement of Beethoven's Third Symphony (*Allegretto*) arranged for piano four-hands. I knew Mutti was deeply concerned about my future, and our emotional interpretation of the music revealed our mutual feelings. I shall never forget that evening and our "concert" together.

The next day I boarded a train that passed through Bregenz to Bludenz, Austria. Upon my arrival in the early afternoon, I made a call from the post-telegraph office to Paris, a last attempt to contact my former classmate. I was told that if I called again at 6 p.m. he would be there. I returned to the post office at the appointed time and placed a second call to him. This time I was able to speak with him. He immediately secured from me all the necessary data for a French visa application, which he volunteered to fill out and submit for me. However, as I left the telephone booth, I saw two men with two huge German shepherd dogs approaching me. I knew at once that they were Gestapo agents. I had been foolish to make the second call from the same telephone and naive to call Paris from the Swiss border so shortly before the war. Either my calls had been monitored, or I had been spotted by someone who thought I looked suspicious. The Gestapo agents placed me under arrest and took me to the local prison.[26]

---

[26] In 1968 while visiting Bludenz with my wife, I was able to show her the prison where I had spent ten days.

Naturally, I was disappointed that my attempt to escape to Switzerland had failed and that I was now sitting in prison once more. In retrospect, however, I realized that with my middling skiing ability, it is quite likely that I would not have survived crossing the steep, rugged mountains without a guide. It may have been dumb luck that I had been arrested and thus prevented from attempting such a treacherous escape. The seemingly unfortunate event had probably saved my life.

In prison I was put in a cell by myself. Fatigued from the emotional stress of the day's events, I quickly fell into a deep sleep. The next morning, the warden of the prison questioned me. He asked me why I had come to Austria to cross the Swiss border, why had I not tried to cross from Germany? I responded that I *was* in Germany, noting that by this time Austria had been annexed by Hitler. At this, the warden became outraged and exploded with furious patriotic fervor, "Bludenz was, is, and will always remain Austrian!"

I thought if Hitler could have heard this, and the manner in which it was spoken, the Gestapo would certainly have put the warden into prison with me. The same thought must have occurred to the warden, because from that moment he became very friendly towards me. His wife even cooked me delicious meals during my stay. I particularly enjoyed her wonderful Wienerschnitzel. I paid a small fee for these special menu privileges, which was not a problem since I had taken along a considerable amount of cash for my journey. The warden also lent me some books, including *Quo Vadis* by Henryk Sienkiewicz. Reading this book, I developed a great admiration for Spartacus, who struggled to liberate the ancient Roman gladiators, and to win rights for the common people of his day.

About forty other men were being held in the same prison. They seemed happy to have me there, especially since I often bought them cigarettes. Each day we were permitted to walk about the prison courtyard, and there I came to know all the prisoners, most of whom were young hoodlums. Many were serving sentences for assaulting and raping young girls. One day the warden confided to me that if the Gestapo ever released me, he would help me cross the Swiss border. I began to hope again.

After ten days in prison, I was finally released by the Gestapo. They instructed me to take a train back to Cologne, and to report to the Gestapo office there. I was expected, it seemed. I was afraid at this point to press the warden to help me cross the Swiss border, as he had promised. I did not fully trust him, or anyone else for that matter. Should he betray me, I would easily be caught. So, I found myself en route to Cologne. It was April, 1939.

In Cologne, I went to the Gestapo headquarters, as ordered. The building reminded me of the Cheka headquarters I had seen in Irkutsk, Siberia. As I entered, the heavy front door closed and locked automatically behind me. I was trapped and could not leave without explicit permission. Someone led me to the office of a young Gestapo officer, who questioned me. In the process I learned that he knew President Ludowigs. I felt certain that a recommendation from Ludowigs would help me a great deal. I suspect the young officer liked my appearance. No doubt the German mannerisms I had picked up during my many years in Germany made a good impression on him.

Building on that, I made every effort to appear strong, confident, and courageous.

During the next six months in Cologne I was obliged to report to the young Gestapo officer twice a week. During these visits I saw other people who were also being oppressed by the Gestapo. They looked completely crushed, with deep, dark shadows under their eyes and fearful, hopeless looks on their faces. During those six months, I spent almost all the money I had saved in the six years I had worked in Wülfrath. Living in hotels was expensive. I also spent a surprising amount of money on telegrams and mailing letters to foreign countries in search of assistance. I wrote to most of my former school friends, but only one of them, Mr. Grassmück, responded. He, however, was not in a position to help me.

Time passed. The imminence of war became more and more evident. I visited the English consulate in Cologne and told the agent I wanted to volunteer for service in the British army. He asked whether I could fly a plane. When I answered no, he was no longer interested in me. Then I went to the French consulate and told them I would like to volunteer for the French Foreign Legion. They told me I would have to apply from outside of Germany to be accepted.

The situation was becoming increasingly dangerous for me. As soon as the war started, I would almost certainly be interned. I was still in contact with President Ludowigs. Mr. Ludowigs tried to help me by visiting relief organizations in Belgium. Although none of them could offer me any help directly, one organization gave him the address of a Mr. Daniloff, who was originally from my hometown of Krasnoyarsk, and who now held an important industrial position in Belgium. Mr. Ludowigs visited Mr. Daniloff and sought his assistance, but without success.

Being in Cologne for so long with nothing to do, I would often get bored. So occasionally I would visit my former landlord and landlady in Wülfrath. It was my practice to take the train to Vohwinkel late in the evening, and then hire a taxi from the station, arriving in the vicinity of their home well after midnight. I walked the last mile alone. To avoid being spotted by the townspeople, many of whom knew me well, I raised the collar of my overcoat, wore dark glasses, and changed my gait. The next morning, I could look through the window and see the familiar faces of former acquaintances as they walked by. I was told that people in Wülfrath believed I had been able to escape Germany and was living somewhere abroad. On one of these late evenings, I was riding to Wülfrath in a taxi as usual, when the driver suddenly switched on the overhead light inside the cab, such that people outside could see me. I asked him why he had turned the light on, and he answered, "No reason." I disliked his answer and suspected he knew who I was. I became quite uncomfortable, but nothing happened. During another visit, I became seriously ill and started running a high fever. My hosts could not call a physician, and they were afraid I was going to die there, in their home. I could hear the couple making plans to bury me in their courtyard if necessary. They were very relieved when I recovered, as, of course, was I.

At the end of August, I went to Dresden to visit my friend, Annaliese Scholz. We spent the evening of August 31st in the park from where we could hear the ominous roar of tanks and heavy equipment rolling along the street. We did not know that what we were hearing at that moment was the movement of the German army toward the front. The war would begin in Poland the next day. My future was certainly hanging by a thread, and I was not sure if or when I would see Annaliese again.

The next day, September 1st, the war started. Now I was definitely trapped in Germany. Tension continued to grow. People were full of fear and hatred, obsessed with the threat of enemies both abroad and within

Germany. Hotels, cinemas, theaters, and stores prominently displayed placards reading "Der Eingang für Hunde und Juden ist strengsten verboten" (Entry for dogs and Jews is strictly forbidden). From time to time, Stormtroopers marched through the streets shouting, "Deutschland erwache, Jude verrecke!" (Germany awake, kill the Jews!) It was tragic that life in Germany, the birthplace of great men like Bach, Beethoven, and Goethe, had come to this.

I now had less than $200, only enough to last me two more months. It seemed as if only a miracle could save me. One day President Ludowigs came to Cologne and invited me and his friend, Mr. Peltzer, to dinner. Again Mr. Ludowigs was putting himself in jeopardy for my sake. Mr. Peltzer was Jewish,[27] although his wife was "Aryan." He had lived in Cologne for many years and knew the city intimately. Mr. Ludowigs asked him directly, right in the restaurant, to help me find a way to leave Germany. Again I was amazed by Ludowigs' courage, to be seen with two undesirables, at a popular restaurant in a locale where many people knew him. A real flesh-and-blood hero in my eyes, he persisted in trying to help me, despite the danger to himself and to his family.

Shortly after this meeting with Mr. Ludowigs, I visited his wife. When she saw me, she said, "Poor boy," with deep sadness in her eyes. Her sincere expression of compassion lingered long in my memory. I remain deeply grateful to her. Mrs. Ludowigs was Belgian. Mr. Ludowigs first made her acquaintance during the First World War while serving as a German army officer with the occupation forces in Belgium. Shortly after the war, he married her, in spite of the extreme disapproval of both of their families. For centuries, France and Belgium had been bitter enemies of Germany. Mr. Ludowigs, a truly great man, was above such prejudices.

To my surprise, Mr. Peltzer agreed to help me. I visited him the next day at his office, where he gave me the address of a boarding house operated by a Jewish family. He told me these people would know how to secure a guide for me who would lead me across the Belgian border illegally. The guide would charge me 400 marks ($100). However, he instructed me not to let the family know I was looking for a guide immediately. I should first rent a room in their house for a few weeks, allowing the family to

---

[27] Mr. Peltzer was the president of a large company, a position which he eventually lost. He later committed suicide.

gain confidence in my sincerity and trustworthiness before revealing my true objective.

The Jewish family who ran the boarding house consisted of a couple and their eighteen-year-old daughter. They were afraid to go out shopping because they faced ridicule from people who recognized them as Jews, so they asked me to go shopping for them, which I did. They were Germans, and as such, felt that Germany was their home. Despite the hardships, they were reluctant to tear up roots and start a new life elsewhere.

It soon became apparent that the daughter was intrigued by me. She was interested in art, painting, and sculpture, and subscribed to arts magazines which contained what I considered to be provocative, sexually explicit pictures. I pitied her loneliness and, indeed, the whole family's plight. I felt they were already doomed, the way the Nazi anti-Jewish program was evolving. Yet I could not bring myself to become sexually involved with this willing girl.

The family probably suspected why I was residing in their boarding house. After a few weeks, I told them what I wanted. At first, they did nothing. Toward the end of September, they told me that they would secure a guide for me who would take me to Belgium.

A few days later, a short fellow, a Dutchman, came to the house to talk with me. During his visit he gave me explicit instructions for our journey together. He told me he would be bringing along an eight-year-old girl. I should only follow them, but never approach them. We would first go to Aachen, a city located near the border of Belgium and Holland. As people were leaving the train and passing through the city gate, I would see a few policemen and Gestapo guards posted at the gate. Anyone who appeared suspicious might be asked for identification papers. He told me that if they quizzed me, I should say I was a native of Aachen returning home.

As it turned out, this is exactly what happened. When I got close to the gate, one of the inspectors asked me, "Why are you coming to Aachen?"

With a strong, surprised voice I responded, "Why, I am from Aachen! I am going home."

Masses of people were standing in line trying to pass through the gate, so he let me go without any further questioning. The trick had worked.

After leaving the train station, I followed my guide and the little girl to a streetcar. They sat at the opposite end of the car. The autumn evening was turning to night and it was already completely dark outside. Since the beginning of the war, all windows in towns and cities had to be covered with black paper, so that the light could not be seen at night by Allied planes. We traveled northwest toward the Dutch border for about twenty-five minutes. Then the streetcar stopped at a small village, and we got off. Many German soldiers were patrolling the streets, so we had to be very discreet. When we managed to be alone for a moment, the guide asked me for the 400 marks. He took the money and went into a house, where he probably hid the money. I now had only three marks, about 75 cents, left in my pocket—the last of my funds. It was just as well. It would have been dangerous for me to carry a lot of money. If I were caught crossing the border with a lot of cash, the Gestapo would arrest me for taking German money abroad illegally, a very serious offense. I'd be in prison again in no time.

After a few minutes, which seemed like hours, my guide returned. He instructed me to follow him at a distance of about eighty feet. Since it was dark, it would have been difficult to follow at any greater distance without losing him. Soon we were out of the village and following a footpath up a hill. Far away I could see a bright reflection in the sky. This was Holland, which had not yet become involved in the war and was not observing a blackout. To get to Holland, we had yet to cross the notorious Siegfried Line, an extended border fortification thickly occupied by German soldiers.

In the darkness we were able to pass undetected through several rows of concrete tank traps. Soon we came to a thirty-foot high railway embankment. The only way to get to the other side was through a narrow tunnel, which my guide entered with the little girl tagging along beside him. The tunnel was so dark I could no longer see them. When I emerged from the tunnel, I continued to walk straight ahead, not realizing he and the girl had turned sharply to the right. After a few steps, I suddenly came face to face with a German soldier. He had two rifles in his arms, and several grenades hanging from his belt. I had almost bumped into him, it was so dark. Aware that I had made a mistake, I instinctively made a quick turn to the right and tried to walk away. But the soldier, probably also surprised to see me, shouted at me to halt. I kept on walking, but he shouted again and turned on his flashlight, pointing its large, bright beam at me. Afraid that he might shoot, I turned around and came back toward him. I saw that he was standing in front of a concrete bunker. I tried hard to make my voice as calm as possible and asked, in my most perfect German, what was the matter and what did he want. He asked me for my identification papers. I knew now that only a calm attitude could save me.

I was very well dressed. With the money I had earned in Wülfrath, I had bought the most expensive clothes I could find in the famous shopping district (*Königsallee*) of Düsseldorf. These well-tailored, expensive clothes and my calm attitude saved me on this occasion. The soldier looked at my passport, finding it filled with many visas from Holland, Belgium, France, Sweden, Norway, and other countries I had visited on business trips. My passport also contained a German exit and reentry visa. Of course, because of the war, none of these visas were valid any longer. If the Gestapo or the police had looked at my passport, they would have realized immediately that all of my visas were out of date, and they would have arrested me. However, this soldier had no such sophistication, and so he assumed that everything was accurate and correct. He looked at me, keeping his flashlight a few inches from my face, trying to read from my expression whether I might be lying. I continued to look very dignified and respectable. He finally permitted me to go my way. He may have thought I was some kind of official inspector, and that I might report his behavior to higher authorities.

I soon caught up with my guide and the little girl; they had stopped to rest. He was very much surprised to see me, having assumed that I had been caught and arrested. Again I was facing a most dangerous situation. Anything might happen. But my innate optimism, my good health, my experience with dangerous explosives, and my work as a coal miner under stressful conditions helped me keep my nerves under control and my facial expression calm. It was a time for bravery and optimistic confidence. These were my only defenses against failure.

We started to move again, my guide with the little girl in front, and I behind. After walking for a few minutes, the guide stopped and called quietly for me to come closer.

In a hurried whisper he said, "About a hundred yards ahead of us is a street, which is the border between Germany and Holland. The lighted houses on the far side are in Holland, and those on this side, the German side, are blacked out. The path we are following goes diagonally towards this street. Between the diagonal path and the borderline street there are several houses with lots that abut the border street. Each lot is surrounded by a fence. Enter the lot of the white house and move through the yard towards the border and hide behind the fence. The fence is made of three-foot wide, four-foot high brick pillars spaced ten feet apart, with wooden slats running between them. Hide behind one of the pillars and wait until I get across the border. The street is heavily guarded by Germans—police and soldiers—who patrol on foot, bicycle, and horseback. Sometimes they have dogs too. I'll watch for the best moment for you to cross. Watch for me to light a cigarette. When you see the flame from my match, jump over the fence and run as fast you can across the street. I'll be waiting for you there."

When I found the designated house and entered the yard, I became aware of other dangers. Someone from the house might come outside and see me. Or they might have a dog and it might start barking at me, calling attention to my position. I thought this risk too great, but I had to go through with it now. I made my way to the backyard fence and peered through the slats at the street. When I reached a pillar I crouched on my knees and hid behind it, tense with excitement, and watched for my guide's signal. At regular intervals I heard the stomp of heavy boots approaching my precarious sanctuary, passing within six feet of me. After many minutes, which seemed like a lifetime, I saw the flame of a match across the street. I vaulted over the fence easily, and in a few seconds I was in Holland. It was October 2, 1939, one month after the start of the Second World War.

My guide took me quickly into one of the houses along the Dutch side of the street. A wonderful feeling came over me—I was safe. No longer in Germany, I was in a country on the Allied side. Now no one could threaten me, arrest me, put me in a concentration camp, or beat me to death. I was a free man again. Relieved and happy, I began to relax. The joy I experienced was similar to when I left Russia and entered Manchuria. Only a man freed from oppression can know what this is like.

My guide brought in some food from the kitchen and offered it to me and the little girl. We were all hungry. After supper I lay down on the sofa in front of the window, overlooking the street where the Gestapo, soldiers, and police were still circulating. But now I watched without fear. I began to revel in my cherished dreams. I would immigrate to the United States, a goal I had set for myself seventeen years earlier when I left Siberia. Soon I was in a deep sleep. Hitler could do nothing more to harm me. Or so I thought.

Boris standing in front of the tunnel to Holland in later years

Chapter 8

MORE LIVES THAN ONE

For he who lives more lives than one,
More deaths than one must die.

—Oscar Wilde, *Ballad of Reading Gaol*

The street dividing Germany and Holland was quite narrow, my haven a mere ten yards from the German border. Peeping cautiously from the window, I could see the Gestapo and German police patrolling up and down the street. Each team seemed to cover about a hundred yards. I could also see the German soldiers and the fortifications along the nearby Siegfried Line.

Awaking after my first night outside of Germany, I felt like a child who knows no fear, who naively feels all is well, and that he is completely safe. In fact, I was far from safe. I had entered Holland illegally, and if caught, I would certainly be forced to return to Germany. I had very little money. But that did not bother me at all. I had been penniless before and had always managed to find a way to survive. I felt certain I could do so again.

Shortly after breakfast my guide came in and said, "You know," he began, "fewer people came across the border last night than we expected. This means that each of you will have to pay more, if you want to get to Belgium."

"I understand your situation," I responded, "but, unfortunately, I really do not have any more money."

"Maybe someone, your friends or relatives somewhere in the world, would pay for you?" he asked.

"I have no relatives. There is no one who will pay my way." I told him truthfully.

My guide approached me several more times, keeping me in that room for three days, hoping I would crack under the pressure and come forward with additional funds. During those three days the Germans built a fence seven feet in height along the entire street. It was now no longer possible to cross the border here. I had been one of the last to do so.

Finally, my guide gave up trying to coax more money from me. He might have held me there even longer, but keeping me in this house, so close to the German border, was dangerous for him too. On the evening of October 6th, he came to me and said, "We shall travel now by bicycle to the other side of town and you will stay overnight there. This move will be risky because this town is so small, and it is crawling with police. Anyone might realize that you are a stranger. But it is dark now, so I hope you will not be noticed."

We crossed the town without incident. Soon I was in another house, where my guide offered me some food and, to my surprise, locked me in a room. He told me that we would start moving again the next day, in the late afternoon.

Late the following afternoon, another man arrived at the house. He identified himself as my new guide, and he told me that we would now mount our bicycles and travel to another, unspecified location. I was to follow him at a distance of forty yards. We made our way through the outskirts of the village and were soon pedaling through the countryside. In the quickly fading light, I caught sight of the modern-looking plant of a coal mine. It appeared to have the most up-to-date equipment available at the time.

Our course turned northward, as we followed a road running parallel to the nearby Belgian border. Every so often we passed concrete bunkers guarded by soldiers. Patrols of six to twelve soldiers would march along the road near these bunkers. Every few miles we encountered road blocks: four-foot-high stone walls with a specially constructed narrow passageway guarded by a Dutch soldier. Travelers had to pass through one by one. The guard could stop anyone he deemed suspicious. We passed through a number of these roadblocks and had ridden by several patrols of soldiers.

All the while, I continued to follow my guide at the specified distance. Suddenly, my guide was halted by one of the patrols. Quickly I turned left into the front yard of one of the farmhouses along the road. I hoped I hadn't been noticed. I waited out of sight for about five minutes. When I returned to the road, the soldiers had disappeared, and so had my guide. I was alone, just a few miles from the Belgian border, with only the Dutch bicycle I was riding.

Looking at the bicycle more carefully, I noticed for the first time that the rear reflector was missing. That meant I was in violation of safety regulations. This added to my worries. Perhaps I would be stopped by the police in the darkness on account of this minor transgression. I also knew that if I were caught within fifteen miles of the German border, I would be sent directly back into the hands of the German police. I hopped on the bicycle and began to pedal as fast as I could away from the German border. I traveled for several hours, passing a number of check points. Each time, as I made my way through the narrow passageway, the guard would check me over. It was clear that each guard was impressed by the handsome, expensive overcoat I was wearing. They may have been reluctant to detain such a distinguished looking person. I had been saved before by my fine clothes, and would be again on several occasions. In European society, good clothes, a neat appearance, and a stately bearing were traits to be respected.

After several hours I began to see the lights of Maastricht, a Dutch city on the Belgian border, emerging over the horizon. As if from nowhere, a tall policeman riding a bicycle appeared and stopped me. At his request, I handed over my passport filled with invalid visas. He asked me where I was going. I told him that I planned to travel to Maastricht and would then go westward into Belgium. I tried to remain completely calm and retain my dignified bearing. The situation was dangerous, and my nerves seemed less steady than I would have liked. Perhaps the hours of physical and emotional strain were taking their toll. The policeman, however, let me continue on my way.

I arrived in Maastricht late in the evening. This city, too, was full of police looking for spies, suspects, and members of the Fifth Column.[28] I was lost and had no idea where to go. As I had very little money and no

---

[28] A clandestine group or faction of subversive agents who attempt to undermine a nation's solidarity.

valid papers, I could not go to a hotel. It was also dangerous for me to stay on the street, or go to the railway station, where suspicious persons were constantly detained and searched by police and security officers. Finally, I thought of a plan.

I went to the first telephone booth I could find. Reading through the names in the phone book, I selected a family whose name seemed Jewish, and I made note of their address. My hope was that if I contacted people who were intimately aware of the great injustice of the times, I might have a chance of receiving some assistance. I called on this family at around 10 p.m. and told them I had just escaped from Germany, had lost my guide, and was penniless. I asked if they could help me reach Amsterdam. At first, they seemed shocked and frightened to see me, a stranger, at their door. In the end, however, their sympathy overcame their fear and they decided to help, like the Good Samaritan of the Bible.

The family knew of a rooming house where I might spend the night safely. However, they warned that I must be gone before 5 a.m., as police inspections routinely took place there during the day. They gave me enough money to pay for a night's lodging and to purchase a train ticket to Amsterdam. I thanked them as best I could, with words surely inadequate considering the risk they were taking on my account. One of the adult men of the family escorted me to the rooming house.

The next morning, I boarded the train, taking my bicycle with me. In a few hours I arrived in Amsterdam. Searching through the Amsterdam phone book, I found the address of a local welfare organization, and I rode my bicycle there. It was October 8th, a Sunday, so the office was closed. While trying the door, I caught sight of a janitor and waved to him.

Upon learning of my need for shelter, the janitor said, "Across the street you will find a hotel. You needn't be afraid to stay there. Nothing will happen to you. Come back here tomorrow and someone will be able to help you."

Following his advice, I spent the night at the hotel across the street. In the morning, after washing, shaving, and dressing, I opened the door, only to see two strong, imposing policemen standing in my doorway. They quickly discovered that my passport was out of date and that I had no right to be in Holland. Without delay they escorted me to the local police headquarters.

I was locked in a large room with various other specimens of humanity, some truly beyond imagination. Among them were some who, like me, had escaped from Germany. But there were also thieves, maniacs, and spies—excellent raw material for any journalist, novelist, or psychologist. Trying to maintain a low profile, I began to observe this unusual collection of people, curious and eager to discern their true natures. The variety of unsavory characters and their ignoble interactions fascinated me, although in some ways the spectacle was horrifying. I felt lucky that I had had a more fortunate heritage and the strength of character to resist taking the low road.

The police officers treated me well, and I received excellent meals. When an officer finally interrogated me, I told him that I wanted to go to Belgium, Brussels being my ultimate destination. The next day I was told that I would be taken by police escort to a point along the Belgian border where it would be easy for me to cross. The police official warned me that if I failed to cross the border, I would be taken directly back to Germany.

Two days later, the clerk at the police station issued me enough cash to pay for my journey to Brussels. Accompanied by two officers dressed in civilian clothes, I traveled first by train and then by streetcar. During our trip, a Dutchman sitting in front of me looked at me suspiciously several times, and, taking me for a German because of my clothes and manner of speech, finally said, "You see that bridge through the window? That bridge was not built by Germans. Neither the parents nor the grandparents of that engineer were German!" He wanted to challenge me by refuting Hitler's theory that only Germans could create remarkable structures. I remained silent.

Near the border we got off the streetcar. About fifty yards ahead of us I could see another streetcar standing on the Belgian side of the border which I would need to board to continue my trip via Antwerp to Brussels. Flanked by the two policemen, I began to walk toward the border. At the second intersection, we turned left and then made an immediate right onto a narrow street. Here one of the policemen instructed to me to continue along this street until I reached the border, which would be marked by a barbed wire fence. I obeyed, and when I came to the fence, which was three feet in height, I jumped over it and was in Belgium.

I continued to walk along the narrow street for about 200 yards more, at which point I entered a large plaza in front of a church. There I saw many soldiers busily digging trenches. I thought this to be a very old-fashioned means of fortification, doubting that it would be of much use in the face of a German invasion. Most of the people in the plaza were watching the soldiers dig the trenches. The diversion helped me cross unnoticed to the opposite side of the plaza, where I boarded the streetcar bound for Antwerp.

A few minutes later the streetcar began to move. After traveling about a hundred yards or so, it stopped again. A police officer came through the car asking for identification papers. Again I submitted my Nansen passport filled with various foreign visas. The officer examined my passport for such a long time that I became concerned that he might realize it was invalid. Trying to remain calm, I assumed an air of impatience. Finally, he returned my papers without saying a word. Soon the streetcar continued on its way. Before arriving in Antwerp I was required to show my passport once more. Once again the inspector did not realize that it was obsolete. In Antwerp I boarded a train for Brussels.

Upon arriving in Brussels, I immediately looked up Mr. Daniloff, whose address I had obtained from Mr. Ludowigs before my departure from Germany. Ludowigs had visited Daniloff personally earlier in the year and had told him my story. Daniloff was also a native of Krasnoyarsk, and although he had never met me before, he had known my parents. Like my father, Daniloff had been one of the richest men in Siberia, a leader in the glass industry. He and his partner, Mr. Furko, had patented a process for making large glass sheets. Daniloff had immigrated to Belgium years earlier, where he had started as a laborer and worked his way up to the highest levels within the Belgian glass industry. He had become the president of a concern of about twelve plants that manufactured renowned, top-quality Belgian glass. In 1938, about a year before I met him, he had had a serious car accident. Already over sixty-five, he decided to retire after the accident, particularly as many of his colleagues were pressuring him to do so.

Daniloff greeted me warmly. He was a strong, handsome man, over six feet tall. He and his young, gracious wife lived in a beautiful apartment. They owned an exquisite collection of Russian porcelain, which was elegantly displayed throughout their home. I stayed for several hours. After supper I hoped Daniloff might invite me to spend the night. Since we were countrymen, I thought perhaps he would favor me with the generous hospitality for which Siberians were known.

When it became quite late he said, "I assume you have no money." I replied that my briefcase contained only a single change of clothes and a little over a dollar.

He continued, "Then I will give you 200 Belgian francs, and more if you need it. But I cannot allow you to spend the night in my home. I knew your father, but I hardly know you at all. I met you for the first time in my life just this evening. You must understand that with the war situation the way it is, and the presence of the Fifth Column, I cannot take unwise chances. Since you have come to this country illegally, you, of course, cannot go to a hotel. I would suggest you find a street girl and spend the night in her room."

I was shocked by this proposal. I considered it most undignified to solicit street girls. But I did not want to be arrested again. It was too dangerous to stay on the streets or at the railway station overnight. I could not take the chance of being caught and sent back to Germany, or of being put into a Belgian refugee camp. I might ultimately fall into the hands of the Germans again, should the Germans attack and occupy Belgium. In the end, I reluctantly agreed that Mr. Daniloff's suggestion was the best solution. Survival was my foremost objective. Choices were limited, and pride seemed a vain thing indeed under such desperate circumstances.

I found a street girl easily and paid her for the privilege of sleeping (and *only* sleeping) in her room. The next day I went to the Russian Welfare Organization and asked for assistance. I was given tickets for free lunches at a local Russian restaurant and was advised to rent a room. They reassured me that as long as I paid my rent, nothing would happen to me. Of course, the police would be watching, but their suspicions would not be aroused as long as I moved about normally.

I rented a room from a lady who owned a three-level apartment. She had two children, a son about sixteen years of age, and a daughter about twelve. Both children were illegitimate and had different fathers, as I later learned. The kitchen and living room were on the first floor. On the second floor were my bedroom and the bedroom of a nurse, another tenant. The bedrooms of the landlady and her children were on the third floor. Although the landlady was polite, there seemed to be an iron curtain between us. Strangers were universally distrusted because of a pervasive fear of foreign spies and the Fifth Column. No one was above suspicion.

The first evening at dinner I was introduced to my new neighbor, the nurse. She was an attractive twenty-two-year-old woman, but we hardly spoke during the meal. When I went to my room that evening, I was surprised to find her in my bed. For years I had been reluctant to become sexually involved with girls and had been considered a "moral athlete" by my friends. However, now, at age thirty-four, having escaped death's grasp several times in the recent past, and fully expecting more danger in the immediate future, I found myself thinking in more liberal and flexible terms. I could be killed at any moment, and yet, I had not enjoyed any kind of sex life. I decided to take this opportunity to discover love's secrets, which until that point had existed mainly in my imagination. My ideals and my dream girl seemed so distant, so remote, as if forever beyond reach. The times seemed to be trampling them to dust. I could not be certain whether my dreams would ever become reality. Since the girl was a nurse, I assumed she would take precautions to avoid pregnancy. She seemed well experienced in love making; I was clearly not her first lover. As a naive beginner, I found I was in good hands. She understood how to excite a man and to give that special feeling of fulfillment that only sex can bring to a human being.

Every day I would go to the Russian restaurant, where a free lunch was served to Russian immigrants, most of whom were refugee aristocrats who had escaped during the Russian Revolution. Although they were now shabbily dressed and poorly groomed, they had managed to retain their dignity and pride over the years. Many had been officers in the White Army, and they continued to address each other formally as "Mr. General" or "Mr. Colonel." In exile, as the years passed, they promoted themselves in military rank, taking into account their "years of service." It was a pitiful and rather ridiculous sight to see these poor people with their proud, solemn faces, taking the utmost care to maintain the formal comportment expected of the highest ranking officers in Czarist Russia. Now they were forgotten outcasts, rejected by the Belgian upper class, even though they had been members of the aristocracy in their homeland.

One of the aristocratic refugees I met at the restaurant exemplified my image of an irrationally superstitious Russian. He told me of a summer back in Russia when the wheat fields near his town were being attacked in a strange manner. Large fields of standing wheat were being mown down waist high. Every few days, a different farm would fall victim to this inexplicable vandalism, and no one could figure out any explanation for it. It was the cause of considerable concern, not only because it was an eerie phenomenon, but because it threatened the crop and the prosperity of the region. One night my acquaintance and a few other men of the town decided they would attempt to unravel the mystery. They had chosen a night when the moon was full to stand vigil among the crops and await the unknown wheat-cutting force. What they saw—and they reportedly all saw the same thing—was incredible: a young woman, completely naked, flew over the fields with a scythe, and mowed down acre after acre of wheat, as she swooped down repeatedly over the land. Local sages reasoned this was the restless spirit of a young village woman who had died the year before under mysterious circumstances. Of course, I did not believe his story, or the vision he claimed to have seen. However, I believed that *he* believed it. The power of Russian superstition is not to be underestimated.

I knew that I was being followed by police each time I left my residence, but they never bothered me. Mr. Daniloff continued to lend me money, which I desperately needed to pay my rent and to buy food. The free lunch I received at the Russian restaurant was my main meal. For supper I usually ate bacon and eggs, which were fairly inexpensive.

During my stay in Brussels, I tried to apply for an immigration visa to the United States, but securing one turned out to be impossible. As a Russian, I had to contend with a strict quota—there was suspicion of Russians in the United States too—and I would be on the waiting list for at least six years. Also, I was required to have a sponsor in the United States; I had none. Trapped in Europe with the war already started, it seemed as if I was on a small island looking out over a bottomless abyss, with nowhere to turn. Everyone distrusted me; I could be a German spy. Even so, I never lost hope or my inborn optimism. I did not yet feel defeated, but it seemed I had as little power over my destiny as a speck of dust caught in a whirlwind.

One of Mr. Daniloff's neighbors was the vice-president of the Belgian

Red Cross. Daniloff asked him to help me if he could. The vice-president contacted an acquaintance, the chief of the Belgian Sûreté de l'État (an agency similar to the American FBI), who told him that there was a desperate need for coal miners in Belgium. Anyone agreeing to work as a coal miner would be accepted as a legal resident immediately and would be issued identification papers. Legitimate papers were highly desirable, because anyone without valid identification papers might be put into refugee camps at any time, particularly in the event of a German attack. Since I had had experience as a coal miner in Germany, I gladly accepted the offer.

Just before my departure for the mine, I saw an announcement in a city newspaper for a series of Bach concerts to be given by the famous pianist Alexander Borovsky. Borovsky was related to my mother (her maiden name was also Borovsky) and had known both of my parents personally. I visited him in his hotel and gave him an account of my present plight. He gave me 500 francs and tickets for all of his upcoming concerts. When I said I had a friend who would also be interested, he handed me an additional set of tickets. My girlfriend accompanied me to the Bach concerts, but I doubt she understood or enjoyed the music much. She seemed to prefer life's more physical pleasures.

A. Borovsky

PIANIST ALEXANDER BOROVSKY, A RELATIVE, WRITES:
"A MON AMI BORIS KOCHANOWSKY EN BON SOUVENIR DE A. BOROVSKY, 1940"

The mine in which I was to work was a few miles from Charleroi. As I left Brussels, I bade a friendly farewell to the nurse. Since my new residence was not far away, our separation was not to be a final one.

When I first arrived at the mine, I was sent to the miners' boarding house and canteen. The boarding house owner was a former Russian policeman, and it seemed to me that he must have been a frightful one. He had the ferocious visage of a wild tomcat: a low forehead, a jutting chin, and a short, thick neck, all attached to a sturdy body of medium height. After giving me some food, he showed me to my bunk in a large communal sleeping room.

The sleeping room measured about fifty by twenty feet in size. Most of the windows had broken panes. It was winter, and I shivered. Along the walls there were dozens of beds with extremely dirty bedclothes and some with bare, soiled mattresses. This was the only home of many of the miners, an odd group whose casual standards of cleanliness alarmed me. At the time, it was widely believed that syphilis could be contracted from a dirty bed, so, being meticulous in my health habits, I bought some newspapers and wrapped myself in them for the night. I was more afraid of venereal disease than of the fleas, of which there were plenty.

The next day, I started to work in the coal mine. It was a particularly deep and dangerous one. I had read about the plight of the Belgian mine workers described in the writings of the painter Vincent Van Gogh. He had been a minister before beginning his career as an artist, and he had witnessed the horrifying circumstances under which the coal miners of his time had to live and work. His observations, however, had been made during the previous century. I was surprised to find that vestiges of these earlier conditions still remained.

The long-wall method of extraction was being used in this particular mine. Each worker had to carry a pick hammer, an electric lamp, an axe, and a saw to the coal face. The total weight of this equipment was twenty pounds. The face was about a hundred yards long, while the coal seam was only sixteen to thirty inches thick, so thin that it was impossible to crawl through the narrow opening. At the beginning and end of each shift we had to slither on our bellies like snakes for about fifty yards, pulling our twenty pounds of equipment behind us. Such maneuvering was strenuous indeed.

Each worker had his own designated working place. Because the thickness of the coal seam was only thirty inches or less, a miner had to work lying on the floor and break the coal off with his pick hammer. Then he would shovel the coal into a steel shaking conveyor. Every so often he would have to cut wood posts and set them up to support the low roof. Each crew was paid by the number of tons of coal they mined. Right from the start, the whole crew and the foreman watched me, the new comer, carefully to see if I could produce the same amount of coal as the other workers. I was not accustomed to working while lying on the floor, and I found it quite awkward. Also, I had not worked in a mine for several years, so I was not in the best of shape. By the end of my first shift I was exhausted and I had a sharp pain in my back. Even worse, however, was the treatment I received from the foreman, who seemed to take a strong disliking to me, perhaps because he knew that I was an engineer. He now had power over someone whom he would, under normal circumstances, have to treat as a superior. He tried to humiliate me as much as possible, in the same way a cruel man might handle his dogs. I remained calm, ignoring his loud, vulgar, insulting remarks. My cool response caused the foreman to become even more arrogant and outraged, but an angry retort from me certainly would have done me no good. Despite the humiliation, I would not let this man break my spirit or subdue the pride of a Siberian, who was now a free working man. At the time, I was actually quite poor, but I never felt that way. I had self-confidence. I was disciplined and still strong physically, and had extensive training and experience in mining. I knew I could do this job, in spite of the hardships.

When I had finished my first shift, I was so tired that I was not hungry, just very thirsty. Because I knew my strength depended on food, however, I forced myself to eat. After a few weeks, I had mastered the routine completely and found it endurable. But it was different for some of the other refugees who had volunteered to work in the mine to escape the refugee camp. Some of them gave up and returned to the camp after just one day because they were physically unable to do the work. Others tried to stay on, but had to quit because of injury or physical collapse. Some, who like me were very thirsty after work, would go to the canteen and drink beer. After two or three beers, especially in their state of dehydration, they would become drunk. The owner of the canteen would then take advantage of their condition and write them up a highly inflated bill. After two weeks, when these workers went to get their pay, the owner of the canteen would show up at the mine office at the same time to collect what was owed him from their paychecks. That way the worker often never saw any of his money—it all went to the canteen owner. This would continue week after week. Some workers, the ones who ran up bills so large they could never pay them off, would try to run away. The canteen owner would then call the police to track them down. Most of the time, the runaways would be caught and brought back to the mine. Feeling trapped and frustrated, the workers would drink even more.

I continued my policy of abstinence. Being concerned about keeping myself physically fit, I religiously avoided alcohol and cigarettes. After about a month, I had saved enough money to leave the dismal conditions of the canteen and boarding house. I rented a room in a private home and began to have a more normal home life at least.

Working conditions in the coal mines were so difficult and dangerous that it was hard to find Belgians willing to work as miners. Most of the mine workers were foreigners. To find enough coal miners, the Belgian government would "legalize" almost anyone willing to work, not only political refugees, but even violent criminals. The workers were sometimes treated as if they were inferior human beings, and worker safety was not taken too seriously. Accidents occurred regularly. Twice I was trapped with my crew when sections of the roof caved in, but we were dug out in time on both occasions. What life had in store for me I did not know, but fate seemed determined that I would not be killed in a mining accident.

On May 11, 1940, Germany attacked Belgium. Many people, including soldiers of the Belgian and French armies, suspected the presence of a subversive spy network. All strangers, particularly those who could not speak fluent French, came under close scrutiny. A great number of people, many certainly innocent, were executed on mere suspicion. One of the White Russians who worked in the mine, and lived in the same rooming house I had started out in, had a very close call. In Russia he had belonged to a distinguished family, his father having been a high official in the Czarist government. Since the sanitary conditions of the rooming house toilets were deplorable, he, like several other men who lived there, preferred to go outside in the fresh air to relieve himself. The coal slag dumps, where there were plenty of hiding places in the bushes, were favored spots.

One evening just after German planes had attacked and townspeople's nerves were particularly on edge, this refugee went to one of the dump sites to seek relief. There, on top of the slag pile, he was accosted by Belgian soldiers, having discovered him in an embarrassing posture behind some bushes. The soldiers arrested him and accused him of giving signals to the German planes, indicating where to drop bombs. Of course, he was frightened by such grave accusations and tried to defend himself. Initially, he did not know whether to laugh or cry because their accusation seemed so ridiculous. Only when the soldiers were reassured by local Belgians, who knew this refugee and of the "custom" of the men in the rooming house, was he released. The incident was the talk of the neighborhood, and everyone got a big laugh out of it. However, the overly suspicious attitude of the Belgian soldiers was very real, and very dangerous. One can better understand why this was so if one considers the extent of German dissembling during the war. For example, in at least one case, German soldiers dressed as nuns parachuted down by night, carrying guns and explosives under their habits in order to blow up bridges and telephone lines.

During the first few days of German attacks, I stayed in my room. Concerned about my welfare, my girlfriend, the nurse from Brussels, visited me for several days. But because of the rapid advance of the Germans, the situation quickly became quite dangerous. It was clear I would have to flee soon. Finally, we heard a radio broadcast asking that all men of military age leave Belgium for France immediately and join up with the French forces. If I stayed any longer, I would surely be captured by the Germans. The next morning, I noticed that a nearby bridge had been wired and charged with explosives. The streets were deserted, the eerie silence punctuated only by the passing of an occasional military vehicle. At that point, I decided that I should leave town at once. I was obviously not a Belgian—my French featured a strong German accent—and I would not be able to avoid arousing suspicion as the situation for the Belgians became more and more desperate.

In preparation for my escape, I went shopping for provisions just a block from my residence. I noticed several French soldiers in the shop, who, when they heard my broken French, became suspicious, thinking I could be a spy. They approached and started speaking to me in an agitated manner, asking annoying questions full of implications. But the owner, who had known me for several months, made them stop. When they let me go, I just smiled, not realizing what a serious situation it had been. I returned to my room with twelve eggs and twelve bars of chocolate.

After hard boiling the eggs, I packed them in my briefcase, along with the chocolate bars and a change of clothes. Soon after I had settled in Belgium, my landlady in Wülfrath had mailed me my Leica camera and Brunton pocket compass, along with most of my clothing. Unfortunately, the camera and the compass were stolen in transit. Otherwise, I would certainly have carried them with me on this journey in hopes of selling them later on. This apparent unfortunate loss actually turned out to be a stroke of good luck.

I hurriedly left my residence that same afternoon. I began my escape on foot, taking the road to Charleroi. The road was already crowded with refugees. After walking about a mile, I heard a tremendous explosion. The steel bridge I had seen earlier wired with explosives had been blown up, either by the French or the Belgians, in order to impede the inevitable German advance. Although I was an experienced blasting engineer, I had never heard such a tremendous explosion before. Everyone was terrified, and many people started running in all directions. It was late afternoon. I arrived in Charleroi quickly, walking the four miles at a rapid pace.

Thirsty from the strenuous exercise, I went to a café on a wide plaza and asked the waitress for a glass of water, "Verre d'eau, S'il vous plaît." I drank the water and started to leave. Just then I heard the click of a rifle magazine and felt the sharp end of a bayonet against my chest. A hysterical voice shouted, "Mains en haut!" (Hands up!)

In front of me stood a French soldier and a sergeant. Both were drunk. The soldier held a rifle to my chest and the sergeant, who was obviously filled with a combination of hate and alcohol, started hitting my face with his fists. I was glad that I had taken boxing lessons as a student, because the training had taught me how to take such blows. Fortunately, since the sergeant was quite small, he was not strong enough to hurt me seriously.

Of course, I was terrified and knew that I dared not defend myself or fight back, or I would be shot.

As the sergeant pounded away at me, more and more of the local people gathered around us. They assumed that the police had caught a German spy and their faces quickly filled with anger and panic. They began to shout, "Kill him, kill the *Bosch*! Kill the German spy!" (*Bosch* means pig, a popular derogatory term for a German.) Spies and traitors were intensely detested by the populace. Most people could not understand how the German army had been able to advance with such speed, as they occupied country after country. They attributed the German success to an excellent system of espionage, and to their advanced paratrooper forces that would disrupt communications and create panic behind the front lines. Now I was suspected of being one of these German agents.

Just as in Wülfrath, when I had been surrounded by forty Stormtroopers out to kill me, I was again standing alone and helpless in the midst of a mob angry enough to tear me to pieces. As I looked into their faces, a feeling of disbelief and shock arose in me. They did not know whether I was innocent or guilty. Sparked by mere assumption, they were eager to do away with me. How frequently injustice arises when fueled by misguided imagination. I understood their fear, hate, and hysteria. In spite of my precarious situation, I held no ill feeling toward them. I realized that they were out of their minds with fear and that their primary motive was self-preservation. Once again, I was not afraid. I simply could not imagine that I would be killed this very instant, when I had come so far and was still so young. Since I had not broken any laws or hurt anybody, such a scenario seemed wholly unfitting and illogical. As before, my attitude was naive, but this is how I felt, the optimist under duress.

I was glad, however, that I was in the hands of soldiers, even drunken ones, instead of civilians. In the end, the soldiers actually saved me from being lynched by the hysterical mob around us. The mob could kill with freedom and anonymity, but the soldiers could not. They were required to take a suspect to headquarters, or to a high ranking officer first for interrogation, unless of course they had been provoked into killing him beforehand in self-defense. Only after interrogation, if it was proven the suspect was a spy, would he be executed. If the soldiers making the arrest were drunk, hysterical, panic-stricken, or full of hate and vengeance, they might kill you anyway, forgetting about the proper procedures. But this is less probable than certain death at the hands of an outraged mob.

The sergeant continued to hit me, blow after blow, until he tired out. After the punches had finally stopped, and I had remained impassive throughout the pummeling, the sergeant asked me for my identification papers. Now I was glad that I did not have my Leica camera and my Brunton compass with me. Such "spying" implements would certainly have incited the crowd, if not the soldiers, to kill me. As it happened, however, the sergeant took me safely to the commandant of the city, who was a Belgian colonel. The colonel looked at my identification papers and the address book I carried in my pocket, and then he released me.

A few hours after I was released, the Germans began to bomb the area around Charleroi. The terrible din permeated the city, and the earth underfoot vibrated with each detonation. Panic spread quickly, especially among the women and children. Joining the cacophony of the explosions began a chorus of uncontrollable crying and shrieking. Never before had I witnessed such a spectacle. It was evening, and the darkness made this scene even more fearsome and macabre. I became quite uneasy myself.

I resumed my escape, walking all night long amongst a continuous stream of fleeing refugees. Of the eight million people in Belgium, one million left their homes in this flight, traveling on foot into France. The roads were choked with the flow of humanity, and military vehicles often had great difficulty making their way through the hordes of refugees. My own plan was to walk northwards to the Belgian coast and to attempt to swim the English Channel, in hopes of being picked up a by a British vessel. I wanted desperately to go to England. But somehow, without realizing how it happened, I found myself walking with the refugees westward towards France.

Late in the evening we met another, smaller group of people running toward us, against the direction of the crowd, shouting, "Bosch! Bosch! Bosch!" These few created such panic that all the refugees in my vicinity turned and started running back, in the general direction of Germany. I could not understand this strange behavior. I knew Germany was behind us, to the east. I could not imagine how the Germans could now also be in front of us, unless they had parachuted in. After a short hesitation, I decided not to follow the other refugees, but to go alone towards the west. As it grew late, it became very dark and terribly quiet. I could hear the sound of each and every one of my steps as my boots struck the road. Alone, I began to feel insecure, and to fear that at any second I might walk right into the Germans, if they really were ahead of me along this road.

At one point I encountered a railroad grade ahead of me which was five feet higher than the road. I had to cross it, but I thought Germans might be hiding behind it, a common practice. So I moved cautiously closer. As I approached I listened carefully for any hint of movement. Hearing nothing, I walked on across the railway. I was afraid to look right or left, but nothing happened. After walking for another hour or so, I turned onto another road which was as packed with refugees as the other road had been. I felt much safer, being with companions, my fears no longer magnified by loneliness.

The night sky was covered with clouds. I could not see any stars, so my sense of direction in the dark became confused. I hoped that I was now heading north, but I did not really know in what direction I was traveling. I asked a woman close to me which direction this road was leading. From her answer I understood that it led directly westward. I was disappointed and exclaimed loudly, "That's impossible!" But I kept on walking. A few minutes later I heard shouting ahead, "Spy! Spy! Spy!" Being curious to see who it was, I walked faster toward the shouting. Suddenly, out of the darkness emerged the silhouettes of a dozen soldiers with their bayonets pointed towards us. They came closer and closer. Finally, they singled me out. *I* was the spy! At that moment I realized that my vociferous reply to the woman in imperfect French, the German clothes I was wearing (a German raincoat), my style of walking with slow, long steps, and my manner of speech and gesticulation all had contributed to their suspicion that I was an enemy spy. Word had traveled quickly up the road about the German agent among the refugees who had just parachuted down from a plane and had momentarily lost his way.

The French soldiers surrounded me, holding several bayonets to my chest and shouting, "Mains en haut!" (Hands up!) I raised my arms high. A French sergeant asked me for my identification papers. I lowered my right hand toward the pocket where my papers were, but several soldiers again started to shout, "Mains en haut!" They were afraid I might pull out a pistol. Quickly I raised my hands again and kept them high.

Here again, as in Charleroi, a mob quickly formed around us, shouting hysterically, "Kill the bosch! Kill the German spy!" The faces of the people projected a now familiar hate and panic. There was no trial by jury in their hearts. I knew that by killing me they would consider themselves patriotic defenders of their country against the Nazis. How strange it all seemed to me. I had been persecuted by the Nazis myself and been almost lynched by Nazi Stormtroopers in Wülfrath a few months before. Now the French and Belgian people were trying to kill me, because they thought I was a Nazi. How crazy and topsy-turvy the world seemed.

It was also strange that I still had no fear. It all seemed like an ugly dream, a nightmare. I simply could not accept this absurdity as reality. My lack of terror in this dangerous situation was not due to courage or heroism, but rather it stemmed from disbelief and the sheer naïveté of a young man who was still full of life and strong in mind and body. This kind of nonchalance is characteristic of youth.

Again, I was glad that I was in the hands of soldiers, who were required to observe rules and regulations. If they had not been in charge, the mob would certainly have beaten me to death. The soldiers' respect for proper procedure once again saved my life. They led me to a house which was serving as their headquarters. There I was required to remove all my clothes. They pierced my boots, ripped the lining and shoulder pads from my jacket, and tore up my tie, looking for evidence of espionage. They found none. Once again it was fortunate that I did not have my German camera and pocket compass with me. Those objects would have implicated me and could easily have led to my execution.

The soldiers then escorted me to the next town, Binche, and locked me in a large room in the town hall. There were about twelve other people there. I was surprised to discover that most of them were Russian emigrants who, like me, had been living in Belgium. As I sat and waited, I pondered over how lucky I had been to have escaped yet another angry mob. After having lived in Germany for sixteen years, no doubt I looked, talked, and acted like a German. Many innocent people were shot during this time because of the emotional panic that pervaded the countryside. The Belgians and the French felt their armies were the best in the world, and their defeat could only be explained by the treachery of spies. The thought of any spy being in their midst infuriated them.

I was tired from the long walk and drained by the ordeal of the arrest, so I was glad that I at least had a roof over my head. We were not permitted to leave the room and there was no restroom available to us, so someone had taken down the large globe from the overhead lamp and placed it on the floor. We used it for a urinal, its acrid odor pervaded every inch of the room. Finding an empty spot on the floor, I lay down and slept soundly the whole night.

Late in the afternoon of the following day, everything became very quiet. The street and plaza in front of our building were completely empty. Suddenly, a Belgian policeman came into the room and announced, "Everyone has left the city because the Germans are expected to arrive at any moment. You are all free to go. If you don't want to fall into the hands of Germans, you had better make haste." Having had a wonderful night's rest, which I certainly needed, I felt able to face another long hike. This time I walked for two days without rest with another large group of refugees, the Germans always close on our heels.

As we proceeded down the road, every so often groups of people around me would start to run. I could never figure out why. I was afraid to ask any questions because of my previous difficulties, so I did not make any inquiries, or even open my mouth. I was normally a gregarious sort, but I felt safer this way. Still, I managed to get into trouble again. On one occasion I took out my address book to look up the addresses of some acquaintances in Paris I hoped to visit when I arrived. A French soldier on a bicycle immediately came up to me from behind and asked me to show him the booklet. He looked at it and then gave it back. Perhaps he suspected that I had a map in my possession, or that I had been making sketches of landmarks along the highway.

The trek from Charleroi to Paris, a distance of over 200 miles, took five days. In Belgium, air raids occurred daily, usually at 10 a.m. and at 3 p.m. Thirty or more German planes would attack at a time, flying low, just over the treetops. They would strafe and drop small bombs on the road. They were not aiming at us specifically. Their main objective was to demoralize the resistance, and to disrupt traffic and communications. Since we could easily see the planes approaching us, we always had enough time to hide in the narrow ditches on the side of the road. Fortunately, I did not see anyone killed or wounded in these attacks. Anything that remained on the road, however, such as cars or horses, was completely destroyed. Once, when I dove into a ditch at the last moment, I realized that I had jumped into a clump of poison nettles. Of course, I had to remain where I was until the air raid passed. The burning and itching was driving me crazy, but I dared not move.

Being a blasting specialist, and having worked in treacherous mines, I was accustomed to danger, so I found my current situation exciting rather than frightening. One night, we passed close to the front, near the north end of the fighting lines that had developed along the French-Belgian border. We could hear the gargling sound of artillery fire and saw continuous lightening-like flashes on the horizon. The whole earth vibrated. Many of the refugees became fearful and panic-stricken. I learned later that some refugees had actually gone mad with fear and eventually had to be put into mental institutions. No wonder.

On one occasion during this trying journey, I saw a battle between two planes. While chasing each other they made huge circles in the air. One of the planes was eventually shot down, and I saw the pilot parachute toward the ground. Another time, we came upon a tank moving toward us. It, too, made the refugees panic because no one knew whether it was German, Belgian, or French. As it got closer, we were relieved to discover that it was Belgian.

As my group of refugees was passing along the north end of the battle front, at one point, we had to run as fast as we could, because the Germans were advancing so rapidly. The allied fortifications were a hurriedly assembled, inadequate extension of the famous Maginot Line. The French had built the Maginot Line, an "impregnable" dug-in fortification, at a staggering cost. But they had built it only along their border with Germany, from Switzerland to Belgium. It did not continue along the Belgian border to the sea. It was said that the Belgian king had objected to the extension of the Maginot Line between Belgium and France, and had promised to defend Belgium himself against any German attack. A few days after Germany attacked, however, the king left the country with his family. The Germans thus did not need to contend with the Maginot Line once they crossed into Belgium, because France was open to them along the full length of the Belgian border.

When the long lines of refugees from Belgium reached the French border, it was impossible for the French police to check everyone for identification papers. Belgian citizens were allowed to cross the border legally, so most of the refugees shouted, "I am Belgian! I am Belgian!" as they shoved their way through the border crossing. I wedged myself in with the crowd and crossed the border without being asked for identification. To avoid suspicion, I continued to remain silent as the march continued through France. On both sides of the road many people were lying exhausted, unable to walk further on their sore feet. I shall never forget an old Frenchman, who was probably over eighty years old. He was lying in the grass crying. He had witnessed three German invasions of France during his lifetime: in 1870, 1914, and now again in 1940. This last attack on his beloved homeland was more than he could bear.

After walking for five days, I arrived in Paris. I had the address of a Baron Ginzburg, given to me by Alexander Borovsky, the pianist I had met in Brussels. I located Mr. Ginzburg, and I was at once permitted, or perhaps it would be more accurate to say required, to take a much needed bath. I was so tired, and my feet were so sore, that I remained in the bathtub for nearly an hour. Ginzburg, fearing that something had happened to me, knocked on the door to inquire whether I was all right. At that precise moment, I stepped out of the bathroom looking much refreshed and relaxed. Ginzburg seemed surprised at my altered appearance, without any shadow of fatigue on my face.

Baron Ginzburg advised me to comply with the prevailing rules by reporting at once to the local military authority. I went, was assigned to a group of Belgians, and, with the quickness and efficiency of a military muster, was packed off by train to a tiny village in the Pyrenees Mountains near France's border with Spain.

Soon after I left Paris, it too fell to the Nazis. France was now divided into two zones: the northern zone, occupied by Germany, with Paris as its capital, and the southern unoccupied zone (zone libre), with its capital at Vichy. I was now in the unoccupied zone, where I could, for the time being, lead a peaceful life. But I had no illusions. I was still a foreigner, with no money, and no way to emigrate legally from France. And the war in France was just beginning.

Chapter 9

NOT A SPECTACLE

Life is not a spectacle or a feast; it is a predicament.

—George Santayana, *Articles and Essays*

I, along with several other refugees, was sent to Coulon, a small village high in the Pyrenees Mountains. Perpignan was the closest large city. In Coulon, I managed to find a room in the home of one of the villagers, a room that I shared with another Russian émigré. The French government gave each refugee a small amount of money to purchase food, making it possible for us to survive in this remote area without any other source of income, at least for the time being. The people were friendly and helpful, and we spent nearly every evening in the warm company of the peasant families. Life was difficult in this region because of the rocky, unproductive soil. I was surprised to see many teenagers, even beautiful young girls, without any teeth, perhaps the result of inadequate nutrition. It was also strange to watch the male villagers pass the time knitting socks, gloves, pullovers, and other garments—a traditional local industry.

The villagers practiced an unusual wedding custom which I had the opportunity to observe. After the church ceremony and a celebratory feast at the home of the bride, the couple would disappear, hiding themselves in one of the houses in the village. Young unmarried men and boys would search for them during the night, and if the couple was discovered, the newlyweds had to arise from their bed, come to the window, and drink a glass of wine in front of the band of young prowlers.

In conversations with my Russian roommate I learned that he had been an officer in the Russian army prior to the Revolution, but since his arrival in Belgium he had made his living as a common laborer. I soon realized that our life views were diametrically opposed. He believed that it was impossible to get a good job, or to be a success in any respect without powerful friends. His attitude reflected that of the old Russian aristocracy. With youthful self-confidence, I disagreed and maintained that nobody could hold a man back who had a good education and the will, drive, and persistence to succeed. Anyone with these qualifications would need no outside assistance.

After four months of living in the sleepy remoteness of the Pyrenees, I decided that the time had come for me to put my dynamic philosophy into action, and to make another attempt to immigrate to the United States. I felt hopeful and ready to fight for my dreams once again.

In September of 1940, I made my way to Marseille on a borrowed bicycle, taking along some food given to me by the villagers. Arriving with less than $5 left of what I had received from a charity (the money from the French authorities had long since been spent), I decided to seek refuge in a sanctuary managed by a Christian order. Approaching the building, I looked through the doorway into a large hall and saw a beautifully sculpted statue of Jesus illuminated by a spotlight. He was holding his arms open, as if inviting all of humanity to find peace and comfort in his embrace. But just in front of the entrance, I encountered an enormous policeman furiously beating another man. I did not know what crime this poor individual had committed, but the contrast between the brutal policeman and the merciful Jesus behind him deeply impressed and disgusted me.

I was given supper and a bed at this asylum. The large sleeping room had many beds lined up along the walls, a similar arrangement to what I had encountered at the coal miners' boarding house in Belgium. But these accommodations were clean and well-kept. The beds had unusually high legs, and each was separated from the next by an aisle. Wearily I crawled into my assigned bed and was soon fast asleep.

When I awoke the next morning, I was surprised to find myself surrounded by several other men who were staring at me with accusing smirks on their faces. Arising from the bed, I quickly discovered the reason. Beneath my bed there was a noticeable puddle. After the long bicycle trip the day before, I had slept so long and so soundly during the night that I had wet the bed. As ashamed as I was, there was not much I could do but to try to clean up the mess.

That morning I set out to visit one of the Russian churches in Marseille. I stopped the first man I saw to ask for directions. He began, "Vous prrrrrenez trrram…." From his rolling pronunciation of the letter "r" I knew at once that he was Russian. After explaining how I could reach my destination, he invited me to visit him at his home later that day.

Following his directions, I soon located the Russian church and its priest. The priest was the spiritual leader of a group of Russian immigrants living in the area. They were in the process of building a new Russian Orthodox Church, the third one in Marseille. I asked the priest if I might remain with him and his congregation and help them build their church, until such time as I could get a visa from the American consulate to go to the United States. I was grateful when he accepted me.

He had rented a large garage and had converted a portion of it into a small apartment for himself and his wife. With the remaining space he had opened up a soup kitchen. Inexpensive meals were served there both at lunch and at suppertime. The kitchen facilities were in a small building in the rear. Right next to the "restaurant," his small Russian Orthodox Church was under construction.

After settling my living arrangements with the priest, I set off to visit my new Russian acquaintance, the gentleman who had given me directions earlier that day. He lived in one of the poorest sections of the city, one of the slums for which Marseille was notorious. When I arrived at his quarters, a cramped, deteriorating apartment, I found him sitting at a small kitchen table. On the table, sitting in an orderly semicircle in front of him, were eight cats, most of them just small kittens. They had wide-spread pointed ears and big, liquid eyes, and were looking attentively and with great respect at him. In a serious tone, he spoke first with one, and then to another. Some of them had particular problems that he discussed with them. One seemed to have a caught a cold; another had a torn ear, probably from a fight with another cat. I saw that the man and the cats understood each other well. The furry little creatures were amazingly obedient. In his manner, I recognized at once the characteristic iron discipline of the Russian military. At the end of his lengthy lecture, he gave each cat some fish.

After dismissing his cats, he invited me to join him at the table. He soon began entertaining me with some exciting stories from his sixteen-year career in Africa with the French Foreign Legion. He also told me of an occasion when he was attacked at the port of Marseille by three Frenchmen.

"When I saw them coming toward me," he said, "I just put my back against a wall, stuck out my chin, and let them hit me until they were exhausted and their hands were sore." A rare defense, to be sure, but I believed him. His unusually large chin was shaped like a horseshoe, and was, no doubt, just as hard. I did not know whether to believe all of his stories, but it occurred to me that he was intensely, almost stereotypically, Russian—romantic, blustery, sentimental, strong as a bull, yet gentle as a puppy.

My new host, the priest, was the first clergyman with whom I had ever had a close association. I worked for him for the next two years. At first my duties consisted of washing dishes and floors, skills the priest taught me. Later on I advanced to waiter, to grocery drayman, and finally to cashier. At first, since I had no bed, each evening I would take one of the doors off its hinges and support it with two chairs, one under each end. On one occasion when I tried to get out of my make-shift bed in the morning, I was unable to do so. The weight of my body had broken through the flimsy door, and I was trapped in it. Other restaurant workers had to help me extricate myself from the shattered pallet. Fortunately, I was eventually given a small room of my own, with a genuine bed.

Little food was available in Marseille. Each person received an official ration of 275 grams (about half a pound) of bread per day, and the following rations per month: one pound of sugar, one half pound of noodles, six pounds of potatoes, half a pound of fat or butter, and a quarter pound of tea. The main dish was always cabbage—cabbage, cabbage, and more cabbage. Working at the restaurant gave me the opportunity to consume some extra meals, but in spite of that, I lost twenty percent of my body weight, approximately forty pounds, during those two years in Marseille.

Although food was scarce, life was livable, and I got into a normal routine. As I did so, and as news of the war continued to be discouraging, I began to consider a moral dilemma which caused me a great deal of anguish. On one hand, I deeply desired an Allied victory in Europe, and a decisive defeat for Nazism. As a leading mining engineer in Germany, I knew certain facts about German industry that might be of use to the Allies in targeting German war production. For example, although Wülfrath was recognized as a major mining center, I did not think many people knew exactly how important it was. In terms of the production of lime and dolomite, two crucial commodities for making steel, ninety percent of the lime and fifty percent of the dolomite available to the Third Reich was mined at Wülfrath. And this is where my moral dilemma arose. Should I contact the Allied authorities and acquaint them with my knowledge of German industry? It was a difficult decision because I could not be sure how they would use this information. It might speed an Allied victory and save innumerable lives. But the bombing of Wülfrath might well lead to the injury or death of many of my old friends and colleagues, perhaps including Mr. Ludowigs, who had saved my life so many times. I knew that if I were to return to Wülfrath after the war and find that Mr. Ludowigs had been killed, I would not be able to live with myself knowing that I might have been the cause of his death. This attitude, though perhaps not the most appropriate for wartime, led me to my final decision. After much consideration, I felt I could not betray my former friends and neighbors, and kept silent.

One day the priest asked me to come to his room. After I took a seat, he gave me a serious, solemn look, and began to tell me a Biblical-style parable in a quiet, calm voice. "Once upon a time," he said, "there lived a man who was famous for his honesty. But, by and by, for unknown reasons, he became more and more dishonest and began stealing things."

I found the story interesting and listened attentively as the priest had a gift for story telling. But I could not understand why he was telling *me* this story. At the end of the tale, when I reacted with vague bewilderment, he, being an emotional man, began to lose his patience. After a few minutes he started shouting at me, accusing me of stealing his cognac.

Known for my calm demeanor in tense situations, I remained unperturbed during the priest's entire tirade. I had never been a drinker, so cognac would not have been the slightest temptation to me. The accusation was absurd, but the priest was extremely upset, and intensely serious, so I tried to help him solve the mystery. I inquired as to when the cognac had disappeared, but he would not answer me. He thought I was trying to feign innocence by appearing to cooperate. As he was already absolutely assured of my guilt, he asked me pointedly if I were ready to confess, to repent, and ask for forgiveness. I replied that no, I had no knowledge of his disappearing cognac, and I had no guilt to confess. This was almost too much for him to bear. Furiously, he took me back to my room, and pulled out from under my bed a three or four gallon bottle of cognac. I told him that I was not in the habit of looking under my bed, that I had never seen this bottle before, and that I didn't know who had put it there. He became even more outraged because of my supposed impudence, and stormed off in disgust.

A few hours later, one of the other restaurant employees admitted that he had put the cognac under my bed because he felt it was the safest place to hide it. No one would think of looking for it under the bed of a teetotaler. The good Father was awfully embarrassed, and asked me to forgive him for his suspicions. Of course, I had no difficulty forgiving him wholeheartedly. I sincerely liked him because I knew how kindhearted he was, having experienced his impressive generosity first-hand. Yet, even so, I was aware that life had presented me with another lesson: How easily even a good man can cruelly misjudge another, thereby inflicting an injustice.

I was now thirty-five years old, in reasonably good shape, and apparently still attractive to women. During my stay in Marseille, two women, one of them married, made serious advances toward me. Both failed to lure me into an affair. I was never the playboy type, and felt no emotional inclination toward them. But they thought me cowardly for rejecting them.

However, I did make the acquaintance of another lady in Marseille, with whom I fell deeply in love. She was beautiful, shapely, intelligent, and always dressed with excellent taste. Unfortunately, she was also married.

Her husband was in the United States at the time. My strong moral principles kept me from showing her the intensity of my feelings. I admired her not only because of her appearance and charm, but also because she, like my brother the physician, served the poor through her work with a Quaker organization. Her visible concern for the most miserable, unfortunate specimens of humanity made a deep impression on me.

I had applied to the American consulate for permission to immigrate to the United States almost as soon as I arrived in Marseille. After a delay of more than two years, I finally received word that my request had been granted. My visa would be ready within a few days. No words can express the excitement I felt. At last, I was to escape the trials of the war in Europe, and my long-held dreams were to be fulfilled. I booked passage on a ship leaving Lisbon for the United States the following month, and purchased my ticket.

Fate, however, was again to intercede. On November 11, 1942, the day after I had booked my passage to America, Francis Miroglio,[29] a young man active in the French Underground who knew of my escape from Nazi persecution in Germany, came to me and brought me some disturbing news.

"Today, the Germans will occupy Marseille in retaliation for the American invasion of Africa. Give me a photograph of yourself, and in a few hours I will bring you false identification papers. Your name will be Jacques Neirinck, and your place of residence will be La Chalp d'Arvieux in Hautes-Alpes." His instructions were given abruptly, but I complied willingly, responding intuitively to the compelling force of this remarkable young man's personality.

I had long suspected that I would eventually have to go into hiding, and I was grateful to have someone looking out for my welfare, but the

---

[29] Francis Miroglio (1924-2005) went on to become a composer of some renown. He studied with Milhaud at the Paris Conservatory in the early 1950's and won the *Priz de la Biennale de Paris* in 1961. In 1965 he founded a contemporary art and music festival at St. Paul de Vence. His works have been published and recorded. In 1977, and again in 1981, Miroglio sent me a signed recording of some of his works for percussion entitled *Extensions 2 de Francis Miroglio* performed by Les Percussions de Strasbourg. He also sent me a recording called *Clavecin 2000*, a collection of original works for harpsichord by Miroglio and other contemporary composers.

whole situation was disheartening for me. Now the ports and borders of France's south zone would be closed. I would have no way to reach Lisbon, to catch my ship to freedom—no way to leave occupied France. Now the Germans would begin increasing their presence and their persecutions in the south. I was again to begin the perilous life of a fugitive.

Later that same day, Miroglio brought me the false documents and instructed me to take the next train into the mountains. "If the Germans ask you where you are going," he warned, "tell them you are going home, as can be seen from your identification papers." There was nothing else I could do. I hurried to the train station and quit Marseille by the next train traveling in the direction of Gap, one of the few sizeable towns in the High Alps region. I took along the addresses of three Protestant ministers in that vicinity which had been given to me by some concerned Protestants in Marseille. Since my departure was so sudden, I had no time to say good-bye to anyone.

Despite being surrounded by many German soldiers on the train, I arrived in Gap without incident. It was after 11 p.m. when I found the home of Reverend Morel, the minister I was instructed to contact first. I rang the bell continuously for several minutes and then commenced pounding on the door. No one answered. Exhausted, I leaned my back against the door, slid down onto the wooden step in front of the entryway, and was soon fast asleep. Winter had already begun by this time in the alpine regions of France. The street was covered with snow and the night air felt frigid. I wore a coat appropriate for the climate in Marseille, but not protective enough for winter weather in the mountains.

The next morning, Reverend Morel opened his door to find me still asleep on his doorstep. He and his whole family had simply slept though my assiduous bell-ringing and door-pounding—sound sleepers every one of them, to my detriment. I awoke almost paralyzed, certain that I was frozen to the bone. I could not move my fingers, and it occurred to me I might lose some of them to frostbite. It took a long time before I could move any part of my body. Finally, I was able to stand and make my way into the house. There I met the family and was given some hot tea. In a short time a warm bath was drawn for me, and as it turned out, that was all the medical attention I required. My Siberian body, accustomed from youth to extreme cold, had saved me. I had withstood the cold night quite well, and emerged from the bath limber and in good spirits.

The minister had a wife and five children between the ages of six and seventeen. All of them struck me as kind people. He invited me into his library where I told him my story, what had happened to me in Marseille, and that I bore false identification papers stating that my residence was in a village close to the Italian border. I also told him that I had the address of another minister living in the region, whom I would be contacting next. I took leave of Reverend Morel and his family later that day, and made my way eastward toward the village of my next contact, Reverend Kierbon.

I arrived at the home of Reverend Kierbon early that evening. A group of people were assembled there. One of the guests greeted me and informed me that a party was in progress and that I should join them. Soon I was able to meet with Reverend Kierbon himself. He was not more than thirty years old and, as I learned later, he was also an excellent athlete, especially adept at skiing. Although he lived in a spacious house, he did not wish me to spend the night there, and sent me instead to a tourist rooming house for the night. I assumed that he would know what was best for me, so I went to the rooming house. In fact, it was a silly thing to do. If the police had checked the identification papers of the guests, as they frequently did, they would have found out at once that my papers were false. My home address listed on my papers was only a few miles away, and from the way I spoke, anyone could tell that I was not a Frenchman. Fortunately, the night was uneventful.

The next day I reached my "home town," La Chalp d'Arvieux, high in the mountains directly on the Italian border. There I met Reverend Picard, my third and final contact arranged by my Protestant friends in Marseille. Reverend Picard strongly questioned the wisdom of sending me to his small village, where everyone knew everyone else. The guards stationed in the area would easily recognize that I had no business in that village, and that my papers were false. Furthermore, because the village was so close to the Italian border, any stranger would be suspected of being a spy. It was apparent to me now that my false papers were only good for *traveling to* La Chalp d'Arvieux, but not for *staying* there. I would have to leave as soon as possible.

Reverend Picard said to me, "I shall help you return to Gap, where you will be able to blend in more easily. But it will not be an easy task to get you out of town. Everyone in this region, especially the police, is suspicious of new faces."

We waited until dark, and then set out on foot, away from the center of town so we would not meet anyone. Trudging for many miles through deep snow and cold forests, we finally came to a deserted railway platform near a small village, where he left me to catch the next train bound for Gap.

When I got back to Gap and appeared once more at Reverend Morel's doorstep, he took it as a sign from God that he should assume spiritual guidance over me, an agnostic. Although he had a large family, he invited me to stay in his home, and I gladly accepted. He gave me a beautiful room where I felt quite comfortable and secure. My life seemed calm and peaceful there with this kind, loving family. Indeed, it almost seemed as if I were living in a kind of paradise.

Several days later the minister sent his eldest son to Marseille to meet with Miroglio and ask him to create new identification papers for me. On these new papers my name was listed as Louis-Jacques Vadiez, born in Abbeville, Somme. Abbeville was chosen deliberately, because it had been completely destroyed by bombing during the past year. Thus it would be difficult, if not impossible, for the authorities to determine whether my papers were bona fide or false.

While Gap and the surrounding area were occupied mainly by Italian troops, it was the Germans who were really in control. A few weeks after I returned, the Germans issued an announcement in the local newspaper stating that all residents, without exception, must report to the local police station, bringing with them their current identification papers and a photo of themselves in profile. Each person would then be issued new identification papers. Since most people trying to escape the Germans would have fled by now, this required registration renewal was a clever move on the part of the Germans. Any remaining fugitives in the area would not dare go to the police station with their true identification papers. But without a helpful contact, it was impossible to get false papers. Consequently, a fugitive remaining in the area without up-to-date identification would be an easy target for the Germans.

My protector and his closest friends, after much thought and numerous long discussions, gave me what they considered to be sound advice. Since thousands of people would be going to the police station for new papers all at once, the police would likely have difficulty maintaining efficient control over the crowd. I might slip by their notice in the resulting mass confusion. I was to report to the police and hand in my false papers, as if I were an ordinary citizen. This is exactly what I did. I stood in line, took my turn at the police examiner's desk, and without asking any questions of me, he handed me my new papers. Of course, my name was still false, but the papers themselves were legitimately issued and registered, and were therefore *genuine*. Now if the Gestapo or police became suspicious of me, they could call the police station in Gap and find out that my papers were indeed valid. This eventually turned out to be extremely advantageous for me. With these new documents I was also able to secure ration stamps required for food, cigarettes, and daily necessities. I did not smoke, so I gave my cigarette rations to my friends.

All in all I now felt considerably safer than before. Considered a part of the minister's family, I benefited from their protection and the respected position they held within the community. I enjoyed attending Sunday church services with them, and participating in evening Bible study sessions the minister held in his home for church members and other friends. All of them seemed to be kind, thoughtful people. Reverend Morel was unhappy about my agnostic attitude, but it was never much of an issue. I had great respect for him, his family, and all the people I met in his home, and I was always careful to avoid saying anything, or expressing any opinion, that might offend them.

Although the Reverend Morel was kind and generous, and I was extremely grateful to him, it disturbed me that he frequently represented his own interpretation of scripture as the only possible correct interpretation. It seemed to me that he was missing many important facets and nuances in the verses, and depriving the Bible of much of its human richness. At this time, I began my own intense study of the New Testament. I learned to respect, and actually to adore Jesus Christ, whose example demonstrated the highest possible standard of humanity and goodness. Although I still doubted the divinity of Jesus, I found him to be an exceptional human being, indeed deserving of the greatest admiration. I also became interested, in this particular time of warfare and persecution, in examining how the Ten Commandments were, or were not, being observed, and whether they were proving themselves valid.

I asked myself if it really was *always* a sin to lie, or even to kill. I asked these questions of several Protestant and Catholic clergyman. One Catholic priest explained that one may lie and kill in *certain cases*, and supported his claim by citing several historical examples in which bishops and cardinals had done so in the defense of what was right. A Protestant minister told me the following story: During the French revolution, soldiers were hunting a girl who had run into a minister's house for protection. There was no time for the minister to hide her before the soldiers reached the house. The minister opened the front door, while the girl stood trembling behind it. One of the officers asked the minister if he had seen the girl, and the minister replied, "Come in and see for yourself." He avoided telling a lie by failing to answer directly. Believing that the minister would not deceive them, the soldiers left. The point of the story was that it is not necessary to lie, even in extreme circumstances. But I was not satisfied with this. To my mind, the minister in the story had actually lied by deliberately deceiving the soldiers, granted for a good cause. So I concluded that right and wrong cannot always be so easily distinguished.

For me, this was a time for thinking about values and virtues. After much reading on the subject of morality and contemplating these issues at great length, I ultimately accepted Albert Schweitzer's doctrine that life itself should be revered above all else. Everything that contributes to the protection or sustenance of life is good. All actions, thoughts and feelings which contribute to the destruction of life are evil. Therefore, if by lying I could save the life of a human being who is being unjustly persecuted, such a lie would not be a sin. Also, the killing of a gangster or rapist for the protection of one's child, or someone else's child, or one's wife, or a relative, or a helpless stranger, can be justified. I was convinced that injustice should not be tolerated under any circumstances. Influenced by reading the New Testament, and experiencing for myself how some people, motivated to do what was "right," could perpetrate horrible injustices on others, I felt that no individual had the right to punish others. This is the domain of God, according to the Bible. Although I had formed my own conception of morality based on the Bible, I recognized that it was indeed difficult to interpret the scriptures. Life is a complexity. Is there such a thing as a simple answer?

On one occasion, I went with the minister to visit his friend in a village not far from Gap, up in the mountains. There he conducted an outdoor service that I shall never forget. The alpine setting was exquisite, appropriately awe-inspiring for the profoundest of spiritual reflection. As the minister spoke of spiritual beauty, I felt as if I were flying over the earth amid the clouds that overhung the lofty peaks of the mountains. At that moment, I felt very close to God. The experience was an extremely positive one, yet at the same time I recognized that it had sprung from the power of my own imagination.

During my stay at Reverend Morel's home, I met a family of Austrian refugees who visited several times. The father was a famous Viennese physician. He had a fifteen year-old son who was later to play a significant role in my life.

Being now "legalized," I was able to find, through the efforts of my ever-concerned protector, a job at a Nestle factory where powdered milk was being produced. Its principal customer was the German army. I actually owed my job to a Mr. Honegger, the Swiss manager of the plant. It was he who had initially agreed to hire me. Only Honegger and the president of the company knew that I was a refugee with a false identity. Because my French was so poor, I made up a story about my past so that my fellow workers would not be suspicious of me. I claimed to have spent my boyhood in several different countries, but ultimately settled in Algeria. I had been vacationing in France shortly before the Germans occupied Marseille and was thus trapped and unable to return home. The story seemed to work well, until one day a new worker told me that he was also from Algeria, and indeed that he hailed from the same city I claimed as my hometown. He began to ask me specific questions. First he asked if I knew of a certain bistro. I said that I never visited bistros because I did not care for alcoholic beverages. He asked other questions, and I began to fear that I would soon be found out. I made my answers as short and evasive as possible. Finally, he got the impression that I didn't want to talk, and he left me alone, apparently satisfied with my replies.

I experienced another close call on my first payday. All the workers gathered in a small room as the cashier called out our names in turn. I was waiting for my name, when suddenly somebody pushed me from behind, saying, "Are you deaf, Vadiez?"

"Why?" I asked.

"The cashier has called your name loudly, several times."

I had absent-mindedly been listening for my real name! Fortunately, nobody's suspicions were aroused.

When we packaged powdered milk rations for the German army on the production floor, it was a common practice among the workers, when no one was looking, to take a ration off the production line, empty it quickly into one's mouth, and return the empty package to the line. This accomplished the dual purpose of obtaining needed nourishment, and of sabotaging the German war effort, if only to a minor degree.

When I discovered that this activity was going on, I decided it was a pretty good idea, and began doing it myself. On one occasion, I had just finished a package of powder, when I turned around to find myself face to face with the plant manager, Mr. Honegger. He stared at me stone-faced. I was extremely embarrassed, and I did not know what to say. Here I was, sabotaging Mr. Honegger's production line, after he had so kindly given me a job and had kept my secret identity safe from the Gestapo. I was more than embarrassed, I was alarmed. He could fire me for this and turn me over to the authorities. He had certainly seen me eating the ration. After staring at me for a moment, he silently put his finger to the corner of his mouth, to indicate that I had slobbered some milk powder onto my face. Then he left without saying a word. As I watched him walk away, I thought to myself that here was another real hero.

While living in Gap, I had a strange love affair with an eighteen-year-old girl. The only relative she had was an aunt who had been ill for many months. Although the girl possessed an extraordinary beauty, she, unfortunately, was also a kleptomaniac. From time to time she would steal things of no practical value or use. She had been put in correctional institutions several times, but to no avail. Once she had escaped from one of these institutions by climbing through a window and over a high fence.

Before long, the girl was caught stealing again, and in despair, her aunt asked several of her close friends for advice, arranging a meeting to discuss the matter. The group decided that the girl must be severely beaten each time she stole, to discourage her from stealing again. They charged one of the men in the group with the execution of the flogging. He had been an army officer, and had spent several years in Africa. He was probably a sadist, as he reportedly took great pleasure in this assignment. He whipped the girl until she was completely broken in spirit. However, the plan did not seem to have the desired effect. The girl continued to steal.

When I learned of this situation, I was disgusted and outraged. I began to develop a deep sympathy and pity for the unfortunate girl. She was impressed by the sincerity of my concern, and fell desperately in love with me. One day her aunt, who had been a professional nurse for many years, asked me to help her niece, to be friendly towards her, and even to make love to her, because she honestly felt that the depth of love the girl had for me, if fulfilled, could cure her and restore her to a normal life. Otherwise, the aunt considered the case absolutely hopeless. By continuing to steal, the girl would be put in prison again and again, and her whole life would be ruined. I was shocked by such a bold proposition, but imagining this young and beautiful girl repeatedly beaten, or put continually into the reformatory—uselessly—made me decide to be friendly towards her, in the hope that I could help her.

I learned from the girl that she had been raped twice in her life. The first time she was raped by an actor when she was only eight years old. The second instance occurred when she was fourteen. She was attacked on the street by three boys late one evening. They had come from behind her, pulled her coat over her head so that she was trapped and could not move her hands. They then gang-raped her; each taking a turn while the other two held her down. Out of pity and sympathy, rather than love, I began to show affection towards this girl. She became very attached to me, and she stopped stealing, at least for the duration of our affair. I know that she did not expect marriage. She knew that I was a refugee hiding from the Gestapo, and that at any time I might be forced to leave town and disappear into the night. Eventually, I did in fact have to leave suddenly. I do not know what happened to her after my departure.

By the summer of 1943 I had been living in Reverend Morel's home for several months. My long stay there was beginning to arouse suspicion, so he decided to move me to another house. My new hostess was the custodian at the church. She lived with her husband and their fourteen-year-old daughter. Again, all of them were kind and concerned about my welfare. I was grateful to find brave people such as these willing to help me. However, the location of their home turned out to be less than fortuitous on the day the Italians made a separate peace with the Allies. That day proved to be a dangerous one for all the inhabitants of that house.

The evening before the peace treaty became final, when Italy and Germany were still formally allies, the German and the Italian soldiers in the area were patrolling the streets together, and eating and drinking in friendly association at the local restaurants, just as usual. I retired at 10 p.m., as was my normal practice. Three hours later I was suddenly awakened by the sound of machine gun fire directly in front of the house. When the firing started, I jumped out of bed and peeked through the curtains. I could see German soldiers with their machine guns, and I could hear them conversing. They were hiding in a copse of trees behind a railroad grade, only twenty feet away from me. I was surprised at their calm and cold-blooded attitude as they prepared to attack their former Italian comrades.

The Germans were firing at the barracks just one block away, where about one thousand Italian soldiers were stationed. Since I could hear machine gun and artillery fire coming from several directions, I realized that the barracks must be surrounded by the Germans, and that they were firing on it from several sites. I also calculated that if the Italians were to return fire, they would be firing directly into my bedroom. I would then be caught in the crossfire. The house was old and had thin wooden walls, which I knew would not even stop the bullets from small arms fire. Because there was no basement and I was on the first floor, I decided to lie flat on the floor and remain in this position until the shooting stopped. The Germans maintained fire continuously from 1 a.m. until 7 a.m. During those six hours I lay helpless and terrified. Although I had faced many gravely dangerous situations before, I had never really felt as frightened as I did that night. Even though I never once considered standing up during those hours, still my knees felt like they were made of rubber. With the gunfire so near, and so threatening, I began to worry that the flimsy house might be blown away at any moment, leaving no trace behind.

Fortunately, the Italian soldiers did not return fire, and at 7 a.m. they marched out of their barracks with their hands in the air. The Germans called to them in French, "Pas peur, pas peur." (Don't be afraid.) That day several hundred Germans disarmed several thousand Italians. In addition to the one near my residence, there were other Italian barracks in town which had been attacked by German soldiers. In some cases the Italians had returned fire. About forty soldiers on both sides, and a few civilians, had been killed. The next day we saw a long procession of Italian and German soldiers side by side, carrying the coffins of their dead through the streets of the town.

Before September 1943, the southeast of France, including the Alpine region where I was living, had been under Italian occupation. Now the area was fully occupied by the Germans. As a result, my situation changed immediately and dramatically. I could no longer remain in Gap and be safe. So began my longest and most hazardous flight from the Nazi authorities.

June 6
1 9 4 1

REGISTERED R.R.R.
VIA CLIPPER.

The American Consul,
Marseille,
France.

Re: KOCHANOVSKY, Boris
16 Rue Roussel Doris,
Marseille, France.
Case #12.571.

Honorable Sir:

At the request of Mr. Francis Hutter, 519 Lincoln Avenue, Rockville Center,
Long Island, N.Y. a friend, we are enclosing herewith affidavits of support
and other documentary evidence submitted in behalf of Mr. Boris Kochanowsky,
at present residing in Marseille, France.

1. - Affidavit of support in duplicate.
2. - Income Tax Return for 1939.
3. - Copy of Income Tax Return for 1940.
4. - Letter of Employment.
5. - Letter from The Equitable Life Assurance Society.
6. - Letter from The Travelers.
7. - Morality Affidavit submitted by Dr. Benjamin Morrow.
8. - Letter from The Irving Trust Company.

We are writing to Boris Kochanowsky advising him that these documents have
gone forward to your office and we are suggesting that he communicate with
you regarding his application for an immigration visa.

We appreciate your very kind co-operation.

Sincerely yours,

Augusta Mayerson,
Acting Director,
Migration Department.

S. Olstein/ms
ENCLOSURES.

LETTER OF U.S. SPONSORSHIP BORIS RECEIVED WHILE IN MARSEILLE

FRANCIS MIROGLIO (1948)

FALSE PAPER DATED JANUARY 3, 1940 (JACQUES NEIRINCK)

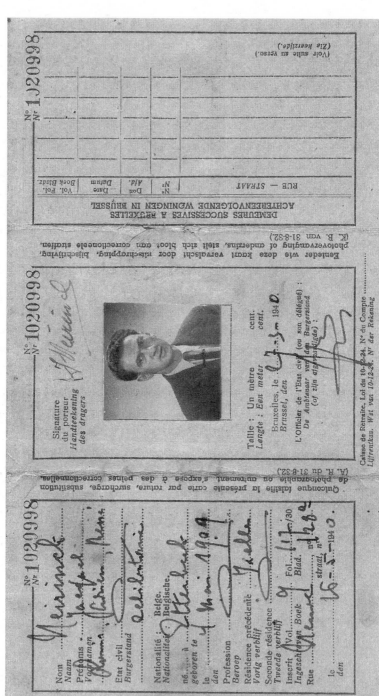

FALSE PAPER DATED MAY 16, 1940 (JACQUES NEIRINCK)

ETAT FRANÇAIS **CARTE D'IDENTITÉ**

Nom _Vadiez_
Prénoms _Louis - Jacques_
Profession _manœuvre_
Nationalité _Française_
Né le _4 Mai 1898_
à _Abbeville_ _Somme_
Domicile _Gap 11 rue des Jardins_

SIGNALEMENT :

Taille _1 m 78_ : Cheveux _châtain_
Bouche _ordinaire_ Yeux _marrons_
Visage _ovale_ Teint _coloré_
Signes particuliers _néant_

Signature du Titulaire : _Vadiez_

Etabli à _Gap_

Le _10 Mai 1943_

~~Le Maire~~ ou le Commissaire,

Empreinte Digitale

Enregistré sous le N° _2567_

Changements de Domicile

Visa Officiel

FALSE PAPER DATED MAY 10, 1943 (LOUIS-JACQUES VADIEZ)

Chapter 10

FALL TO RISE

One who never turned his back but marched breast forward,
Never doubted clouds would break,
Never dreamed though right were worsted, wrong would triumph,
Held we fall to rise, are baffled to fight better,
Sleep to wake.

—Robert Browning, *Asolando*

A few days after the Germans occupied Gap, the Gestapo and the French police came to my house to arrest me. Someone, probably someone I knew, had denounced me. Fortunately, my friends had warned me in advance, and I managed to get away before the Gestapo arrived. Since I could no longer go back to my former residence, one couple I knew, despite the considerable risk, took me into their home. I knew how dangerous it was for these people to hide me, so I decided to act quickly and try to flee from France. Since I was closer to Switzerland than to Spain, and the Swiss were known to be anti-fascists, I decided to try to escape to Switzerland.

My plan was to swim across Lake Geneva. I would have to swim at least four miles to come ashore sufficiently far from the city not to be noticed. The streets of Geneva were no doubt well guarded by the police. For several years, I had had no opportunity to swim, so I decided to go to Annecy and train there before making my attempt.

I arrived in Annecy, and went to the home of a Protestant minister, whose name my friends in Gap had given me. I asked him if he could arrange to hide me for a few days. He contacted a friend who agreed to take me in.

After training for only one day, I easily swam across the two-mile wide lake. Since I was not tired at all and believed I could have swum even further, I concluded that I was in good enough shape to cross Lake Geneva. But to be absolutely certain, I wanted to continue training for a least another week. However, after just a few days, in order not to endanger the lives of my host family, I decided to go to another lake not far from Chambéry, near the Swiss border. Again, through the local minister, I found a family willing to hide me for a few days. I was deeply grateful to them, knowing that hiding a stranger was becoming more and more dangerous, as the Germans were intensifying their occupation. As soon as I was settled, I started swimming daily in the lake. This time, my host was a Mr. Zdenek, who had a wife and three school-aged children. The father worked a regular eight-hour shift daily, and the children came home late in the afternoon from school, leaving me alone with Mrs. Zdenek each morning, and a for a few hours in the afternoon. After a couple of days, I noticed that she remained in her nightgown, actually a mere negligee, all day long, and I began to sense she was trying to seduce me. For several days, I did not respond to her flirtations, until one day she actually removed the negligee in my presence. At this point I felt I had to say something. As tactfully as possible I tried to point out to her how grateful I was to her husband, who was endangering himself on my account, and that I felt I could not betray him in such a selfish manner. Apparently, I was not tactful enough, because she became furious with me, concluding that I was "stupid." I decided that it was time to take my leave.

As luck would have it, on that very day my friends in Gap sent me some good news. Through the efforts of certain Protestant ministers, I was soon to obtain permission to enter Switzerland legally. It was fortunate that I had not taken the risk of swimming across Lake Geneva. Since leaving Gap, I had learned that the Swiss were now routinely expelling refugees who crossed their border illegally.

During my stay in Chambéry, I had heard the story of a certain young Catholic priest who had been actively helping people persecuted by the

Germans. He was finally arrested and beaten by the Gestapo. They broke several of his ribs and deported him to Germany. He disappeared, never again communicating with his friends, or returning to his home—another hero of the day.

Because most of my friends were in Gap, I wanted to return there and hide out while I waited for my chance to enter Switzerland. Although my former hosts, the church custodian and her husband, were still willing to house me, some of my friends convinced me that it really was too dangerous for me to remain in Gap. They advised that I leave town and hide in the mountains, and I was given the addresses of several sympathetic ministers and priests in nearby villages. So, I set out once again.

The most dangerous part of the journey was getting out of town. Taking my chances, I boarded a bus headed for the countryside. By now I knew that the French were a talkative people. I was afraid the passengers, if they conversed with me, would discover from my accent that I was a foreigner, thus jeopardizing the obscurity in which I hoped to travel. They might even think, as the Belgians had, that I was a German spy. I was spared this distress, oddly enough, when a portly policeman boarded the bus shortly after I had. Since all the seats on the bus were taken, I gestured to him to sit on my lap, which he did. He covered me completely with his broad body, so no one could see me, and no one could talk to me for the length of the journey. How fortunate I felt to have been provided with such a safe hiding place from an unexpected source.

It was Sunday. After riding the bus for several hours I reached my first destination. Leaving the bus, I went directly to the village church. The minister was out in front, cleaning off the gravestones in the cemetery. He was blond and had a pleasing general appearance. His face bore the features of a sympathetic person of strong character. I regretted not being able to capture his likeness with a photograph, but I had no camera with me.

After I introduced myself, the minister took me into his home and gave me some food. His fearlessness in helping someone he had never met before surprised me. It was dangerous for anyone to befriend strangers. The letter in my pocket could easily have implicated him, as well as the minister in Gap. If I had been a Gestapo spy impersonating a refugee, he would have fallen into a terrible trap. I pointed this out to him, and he replied that he was aware of that possibility, and that he expected one day he would inevitably be faced with such a grave misfortune. The awareness of the dangers did not keep him from what he saw as his duty: to help those who were being persecuted. I never forgot this wonderful man, whom I considered in my heart of hearts to be a genuine hero. I later learned that he was eventually arrested by the Gestapo and deported. He may have perished in one of the German concentration camps or may have been beaten to death somewhere along the way. Such heroes exist in the real world, not just in works of fiction, or in legends, or movies; not just in the distant past, but now, right here, in the present. The next day, the blond minister sent me on to another village.

On the outskirts of the next village, the first person I encountered was a young boy. When he saw me, he ran away in fear. A few minutes later four men appeared carrying axes, sickles, and other formidable farming tools. Armed with their "weapons," they kept their distance from me. I knew they were watching me closely, but when they saw me enter the village church, they disappeared. Again, I found comfort and a night's rest within the walls of a religious establishment.

The next day, I reached my final destination, a tiny, remote village high in the mountains. Only seven families resided there. Far from civilization, this place had served as a retreat during the First World War for conscientious objectors who wanted to avoid military service. It was winter, and during that part of the year it was impossible for outsiders to reach the village unguided. The road and the slopes of the surrounding mountains were completely covered with snow. Many frozen creeks and waterfalls lay beneath the snow, so a hiker might at any point encounter hidden ice just below the surface of the soft snow. If someone unfamiliar with the region tried to climb the slopes of the mountains, he could easily slip on the ice and slide helplessly down thousands of feet into the valley below. Only natives, the itinerant minister, and the mailman knew exactly how and where to traverse these treacherous mountains in winter.

After a couple of weeks in this remote village, I received a message from my friends in Gap urging me to return as soon as possible, as it seemed likely that I going to receive permission to go to Switzerland any day. I decided to travel by foot over the mountains, following the sheep drivers who knew the terrain intimately. Late in the afternoon, we began our trek down the mountain, a slope that descended over 3000 feet. It was so steep that I could neither stand still without clinging to something, nor lie down without fear of falling or sliding. This particular stretch seemed to me to be like one long, slow fall. I carried a thick, heavy stick in my hand, which I dug deeply into the snow with every step to prevent myself from slipping down the treacherous slope. After descending over 1,000 feet, I began to regret having started this dangerous journey, for which I was woefully unprepared. The sheep herders were descending with amazing speed, but I was moving slowly and cautiously. It would be dangerous for me to stay on the mountainside overnight because of the severe cold, and it was too late to return to the top. It was already completely dark. Under these conditions, one false step could mean death. I continued to descend, however, and at long last I finally reached the village at the foot of the slope.

As usual, I went directly to the local minister, who immediately provided me with a bed. The next morning, I could not move. I felt excruciating pain throughout my entire body. Strained muscles I did not even know I had made their presence all too clear. I stayed with the kind minister for three days, until I regained my ability to travel.

When I returned to Gap, Mr. Honneger, my former manager at the Nestle Company, put me up. It was more dangerous in Gap than ever, and Honneger was taking a serious risk housing me. I learned that while I had been gone, quite a few people I had known in Gap had been killed by the Gestapo or arrested and deported to Germany. The family from Vienna with the fifteen-year-old son had disappeared too. At first the Gestapo had engaged the boy as a translator. It was probably he who had betrayed me, no doubt hoping to save himself and his parents by "cooperating" with the Germans. The Gestapo had treated him well while they were trying to extract information from him, but after squeezing out all they could, they arrested the whole family and deported them to Germany. They were never heard of again.

One eighteen-year-old son of a minister who had been living in a neighboring village was able to escape out the back door of his home just as the Gestapo was entering the front door. He was wanted as an active member of the famous underground resistance. These resistance fighters were brave people, the compassionate patriots of the mountains—more unsung heroes.

It was December 1943. After several days of hiding out in Gap, I was finally notified that I had received permission to enter Switzerland legally. My first stop on the way would be Lyon, where I would contact a Reverend De Purry. I had purchased my ticket and was standing on the platform waiting for the train, when all at once I spotted two men, each one with a large German shepherd dog. I realized right away that they must be Gestapo. They were heading straight towards me. My mind raced. They had appeared so suddenly, I had had no time to run or hide. A feeling of doom crept over me; I would be caught trying to escape, just as I had been in Bludenz when two Gestapo officers and their dogs had cornered me. But now the situation was far worse. The Germans were starting to lose the war. They were desperate and frustrated, and much more likely to put suspects to death immediately than to deport them. In Bludenz I had been released; I doubted that would be the case here. How tragic it would be for me to be caught by the Gestapo now, after having been miraculously saved so many times during the past five years. I was so paralyzed with fear that my heart nearly stopped beating. My eyes widened as they approached. With their arms outstretched they rudely accosted the man standing right next to me. Shocked and stunned, I slowly backed away from the commotion. I had once more cheated fate.

I arrived in Lyon early on a Sunday morning. My contact, Reverend De Purry, took me immediately to his church where he was to conduct that morning's service. The large church held several hundred parishioners who were listening with great interest, respect, and reverence to his excellent sermon. Afterwards, however, when we had returned to his house for the noonday meal, I was taken by surprise, when during our conversation his wife remarked to him, "But you are a big, silly, stupid child." I knew she was just teasing him, because of the charm with which she expressed herself. Yet her choice of words shocked me in a way. At church earlier in the day, hundreds of people had been clinging to Reverend De Purry's every word with the highest respect. Yet his wife felt he was a "big, stupid child." That style of repartee between husband and wife was new to me, but in a way it was gratifying to observe. The understanding between them was so great, that critical words, spoken in a loving way, were easily accepted.

Reverend De Purry was of Swiss origin. He too, had the qualities of a hero, and I came to admire him tremendously. Not many people have the courage and personal conviction to help others despite personal risk. Even fewer are willing to sacrifice their lives for a just cause. Once again, I was fortunate enough to encounter such a courageous and rare individual.

De Purry, who was heavily involved with the underground movement, had already rescued many refugees fleeing German persecution. He knew what he was doing, and he must have known that one day the Gestapo would catch up with him and arrest him. That is indeed what finally happened. One Sunday, as he was giving a sermon to his congregation, the Gestapo entered the church. He had been warned beforehand, but he had not tried to escape. At the close of the service the Gestapo arrested him, and put him in solitary confinement in a German prison. Later, however, the Swiss government exchanged him for several important German spies who had been trapped in Switzerland. His arrest occurred shortly after I left Lyon.

Before my departure, De Purry filled me in on all the particulars of my escape. I was to board a certain train on a particular day and time. There I would encounter another refugee who would find me on the train. We were to travel together to Switzerland. At first all went according to plan. I took the designated train. A man riding in the same coach eventually approached me and asked me if I were Jacques Vadiez, my false name. My contact was a thirty-five-year-old physician. It was he who later located our guide, who was also traveling on the same train with us. Our guide was a marquis who belonged to the underground movement. He looked about eighteen years old.

After we disembarked, our guide took us to a nearby house, where a light supper was waiting for us. He told us he would take us across the Swiss border the next day. Realizing we had many hours to wait, we tried to relax. While we were eating, the guide explained how we would cross into Switzerland. My understanding was that he would take us by streetcar to a point not far from the border. There the three of us would continue on foot in the same direction, toward the Swiss border. At a certain point, our guide would turn back and leave us on our own to take the final step. We were then to take an immediate left and pass through a field. By continuing in this direction for several hours we would eventually reach Nyon, on the shore of Lake Geneva.

I found the explanation quite simple, but did not give it much thought, believing that our guide would instruct us again in the morning. I felt certain that I would be able to ask him any necessary questions then. Also, I found myself too exhausted at this late hour to listen attentively. About half an hour after our supper, to our great surprise, our guide announced, "We are going to Switzerland now. Let's go." Later I realized that this had been a clever way to handle such a tense situation. Thinking that we had the whole night ahead of us, we had been able to eat our meal quietly and stay relaxed up until the last minute.

Soon we boarded the streetcar. It was quite crowded initially, but it emptied out gradually with each successive stop. As we approached the end of the line, only the three of us and several German soldiers remained in the car. The soldiers carried machine guns and ammunition with them. They probably were among those assigned to guard the border and to prevent people like us from crossing it.

It was about 10 p.m. and quite dark. It had been snowing heavily for the past several hours. After a long, slow ride, we finally reached the end station, about two hundred yards from the border. Everyone got off. All the soldiers entered the station, but we stood outside for a while. Then we started to walk down the road toward the Swiss border. Looking in that direction, I could plainly see a German soldier at his post, standing under a streetlight which, much like a spotlight, shone directly down on the top of his helmet.

When we were about seventy yards from the German guard, our guide suddenly stopped and said, "Now!" He turned back, leaving us alone. At once I turned left, jumped over a snow-covered ditch, and, keeping down low, started climbing through a low barbed-wire fence.

At that moment the physician, who had remained on the road, called to me in a hoarse whisper, "Where are you going? That's the wrong way! We are supposed to go to the *right* of the road!"

I stopped in amazement. I knew we could not linger on the road debating questions of left versus right. We had to get out of sight fast. Since

I was convinced I was correct, I whispered back, "You do what you want, but I understood that we had to go to the left, and that's where I'm going."

I slipped between the strands of barbed wire, in my haste tearing a little bit of material off my overcoat. I was glad I had left the road and was in darkness now, away from the streetlights. Although the road was badly lit and the weather poor, the German soldier might still see us. We were clearly in danger of being caught. My companion remained standing on the road only a few more seconds and then decided to follow me.

It was difficult to walk with any speed through the field because of the deep snow. We sank knee-deep with every step. In the dark, we soon realized we were walking up a steep hill. After traversing only about fifty yards, we suddenly noticed a man walking in the distance. We immediately fell flat onto the snow and remained there motionless. The lights from nearby houses revealed he was wearing a green uniform, and from this we assumed he was a soldier. From our vantage point, it first seemed as if he was moving towards us in a perpendicular direction to our path. But, it soon became apparent that he was actually heading in the direction of the German border guard. We watched as he continued to walk towards him. After reaching his destination the soldier began speaking with the guard. We assumed he was telling the guard that he had seen us. This was our last chance. We had to get to Switzerland before we were apprehended. Lying in the snow for many minutes had provided us with a necessary respite. With renewed energy, we got up and bounded away as fast as we could towards the edge of a forest about eighty yards ahead. I was pretty sure, but not completely, that that forest was rooted in Swiss soil.

Maintaining our forward pace, a sort of high prancing gait through the snow, we glanced aside occasionally at the German soldier in the distance. Finally, we reached another barbed wire fence. This confirmed my belief that we probably had crossed the one-hundred-yard no-man's land, and soon we were in the forest. My companion asked me if I thought we were in Switzerland. I said yes, but in reality, I was not quite certain myself anymore if we were in Switzerland or still in France. Had we indeed taken the wrong turn back at the road?

We waded through snow for about an hour in the forest, exhausting ourselves in the deep drifts. We then came upon a road in the middle of the forest. Following it made traveling a little easier, though it was still a long, difficult hike. We walked for two more hours and then noticed that we were now going downhill. This again confirmed my belief that we were actually in Switzerland, descending the mountain at the edge of Lake Geneva.

As we continued moving downhill, we suddenly heard the click of a rifle bolt, and a voice shouting, "Mains en haut!" (Hands up!) We were caught, but by whom? I had both false and genuine identification papers in my pockets. I needed the false papers to move through France. The genuine papers I needed to show the Swiss authorities to be admitted into the country. My plan, if captured by the Germans or the French, was to throw away my genuine papers. I would be lost if they discovered my true identity. However, when I heard "Mains en haut," I had no time to think or to do anything. If I had tried to reach for my papers in my coat pocket, the soldier would probably have shot me, thinking I was reaching for a pistol. If I had had the time to throw away my genuine papers, I might never have been able to recover them again, making it difficult for me to try to immigrate to Switzerland again, or anywhere else for that matter.

Instinctively, I raised both of my hands. My heart froze with fear. To fall into German hands now meant arrest and probably death, either immediately, or in a Nazi concentration camp. The Germans had started persecuting me in March 1939. Now it was the end of December, 1943. For nearly five years I had miraculously escaped death again and again. How horrible it would be to fall into German hands now, when I was so close to freedom.

With our hands raised, my companion and I turned around to face our captors. For the first moment we could see nothing, it was so dark. Soon two men on skis emerged out of the darkness. They were dressed in white outfits, which were impossible to distinguish from the snow. Their rifles were aimed directly at us. They asked in French what we were doing and where we were going. I tried to remain calm. Instead of answering their questions, I asked, "Where are we, in France or Switzerland?" One soldier said, "In Switzerland." Hearing those words, I immediately felt as if I had arrived in paradise.

To our surprise, the soldiers escorted us back toward the French border, precisely where we had crossed it a few hours before. We learned that early in our trek we had passed close to a Swiss border station. One of the Swiss soldiers had discovered our footprints in the snow, and he and the second officer had been sent out to track us down—probably no difficult task, since we had made no attempt to disguise our footprints.

It took two hours on foot to get back to the Swiss police station, less than a hundred yards from where we had crossed the barbed wire fence into Switzerland earlier that night. On our way back we could hear singing and happy yodeling accompanied by the zither coming from the chalets we passed. I had an ecstatic feeling, listening to this music—it seemed to be the voice of freedom and peace. Although the soldiers were guiding us back toward the border, I felt safe, assuming that there would only be a few formalities and we would be admitted into Switzerland.

At the station, one of the officers asked us where we had come from and what we were doing in this area. My companion and I gave him our genuine identification papers and said, "We have permission to enter Switzerland. Our names are on the list." We knew that each police station on the Swiss side of the border had such lists. This method of identification had been set up by French Protestant ministers who, as part of the resistance, were actively assisting refugees. The officer said that he knew nothing about such a list. But after several minutes of argument, convinced that we were emphatically confident of its existence, he left us by ourselves in the interrogation room. This was not as simple a formality as I had at first envisioned.

A few minutes later, the officer returned. Pointing his finger at my chest, he said, "You may stay in Switzerland, but," pointing to the physician, "your companion may not. He will be taken back to the border, where he must cross back into France." The physician's face turned white as a sheet. I started to defend him saying that it was only thanks to him that I was able to locate my guide, making my escape to Switzerland possible. I was certain he had permission to enter Switzerland too, just as I had. But it was no use. They did not even permit him to call his friends in Switzerland, who knew that he was on his way and that he had permission to enter the country.

The Swiss police took the poor man, now completely exhausted, and escorted him to a place where he could cross the border. I had tremendous pity for him, and I could not understand why he was being sent back after he had succeeded in making his way to Switzerland under such difficult conditions. By returning to France now, he would be in even greater danger of being persecuted or killed by the Nazis.

After my companion had been taken from the interrogation room, one of the police officers gave me some hot chocolate and then led me to a hotel. It was quite late already. Our path to the hotel passed only a few feet from where the German soldier stood beneath the streetlight. He looked at me, and I calmly looked back at him. He had no idea that I had slipped past him only five hours earlier. This was the first time in years I had looked at a German soldier without fear.

When I undressed in the hotel, I found, to my surprise, that my underwear was frozen solid. While racing through the snow away from the border, I had perspired heavily, but on the return route with the Swiss soldiers, I had walked slowly, producing less body heat, and my thin overcoat did little to help me retain it. Thus my perspiration-soaked underclothing had frozen. I had been so excited, I hadn't even noticed! Now, however, the excitement was over for the day. I managed to undress and slip into the feather bed, and in no time I fell into a deep, sound sleep.

Here was a strange coincidence: I had left Krasnoyarsk on December 25, 1921, and Harbin on December 25, 1923. Now I had successfully crossed the Swiss border on Saturday, December 25, 1943. It was truly a memorable date for me—a Merry Christmas! I was now, without doubt, safe and secure in a free, neutral country.

Chapter 11

THE POWER OF DREAMS

Imagination rules the world.

—Napoleon

When I awoke the next morning, a feeling of deep relief and indescribable happiness came over me. For the past five years I had been living fearfully in hiding, or running for my life. Had I been caught, the Nazis might have killed me on the spot, or done away with me in their infamous gas chambers. At long last I had escaped their persecution. Finally, I was truly free.

But to what or whom did I owe my freedom? Was it only a matter of luck, or certain innate qualities, such as courage or perseverance? Perhaps a Divine Power had been guiding, instructing, and protecting me all along, saving me for some special unknown purpose? To anyone of faith, the answer clearly lies with God. But even from a scientific point of view, the odds of successfully cheating death so many times are improbably high, if not completely absurd.

Coincidence or miracle, I realized that two main factors contributed to my survival. The first was my great fortune in finding so many brave people willing to assist me, despite potentially dangerous consequences. Without the help of these heroes I certainly would not have made it. I will remain grateful to them for the rest of my life. Second was my own strong inborn will to live. During those years of persecution, I simply could not reconcile myself to the idea of failure. I was simply too young to die! This feeling nourished my will to survive despite overwhelming odds and misfortunes. I was healthy and strong, had a positive mental outlook, and the possibilities I imagined for my future fascinated me. From childhood I had wanted to grow mentally, physically, and spiritually. *Life* meant developing my inherited capacities and using my talents to the greatest extent possible. I felt, even at a young age, that the more a person uses his talents, the greater his involvement in life, and the richer and more interesting his world becomes.

I had certainly made some serious mistakes along the way, but I had also taken some wise steps. I had suffered much misfortune, but had also encountered a lot of good luck. Certainly the experiences of the last few years—suffering under oppression, and witnessing the suffering of others—had made me wiser and more mature. I had seen the worst weaknesses in human nature—hate, cruelty, and injustice. I myself had been a victim, and had witnessed the darker side of mankind.

I concluded that most men subscribe to one of two diametrically opposed philosophies. Some achieve their goals by selfish, ruthless, and dishonest means. A man without a conscience might attain happiness this way. He may even believe that he is being smart. However, a man with any degree of inner goodness cannot lead that kind of life and be content. Subconsciously, if not consciously, he will be miserable, having to constantly rationalize his avaricious ways.

An honorable life philosophy is based on solid virtues, such as honesty, respect, kindness, and justice, which go beyond mere survival instincts. I sincerely wished to strive for this kind of greatness and to rise above selfish, primeval urges. Having *greatness* means overcoming baser human instincts to follow more virtuous paths: striving for peace, justice, and truth; helping your family, your community, and mankind as a whole.

Great people had always fascinated me. When you travel extensively, you may see many mountains. But only a few really high mountains, like Everest, McKinley, Mont Blanc, and the Matterhorn, impress and inspire you so much that you never forget them. You might notice the smaller mountains, but they leave no lasting impression. Those greater mountains cannot properly be seen in the valley. One needs to climb up and stand on a higher plateau to view those higher peaks. So it is with people. You recognize people with true greatness at once and never forget them. Less exceptional people you may notice momentarily, but they are quickly forgotten. But you yourself must possess a higher spiritual level to be able to recognize these exceptional people for what they are. It is through your own capacity for goodness that these giants are able to impress and inspire you.

In my professional life I had been proud to be a front runner, a leader, and an innovator. This required foresight and courage. I felt that the challenges I had faced in my life until now had been extremely interesting and worth the struggles I had to endure. However, to be completely happy I knew that I needed to love and be loved. Now that I was free, I realized that I needed a wife and family, whom I would care for and try to make happy. I also needed the love of my family in return. Most important, of course, was my future wife. Children, when they grow up, naturally and rightfully leave their parents. But a wife stays with her husband until death separates them. I hoped that my future wife and I would inspire and help each other to achieve mutual goals. Doing so would bring us both happiness.

Switzerland is the oldest democracy in existence. The Swiss people fought for freedom and won their independence in the thirteenth century. These brave people, surrounded by their majestic mountains and beautiful lakes, possess a great love of freedom, which I too had cherished as a boy, and cherished even more so now, after my most recent escape from the Nazis. I thought that this should be the ideal place to find the girl of my dreams.

At the age of thirty-eight, finally free from persecution and oppression, I was ready and eager to start life again. I would renew my pursuit of long-held goals. I was ready to fight again, to meet any challenge. Breathing the fresh Swiss air, I felt exhilarated, just like a runner feels when he approaches the finish line certain of winning the race.

After my first night of good, sound sleep at the hotel near the border, two policemen took me to a camp in Lausanne, where about one hundred other refugees were residing. It was interesting to make the acquaintance of these people, who had come from all over Europe. One sentiment common to all of us, regardless of origin, was a sincere gratitude to the Swiss people for their hospitality, and for saving our lives. After surviving persecution and the harrowing dangers we all had experienced trying to reach safety and freedom, we felt as if we were living in paradise. We held everyone and everything Swiss in the highest regard.

Among the many refugees, I even met two Russian girls. The Germans had taken them during the Russian campaign and brought them back to Germany to work as laborers. They had escaped to Switzerland by a daring and creative ploy. One afternoon, they managed to slip away from their work detail, taking with them a quantity of a special kind of industrial powder. When they reached the border, two German guards stopped them and asked to see their identification papers. Instead of producing their papers, they threw the powder into the soldier's eyes, blinding them for a moment and causing great pain. The girls used this fleeting moment of opportunity to dash across the border.

As it happened, I had to sleep on the floor of a large room along with twelve British soldiers. They had escaped from a German prison camp by digging a tunnel under the high barbed wire fence. One of these soldiers had fallen in love with a refugee girl from Yugoslavia. Some nights he would bring his girlfriend to our room to sleep with him, and since I slept right next to him, she would often be lying between him and me. Often late at night, when he thought we were all asleep, he made love to her. If I were awake, or awoke due to the commotion, I found this to be most provocative, and more than a little frustrating.

Within a short time, I decided to organize a chorus. There were several excellent singers among the refugees. We usually sang Russian folksongs that I taught to the others. Everyone in the camp and the neighboring community enjoyed our impromptu concerts.

Soon a theater group was established, which I joined. We set up a stage such that the audience could see only the silhouettes of the actors behind a large screen made out of a bed sheet. In one of our shows we portrayed a sick refugee lying in bed. A doctor was summoned who anesthetized him by striking him on the head with a bottle. Then he started to pull out head after head of cabbage from his patient's mouth. This satirized the cabbage-heavy diet we were served at the camp, and it got a good laugh. Another show featured a camel played by two men, one at the front and one at the rear. As the camel walked, its sex organs, of tremendously exaggerated size, swung violently back and forth. This got an even bigger laugh for more than one reason. The skit poked fun at the camp's female physician, who was sitting in the audience, because she was famous for her excessively thorough examinations of us. Such precautions were no doubt necessary to avoid the importation of venereal diseases, but we would have preferred, in any case, to have been examined by a male physician.

After a few weeks, I was transferred to another refugee center in a luxurious resort hotel in Les Avant sur Montreux. About four hundred refugees from France, Italy, Austria, Germany, Yugoslavia, and other countries were residing there. No refugee could have hoped for better than what we received at this hotel—much better food, and excellent accommodations and treatment. The resort itself was now closed to tourists because of the war. Among the refugees were some highly educated and talented people, and again we soon organized a series of concerts and lectures, with refugees serving as performers and speakers. I myself gave a lecture in French. My topic was "The Goal of Life," and my thesis was that one should strive for self-conservation, self-development (physical and spiritual), perfection, and creativity.

Most of the refugees were under the impression that they would have to remain there for the duration of the war. We were not allowed off the premises, nor had we permission to seek employment in Switzerland. This was only minimally acceptable to me, as I was eager to start living a real life again. After two months at the hotel, I discovered an opportunity that might ultimately release me from the camp. If I could appear in person at the office of a certain welfare organization in Geneva, I might be granted a scholarship to continue my graduate studies at a Swiss university. Unfortunately, I could not get permission to leave the camp, even for a single day. Faced with this impediment, for some reason, I recalled my time in Irkutsk, and how I had managed to escape from Russia. This gave me an idea: I resolved to give a piano recital.

From 1921 until 1938 I had not practiced the piano seriously at all. In 1938, in Germany, I had purchased a piano, but because I was so occupied with my career, I played little, and only for a few months, until March 1939, when I had had to flee. Here at the hotel, we had several excellent pianos at our disposal, and I began to practice many hours each day for several weeks. Not having any music with me, I struggled to recall the pieces I had played best in Krasnoyarsk: Mendelssohn's *Concerto in G minor*, opus 25 and *Caprice Espagnol* by Moszkowski. Again and again I would attempt to play these pieces, trying to resurrect them from my memory. Often I would play with my eyes closed. Slowly, I began to remember, first only a few scattered passages, but gradually more and more, until finally I was able to play large portions of both compositions. To fill in the sections I just could not recall, I had to compose transitions from one part to another, to construct what seemed to be a whole piece, suitable for a performance.

Besides these two pieces, which I played from memory, I played from an available score of the *Egmont Overture* by Beethoven, arranged for piano, four hands. My partner pianist was an Italian who had been a dentist. We played with great emotion, expressing our own deep feelings through Beethoven's music. A third man working with us, another Italian, was a professional cellist who had been professor at a music conservatory in Italy before the war.

After several weeks of practice, we were ready to present our concert. It was publicized in the nearby towns, and the members of the audience, townspeople from Montreux, Vevey, and other nearly locations, were charged an admission fee. As I was playing, I noticed a group of Swiss officers in the front row. After I finished my solo pieces, which I felt I had played quite badly, I thought I saw disappointment in their faces. They probably knew the music well, and had expected something special from me, maybe because of my artistic-sounding Slavic name. They did not know, of course, that I had been handicapped by many years of pianistic inactivity. My last pubic performance had been in 1921.

However, in spite of some artistic disappointments, the concert was a great success overall, and the three of us were instant celebrities. Before the concert, I had asked our camp director several times for permission to go to Geneva, and he had always refused. However, after this concert he immediately granted my request, and gave me a three-day leave. My plan had worked. As in Irkutsk, the piano had rescued me once again.

In Geneva I met with Mr. Freudenberg, Secretary of the Ecumenical Council. He gave me an excellent letter of recommendation, believing, without verifying from any other source, what I told him of my qualifications. With this recommendation I was able to obtain a scholarship—200 Swiss francs per month plus tuition—enabling me to enroll in a graduate program at the Federal Institute of Technology (Eidgenössische Technische Hochschule, or ETH) in Zurich, where I was accepted without any difficulty.

In the meantime, until the semester started, I was transferred to a different, smaller refugee center. In this center, the refugees had to work outdoors on an earthmoving detail. However, the center director, a sympathetic and sensitive man, permitted me and another musician, a good violinist, to stay inside and practice. I enjoyed my time at this center considerably.

I met a Polish officer with a German-sounding name there. He was twenty-eight years old, about five feet, ten inches tall, and had a fine athletic build. Later he too obtained permission to attend the ETH in Zurich. One day, he told me a dramatic and shocking story about how he had escaped to Switzerland. He had been in Italy during the war. Shortly after Italy signed an armistice with the Allied Forces, but before the Germans had left the country, some Italian Air Force officers visited him. They knew that he was a trained Polish officer, and they told him of their plan to kill some members of the Gestapo living in a certain house that night. They added that they would be pleased if he would join them. He replied, "Why not?" That same night, at 3 a.m., they all arrived at the designated house. They broke in, awakened the Gestapo officers, and held them at gunpoint. But at that moment the Italian officers got cold feet, and would not go through with the plan. The Polish officer had to kill the Gestapo officers single-handedly with his pistol, one by one. They then took the Gestapo uniforms from the corpses and put them on. Taking the Gestapo officers' staff car, they made their way toward the Swiss-Italian border. On route somewhere in northern Italy, they were trapped by Germans, and a gun battle ensued. My acquaintance, along with several of the others, was able to escape with only a few flesh wounds (now scars) on his face.

Near the Swiss border, the group decided to separate. My friend continued on by foot, but soon ran into a German soldier. The soldier did not draw his gun, and was not immediately suspicious, but my friend knew he could not explain his presence in that area, or pass for a genuine Gestapo officer, so he frankly explained that he was a fugitive, and offered the German an expensive ring in exchange for his freedom. The German took the ring and let him pass. If the German had resisted, my friend would have killed him. He still had his pistol in his coat pocket, and he would have used it if necessary.

I did not know if his story was true, but the man seemed sincere. It amazed me how this seemingly gentle person, who spoke with such a soft, pleasing voice, could kill several Gestapo officers single-handedly in cold blood.

My three semesters in Zurich were quite enjoyable. I rented a pleasant room on the Breitenhauptstrasse. After being on the run for five years, it was wonderful to be following a normal routine and using time in a productive way again. I started attending lectures and doing laboratory work at the ETH. However, I had not been a student for fifteen years and found the academic work quite challenging. I had difficulty following the lectures and could not understand instructions as easily as the younger students. Although I had been accepted at the university without difficulty, my credentials as an expert in mining were questioned—a situation that limited my opportunities at the university. Fortunately, at the local textbook store I found two books on open pit mining that I had written while in Germany. I bought one of them and showed it around to establish my credibility.

I enjoyed my courses in material science, and the courses in economic geology taught by the famous Professor Niggli. But my favorite lectures were those on physics given by Professor Scherrer. I was one of about 500 students in the class, yet I remember a great deal, even now, of what I heard and saw demonstrated in his lectures. Two or three assistants were always busy preparing instruments that lay on a long table at the front of the classroom. Each physical phenomenon was meticulously demonstrated, and a mathematical explanation of each experiment was given thereafter. Movies were also shown, and special lighting techniques were used to project ongoing experiments onto a screen, so that they could be seen clearly by all of the students in the class.

Of greatest importance to me was my work with Professor Stussi, who taught bridge design. He had previously been an assistant director to the famous bridge designer Othmar Ammann, the head of engineers for the Port of New York Authority. Professor Stussi's hobby, however, was blasting. I learned much from him in this field, a field in which I was later to become internationally known myself.

During my stay in Switzerland I became acquainted with several families. I shall always remain grateful for the affection and kindness they showed me. Although I had enough money to live in a modest way, my new friends showered me with many gifts: an expensive suit, shoes, and many other fine things. They frequently invited me into their homes, trying to make me as comfortable and happy as they could. But my freedom was the main source of my happiness at this time. Freedom is a person's most precious possession. One knows better how to value it, if one has lived without it.

While I was in Zurich, the war ended, and I was able to contact my old friends and colleagues in Wülfrath. All of them were still alive, much to my joy and relief. Their survival, however, awakened my old moral dilemma—whether I should have informed the Allied military command of the industrial importance of Wülfrath. Wülfrath had survived the war without a scratch. Not one bomb fell on the entire enormous mining operation during the war. Was this because the Allies did not know about Wülfrath, or of its importance? Could my information have made a difference? Or did the Allied forces simply choose to ignore mining operations, concentrating instead on factories? I still do not really know, but at that time, knowing my old friends were still alive, I was sure I had made the right decision.

I heard from my old friends in other parts of Germany too. Fortunately, most of them had also survived the war. In fact, all were still alive but one. Dresden had been heavily firebombed in 1945. My dear friend, Miss Scholz, was killed in that tragic eleventh-hour attack. The bombing had been much criticized, even by some Allied leaders at the time. The Allied air force ruthlessly destroyed the city, a beautiful and historic old town of no military importance, solely to punish an already defeated Germany. I had seen Miss Scholz last on August 31, 1939, the day before the war started.

One day I read an announcement posted at the university inviting interested students to take part in a religious study group at Heimstätte

Gwatt. Gwatt, a small community on the shore of Lake Thun, boasted fantastic panoramic views of the Monch and Jungfrau mountains. The Heimstätte (homestead) was a home for young women, run by the Reformed Church and directed by a minister who lived there with his wife and three small children. Courses on a variety of subjects were regularly offered there. Although still an agnostic, I was interested in learning more about religion, so I signed up for the course.

Throughout my life I had often dreamed of the girl who would someday be my wife. Because of this dream, I had generally been conservative and self-disciplined in my relationships with women. I always felt certain I would eventually meet the right girl. At the Heimstätte in Gwatt, I met one of the young ladies residing there. I was thirty-eight, and she only eighteen. Yet when I first saw her, as she stood shaking a plum tree, trying to get the ripe plums to fall, I felt a special "click" in my heart. I immediately became fascinated by her, and quite soon I realized that she was the one—my future wife, about whom I had been dreaming all my life.

Her name was Anna, or Anneli, as I would learn to call her. The more time I spent with her, the more convinced I was that she really was the object of my long search. She had charming ways, and possessed a beautiful face and figure, and a lovely, gentle, warmly responsive personality to match. She also was an intelligent, capable person, curious to learn all she could about culture, history, and the arts. She asked me many questions about these and other topics, for which I often had to do extensive library research, sometimes hours at a time, to give her a satisfactory answer. Every day I admired her more and more, and I soon was deeply in love with her. Everything she did was exciting to me.

In two weeks, the religion seminar was over, and I left Gwatt. But each day thereafter I wrote Anneli a long letter. This was unusual. I had always hated writing letters, and wrote only in exceptionally urgent cases, but to her I wrote gladly. In each letter, I enclosed a beautiful picture postcard of a composer, or another famous or historically important person. I also enclosed a small cake. I later found out how much this irritated the postman. Some of the cakes I sent were cream-filled, and sometimes the envelope would break, causing his mailbag to become a smeary, creamy mess.

After one and a half years of graduate study in Zurich, I got a job as the manager of a coal mine in the canton of Wallis. Later I became a consultant at a coal mine in the canton of Bern. At last, after a six year hiatus, I was working in my field again and earning good money. Every weekend I would try to go to Gwatt to visit Anneli. She was nearing the end of a three-year apprenticeship in sewing and upholstery in Thun. Soon after I had begun working professionally, we decided to marry.

My bride's father, Johannes (Hans) Stahel, however, would not consent to our marriage. I understood his objections—I was twenty years older than Anneli, and I was a refugee with an uncertain future who could offer his daughter little financial security. A foreigner, I hailed from an area in Russia often misrepresented as nothing but a primitive wasteland populated by criminals and ruffians. No doubt he would have preferred a Swiss son-in-law. Anna's step-mother, Martha, tried to ease the tensions, realizing that the more opposition they showed to our marriage, the less likely it was they would dissuade us. I was grateful for her tolerance, but her lenience did nothing to sway her husband.

In 1922, I had left Siberia with the specific aim of going to the United States. In 1923, while in Manchuria, I decided to follow Mr. Skorochodov's advice instead and study at the world-famous Freiberg School of Mines. After graduation, I delayed making arrangements to immigrate to the United States because I had been offered an excellent position in Germany and had become increasingly fascinated with my work. That delay cost me dearly. In 1939, upon leaving Germany, I had immediately requested an immigration visa from the American consulate in Belgium, but to no avail. Again in 1943, when I was in Marseille, I applied for a visa and was at the point of receiving it when the Germans occupied Marseille, and my hopes were dashed once more. But I continued to cling to the distant hope of one day reaching the United States even so.

Now, in 1946, the American Consulate in Switzerland was attempting to secure an immigration visa for me once more. However, my upcoming marriage complicated the process, because finding a sponsor (required for immigration) for two persons was much more difficult than for one. While attempting to address these problems, I received an offer from a British mining company for a position at a remote mine in the mountains of Argentina. My old friend Grassmück had recommended me for the job. Since I could see little opportunity in Switzerland, where mining was only a wartime industry, and because I had no assurance of getting an American visa any time soon, I decided to accept the offer in Argentina, and to apply for an American visa from there.

Anneli and I then decided to marry immediately. Our marriage took place on July 30, 1946, in her home town of Winterthur, in a civil ceremony, followed by a religious ceremony in a Protestant church in Zurich. To my regret, Anna's parents did not attend our wedding, because of her father's disapproval of me. Particularly, I was sad for Anneli.

We spent a joyful honeymoon week in Silvaplana, a beautiful spot in southeastern Switzerland. Elated to be married to such a charming, young, and beautiful wife, I was nevertheless uneasy, because I now carried the responsibility of providing for her needs and ensuring her happiness. I worried because my financial situation was so miserable for a man of my age. I was beginning a new life once more—again starting with nothing. This time, I hoped, it would be a life filled only with good fortune.

Concert
Instrumental

ORGANISÉ PAR LES

Oeuvres sociales du Camp de Réfugiés des Avants

EXÉCUTÉ PAR LES RÉFUGIÉS :

Mr le Professeur VITTORIO BASEVI
violoncelliste

Mr l'Ingénieur des mines BORIS KOCHANOWSKY
pianiste

dans la Salle de Théâtre du GRAND HOTEL des Avants s/Montreux

Mercredi, le 15 mars 1944, à 20 h. 15

Programme

Première partie :	Cello	Antoniotti :	**Sonate en sol min.** (Adagio-Allegro-Largo-Finale)
		Saint-Saëns :	**Le Cygne**
		Van Goens :	**Scherzo**
		Hændel :	**Largo**
Deuxième partie :	Piano	Grieg :	**Sonate en mi min.** (Allo Minuetto)
		Moszkowski :	**Caprice Espagnol** (A. moll)
	Cello	Gounod :	**Ave Maria**
		Schumann :	**Träumerei**
Troisième partie :	Piano	Rachmaninoff :	**Prélude** (op. 3 n. 2)
		Grieg :	**Scène du Carnaval** (op. 19 n. 3)
	Cello	Gabriel Marie :	**La Cinquantaine**
		Valensin :	**Minuetto**
		Albeniz :	**Malaguena**

ENTRÉE : Fr. 1.20 par personne   —   Militaires et Enfants : Fr. 0.60

Les bénéfices nets seront destinés aux réfugiés nécessiteux du camp des Avants

Train des Avants pour Montreux à 23 h. 50

PROGRAM FROM THE REFUGEE CAMP CONCERT, MARCH 15, 1944
BORIS WAS ABLE TO SECURE A THREE-DAY RELEASE FROM
THE CAMP AS A RESULT OF THIS PERFORMANCE.

HEIMSTÄTTE GWATT, ON THE LAKE OF THUN

ANNA STAHEL AT THE LAKE OF THUN, SWITZERLAND

Anna (1946)

BORIS (1946)

Chapter 12

ALWAYS AN ARARAT

There's always been an Ararat
Where someone someone else begat
To start the world all over at.

—Robert Frost, *A Wishing Well*

My employer in Argentina insisted that I take up my appointment immediately, but booking passage for the two of us during the summer of 1946, so soon after the war, was not easy. With the assistance of a friend at the British consulate I was able to purchase a plane ticket for myself, and to arrange passage by ship for Anneli three months later. Thus, after only a brief ten-day honeymoon, was I forced to leave my dear wife behind. Separating was heartbreaking for both of us. She cried when I left her, but she showed unwavering courage, which only increased my admiration for her.

My new job was at the Minacar asphaltite mine in the state of Mendoza, not far from the Chilean border. High in the Andes Mountains, the remote mining community stood two hundred miles from the nearest city and sixty miles from the nearest police station. The frequent violent wind storms there made it impossible for any vegetation to grow. The landscape was totally barren; only rocks were visible as far as the eye could see. Forsaken by nature and neglected by man, the area was forbidding and desolate. I could not imagine a more inhospitable or isolated environment. I was afraid Anna would be disappointed when she arrived, and would want to return immediately to the beauty of her homeland. But, to my surprise, she considered everything—the mountains, the sky, and the terrain—beautiful and colorful. She loved the newness of the adventure, and found the people associated with the mines fascinating. When I started looking through her eyes, simply by being near her, I found that there was much to admire in my surroundings that I had not noticed before. I was forty years old and she twenty, yet she was a keener observer than I. In many respects, she also proved to be cleverer. I was learning to adore her more and more. I was proud of her and extremely happy finally to have the reality of love, instead of just the dream. The misery of the past made these moments of happiness even more precious.

Gerhard Grassmück, my friend since our student days in Freiberg, had helped me find the job at Minacar. He had accepted a position in Argentina as well, in Buenos Aires. He, his wife Karin, and their young daughter Rita would visit us often at Minicar, and Anna and I would relish the chance to visit them from time to time in the city. Anna soon formed a fast friendship with Karin, who was closer to my age and also Russian by birth.

During our stay in Argentina, six years in all, I formed a favorable impression of the country and of the Argentine people. I admired their intelligence and quick-mindedness. No wonder they made such formidable competitors in polo, soccer, and chess. Their race car drivers were superior too, and foreign nations often purposely sought out Argentines for intelligence work. I was treated to an example of their quick wit on the occasion of an election. I had expressed shock to learn that it would take several weeks for the ballots to be counted and the results to be announced, and I remarked that in Europe, the outcome was known twenty-four hours after the polls closed. One clever Argentine replied, "In Argentina, we know the results twenty-four hours *before* the polls close."

Minacar employed about 500 mine workers, while the total population of the mining community was about 1,000. We had our own school, church, prison, and police force, all staffed by employees of the mine. During my first year, there were two explosions in the mine which resulted in dangerous fire outbreaks. We also had a cave-in that killed two miners. Asphaltite when broken is like coarse sand or small pieces of gravel. During the cave-in, the asphaltite fell in so quickly that when we dug the bodies of the miners out, they were still in a standing position.

After serving as an engineer for one year, I was promoted to site manager. I immediately made safety the number one priority, and after adopting several new safety regulations, I began to focus on other issues as well. When I took over, the management was relying on a secret police force of informers recruited from among the workers to report any incidence of criminal activity or labor unrest. It was crucial to maintain order, because we were so far from civilization and had to contend with a rather rough breed of men, many of whom had questionable backgrounds. I abolished this secret police system, and openly appointed a corps of labor representatives, one from each camp barrack. Each representative wore a special white hat, so there was no doubt as to who they were. The men selected for this position were those with the best work records, and they were honored to serve in this capacity. Their duties remained the same—to report any unrest or other type of trouble. But they also served as spokesmen for the workers. The workers knew they could report any legitimate concerns or grievances to the "white-hats," and they would get a fair hearing.

By far the biggest change I made was in the employee wage structure. When I started at the mine, there was a complex system in place for calculating wages, based primarily on seniority. Productivity was low, and the foremen struggled constantly with the workers to get them to do any work at all. One day I decreed that all workers, from that day forward, would receive the same pay, the lowest starting rate for a new employee. In addition, foremen were no longer to nag the workers to work any harder than they wanted to work. Confused by this, most of the foremen seriously doubted this system could work.

But I insisted, "If a worker wants to sleep, let him sleep." If any worker wished to earn more than the minimum pay, he would have to come to me and sign a formal agreement to produce a larger output.

As might have been expected, there was quite an uproar. A few workers—not many—quit on the spot, and there was considerable grumbling from the rest. Productivity dropped even lower for a few weeks, but eventually the first volunteer came to my office.

"I want to make more money." he said.

I replied, "That's fine, but you can't work alone. You need a team of at least four."

"I'll get them," he said, and soon returned with three friends. We agreed to an increase in pay for the four of them, in return for a certain number of tons of yield per day from that team.

It was not long before several teams came to me to make similar deals. Then established teams started coming back, agreeing to produce even more, for further increases in pay. Within a few months, productivity was sky-high, and every worker, without exception, was making considerably more than he had under the old system. I gave out blue ribbons to the teams that produced the most, and the recipients wore their ribbons on the job, as badges of honor.

After two years at Minacar, I accepted a professorship at an Argentine university in San Juan. Another year later, I received an additional post as professor at a branch college of the same university. Two years after that, I also became an advisor to the Argentine federal government in Buenos Aires for coal and uranium mining.

After all I had been through—revolution, war, persecution, fleeing for my life, hiding from the Nazis—nothing prepared me for anything as terrifying as the earthquake that hit us in San Juan. Once we had settled in San Juan, Anna and I had decided to build a home on the outskirts of the town. I was sitting in the living room of our house and Anna was seated across the room from me, when things started to shake. Long, powerful jolts continued for several minutes. I thought I saw Anna, the chair she was sitting on, and the floor under her, rise up four or five feet and then come back down again. Thinking back, it seems unlikely that the vibrations could have been that large, but, in my terror, that is what I thought I saw. It seemed to me as if the earth was going to swallow us both up, and that there would be absolutely no hope of survival. The earthquake was quite severe. Our house sustained heavy damage, and most of the town was completely destroyed. There were many injuries and several deaths. Of course, natives of that earthquake-prone region had not been as frightened as we were. But this had been our first encounter with an earthquake.[30]

Although I admired the intelligence of the Argentines, I was dismayed by the depth of corruption in their society. After the earthquake, I and all of my friends sought out loans from the government to repair or rebuild our homes. I appeared at the bank's disaster loan bureau where a bank

---

[30] The San Juan earthquake of June 11, 1952 registered 7.0 on the Richter scale.

official asked me several questions as he filled out a standardized form. The questions were logical, like how much money I wanted to borrow, my annual salary, and how large a monthly payment could I make. Then finally, after he had completed the form, the official turned to me and asked, "And how much for me?"

I thought he was joking, and so I just laughed. But, a few days later I received notice that my loan application had been rejected. When I told a friend, who had been approved for a loan, he seemed puzzled that I had been turned down. "Didn't the officer ask you some questions?" he asked.

"Yes," I replied, "about the amount of the loan, my salary, and so forth."

"Ah," said my friend, "but didn't he ask you one very *special* question?"

I learned then what the appropriate answer to that question was, whereupon I returned to the loan bureau, offered the proper amount of bribe, and was soon granted my loan.

My salary as a professor was 2,200 pesos per month, the equivalent of $450. In comparison, mine workers at Minacar had earned $40-60 a month, mine managers $300-500 a month. From time to time I could supplement my income by working as an industrial consultant, which boosted my earnings to as high as 10,000 to 13,000 pesos ($2,600) a month, four to five times the salary of a full-time professor. It was fantastic money, considering that dinner in a good restaurant in Buenos Aires cost only about a dollar at the time.

In spite of my secure position and high income, when I was notified by the U.S. consulate that our immigration visas were ready, we left Argentina as soon as we could. It had been my constant dream since 1922 to live in the United States, and now after thirty years, thirteen years after I had first applied for a visa in Brussels, I would finally be able to realize this long-envisioned goal.

We had invested most of our money in our house in San Juan. Unfortunately, the economy had taken a downturn and I was not able to get the price I wanted for it before we left. So I asked a friend to sell it for me. When it finally sold a few years later for the price I had originally sought, the Argentine currency had been so devalued, that the money was worth only one-fifteenth of what it had been. I received less than $3,000 from the sale. Again, I had lost nearly everything in making this move to the United States, but I had no regrets. Free from persecution, with the girl of my dreams, I was ready to preach to anyone who would listen that dreams really can come true if one only has the patience and perseverance. Again, I would be starting over in a new country, but I felt rich and happy.

MINING SETTLEMENT MINACAR, ARGENTINA

MAIN ENTRANCE TO THE MINE AT MINACAR

GERHARD GRASSMÜCK, ANNA, AND BORIS AT MINACAR

Anna and I boarded a ship bound for New York City. We arrived on January 5, 1953. Because we had not been able to sell our house in Argentina and because of the devaluation of the peso, our entire savings amounted to only $2,500. For the first several months, as hard as I tried, I could not find employment. Nobody seemed to want me, a foreigner, and worse than that, a Russian. With the Red Scare in full force, Russian immigrants were looked upon unfavorably at the time, particularly because of the on-going war in Korea. In addition, I was a blasting expert, trying to get a job in the explosives industry. In some quarters, this combination may have aroused suspicion that I might be a Russian spy looking for the means to wreak havoc and destruction on American soil.

My other handicaps were my age and my poor command of the English language. I was struggling to learn my fifth language at the age of forty-eight. Employers might have been willing to risk hiring a younger person, but I sensed their reluctance to bring a senior staff member on board with so many unknown factors. I had been a leading mining engineer in Germany and in Argentina, but had no viable reputation in the United States.

My Swiss wife, on the other hand, was considered a "good" kind of foreigner. Only twenty-seven years old, attractive, and personable, Anna landed a job as a receptionist in one day. We could not, however, live on her wages alone. Prices in New York City, even then, compared to the cost of living in Argentina, seemed astronomical. As the weeks and months passed, we spent down our tiny savings, and hoped for a change in our fortune.

We were down to $450, when I was invited to interview for a teaching position at the Pennsylvania State University[31] in State College, Pennsylvania. My interview was with the head of the mining engineering department. The man seemed hostile towards me for some reason. In spite of my extensive international experience, nothing I said seemed to interest him, and as the interview concluded, he said, "I'm sorry, but we do not have a place for you here." This confused and confounded me, because I was desperate for work, and I knew I was more than qualified for the job. I went, uninvited, to the dean's office, and asked for a few minutes to speak to him. In sharp contrast with the department head, the dean was very interested in my background, and we had an excellent conversation. When I told him that I had not been offered the position, he seemed shocked. He led me back to the department head's office, and from the doorway pointed to me and said, "Take him." Then he walked away without saying another word. So, in that quite inauspicious manner, I got the job.

Anna and I would make the move to Pennsylvania in August, just prior to the start of classes. On the day before our departure, I decided to visit the library of the American Institute of Mining, Metallurgical, and Petroleum Engineers (AIME) one last time. I had often gone there during our stay in New York to read some of the latest journals in the field in the library's large public reading room. There on the wall I had noticed three huge portraits, presumably of distinguished engineers. The middle one I had recognized as former President Herbert Hoover, who had also been a famous mining engineer. But I did not know who the other two persons were, and, until then, I had not bothered to find out. I realized that this would be my last opportunity to do so for quite some time, so I made my way toward the wall where the portraits were hanging. I passed a series of long reading tables covered with journals that were standing parallel to the wall. As I approached the paintings, looking up intently at the inscriptions

---

[31] The institution changed its name from The Pennsylvania State College to The Pennsylvania State University in 1953.

to make out the names, I suddenly lost my footing and fell through the floor. Concentrating on the pictures, I had not noticed the open stairwell beyond the last reading table.

My pelvis took the major force of the blow, striking the sharp edge of a step about halfway down a steel staircase. From there I rolled to the bottom, falling a total of ten to twelve feet. I weighed about 200 pounds at the time, so the effect was about the same as a 200-pound weight falling on my body from a height of several feet. I lay on the floor without moving for several minutes because I thought I had surely broken some bones. Since my fall had created quite a clatter, a man soon came to investigate. He looked down at me in horror, but instead of helping me, he ran away. After a few more minutes had passed, I realized that no one was coming to assist me, so I cautiously began to try to move. Finally, I succeeded in standing up. Painfully I made my way to the elevator and exited the building. I flagged a taxi and asked to be taken to the nearest hospital.

Miraculously, the x-rays showed no fractures. But I suffered from a major concussion. The doctors told me that if I had struck my back one inch higher, I would have broken my spine. That fall was the worst accident I ever experienced. After surviving so many dangers, running from the Nazis, working with explosives, and coming close to death several times in mining accidents, it is ironic that I was almost killed in a library. I thought of the great soldier Lawrence of Arabia who, after staring death in the face so many times in hand-to-hand combat, finally met his end in a motorcycle accident. Later I was reminded of this incident again when astronaut John Glenn, after orbiting the earth, nearly died from slipping in his own bathtub.

Because the open stairwell where I had fallen had had no protective railing, I received a small sum in compensation from AIME's insurance carrier. Forty percent of it went, of course, to my lawyer. However, the money mattered little to me. I was happy to have survived the fall. This escape from death, or certainly serious injury, was one of the many "miracles" in my life.

Shortly after arriving at Penn State, I experienced another close shave in my office. A heavy seven-foot steel bookcase stood directly behind my desk. One day, as I was reading at my desk, the bookcase suddenly fell forward unexpectedly, impelled by the weight of the heavy books. It whisked by my left ear and landed on my desk. The steel frame dug into the wood like a sharp knife, leaving an indention of about one-third of an inch. Had it fallen a little more to my right, my skull would have been crushed.

The regular presence of fateful events in my life such as these had become nearly a normal expectation. I was grateful to have been spared so fortuitously so many times, but surely I had now been through the worst. I felt that fate had held a kindly concern for me, since I had been able to survive so many adversities, and I continued to face the future confidently, convinced that I would be able to convert my dreams into reality. All I needed was to rely on the innate drives that had served me so well over the years.

Although I was happy to be living in the United States and to have finally found a job, one thing really puzzled me, and that was the strange relationship the Americans had with dogs. First, while I was still residing in New York, I was shocked to discover that street vendors sold *hot dogs*, and that people would actually buy them and eat them. I was appalled that the citizens of the world's most modern country would consume dog meat. I had never heard of such a disgusting thing.

Even worse, many people seemed to be calling *me* a dog. This was hard to take, because in Russia calling someone a dog is the worst possible insult one can level at another person. One day I was teaching a surveying class outdoors, allowing the students to practice using surveying equipment to map out large areas around campus. One student across a wide lawn needed my help, so he put his fingers between his teeth, gave a sharp whistle in my direction, waved, and said, "Hey dog, come over here!" Such disrespect from a student! This would never have been tolerated by my dignified professors in Germany.

Finally, one day in my office, one of my students called me "dog" again, and I decided I had had enough.

"Why does everyone call me dog?" I demanded. "I am not a dog!"

Then it was explained to me that I was being addressed as "Doc," short for Doctor Kochanowsky, and I felt much better. I also eventually learned the true contents of hot dogs.

In 1953, when I first started working at Penn State, my salary was $440 a month. Anna worked too, behind the fabrics counter at a small department store, until 1957 when our daughter was born. My salary in 1959, after six years of teaching, had only risen to $550 a month, despite my considerable qualifications. I had two masters degrees and a doctorate from reputable mining schools. I had conducted graduate research at four German universities—Freiberg, Clausthal, Köthen, and Jena—and at the Federal Institute of Technology (ETH) in Zurich, Switzerland. I also had held prominent positions in industry. I had been the top man in blasting and open pit mining in Germany and had served as an advisor to the highest mining official in the German government. I had also advised the Argentine government on the mining of coal and uranium. Yet I just could not seem to advance at the university, nor was I receiving the recognition I felt I deserved.

Most people spend all their working lives, maybe forty years or more, building their fortunes. I had started building mine in several different countries, but had lost nearly everything each time. In 1970 I would be sixty-five years old and would have to retire from the university, so I had only eleven more years to establish financial security for my family and make provisions for my daughter's college education.

I began to feel trapped and frustrated. Finally, I lost my patience and began to look for consulting opportunities with American mining industries. Business leaders recognized at once that they could use my ideas, and although these same people might have balked a few years previously at hiring an unknown foreigner, they had no misgivings now about engaging an American university professor. Again, as in 1929 and in 1933, when I obtained jobs in Germany at a time when unemployment was high and foreigners were barred, I found I could create work for myself. Soon I was being offered more and more consulting work in some of the world's largest manufacturing and mining companies. My earnings from my work in industry in some years were so high that my salary at the University was not enough to pay my income taxes. When the University eventually became aware of my reputation in industry, I was only then given academic recognition and my salary there started to grow rapidly too.

Two of my inventions became particularly successful, such that I became known semi-humorously as "The Father of Angle Drilling," and

"The Mother of the Mobile Crusher." Angle drilling[32] is a blasting method in which the drill holes for the explosives, drilled downward into the flat surface at the top of a cliff (or *bench*), are drilled at an angle, rather than straight down. This makes the blast more effective, and increases its efficiency. I researched this concept, and invented equipment to do the drilling. I also invented a mobile crusher, which made it possible to bring the crusher to the rock, rather than having to haul the rock to a traditional, stationary crusher.

By 1962 I was internationally known. I presented numerous papers at national and international congresses, and my papers were being printed and reprinted, both in the United States and abroad. The new methods I designed and the machinery I invented were being used in many countries. In three years, I once again had advanced from the bottom to the top. My life had been like the ebb and flow of the tide, and each rise had swelled larger and larger. As a United States citizen, I now felt safe and secure. I was convinced that nothing disastrous could happen to me to cause another downfall. There was only one way I could go—up.

I now had a charming wife, of whom I was proud, and we had a beautiful, talented daughter, who was born in 1957 and whom we named Vera. My income was such that we were even able to afford some luxuries. With Anna's excellent taste, we built a beautiful home on a hill among tall old oaks and cherry trees, with a magnificent view of the nearby mountains. I had figuratively moved mountains like these to fulfill my dreams.

I had succeeded in all respects. I was living in the country I had admired since I was a young boy in Siberia. I had worked thirty years to get here, residing in five countries in the meantime, and learning to speak

---

[32] Boris' daughter, Vera, remembers: "My father would visit various open-pit mines around the country where his blasting method was being used, and film the resulting explosions with his hand-hand camera. He used the same camera to make family home movies. Most often the subject of these home movies was me, his only child. Scenes of me playing in the garden, swinging on my swing, running around with a broom, etc. would alternate regularly with views of some peaceful mountain that would suddenly be blown to bits. My father would always react to these filmed explosions with great enthusiasm and make some comment about their extreme efficiency, or the like. I, on the other hand, could not watch these movies without bursting into uncontrolled, hysterical laughter."

four languages besides my native Russian. For all those years, I had been a refugee without any national identity. As an American citizen I could now live as a free man, without fear of being unjustly arrested, humiliated, or persecuted. I was protected both at home and abroad by the most powerful nation in the world. With my American passport I could travel easily, to almost any country in the world, and feel secure. American citizenship and my American passport were worth a fortune to me.

I admired the American people too, because they did not seem to have impetuous feelings of hate, jealousy, or vengeance. Of course, Americans like to fight, and they know how to fight effectively. They fight for principles like freedom, but also just for fun—football, boxing, and other rough contact sports are extremely popular. Americans consider the right to argue a birthright. They express their opinions openly, without fear, no matter what the opposition. But whatever the fight is about, when it is over, Americans shake hands and hold no grudges. The loser in an election even congratulates the winner. During a boxing match a fighter might break the other contestant's nose, but when the fight is over, they are friends again. I had not seen this prevalent strength of character in the people of any other nation. A good example of this was the Marshall Plan. The Americans sent money to Germany after World War II to help rebuild the country, even after so many Americans had fought and died there. What a people! I was proud to be an American citizen.

By the 1960's I had renewed contact with my former employer in Germany, the Rheinische Kalksteinwerke Company in Wülfrath. My old colleague, Dr. Flachsenberg, who was now president, hired me to do consulting work on a regular basis. Often these and other assignments required me to travel extensively and spend large periods of time away from home. During my first eighteen years in the United States, I made twenty-one trips abroad. Because our daughter was in school, Anna rarely was able to accompany me, except during the summers, when all three of us would go to Europe together. Whenever I was on a trip alone, I could not wait to return home to enjoy my family.

On one of our summer trips to Europe, I finally resolved to tend to my old skiing injury, which I had sustained forty years earlier. By 1967 the pain in my toe had become so severe, I decided that surgery was finally warranted. Because skiing accidents were so common in Switzerland, I supposed one would find the best, most experienced physicians there for this type of surgery. I sought out the most reputable foot specialist I could find, who also happened to be a professor at the University of Zurich, and I arranged to see him. This doctor was a strange man. He did not look me in the face once during the entire appointment. Twice he passed quite close to me on his way to the wash basin and back to his desk. Each time I extended my hand, attempting to shake his in greeting. Each time he ignored me, an arrogant thing to do, especially in Switzerland, where hand shaking is an ingrained social custom. I was quite put out by his snobbish attitude. After examining my toe, the doctor gave me the names of two American surgeons, one practicing in Philadelphia, and the other at the John Hopkins Medical Institute. Both in the United States! He told me that if I wished, they would be able to perform the operation. I left his office quite disappointed. Miraculously however, from that moment on my toe never hurt me again. I was able to walk for miles without the slightest trace of pain. That doctor, for all his rudeness and disinterested manner, turned out to be the best doctor I ever had in my life.

I had another amusing experience, involving yet another trip to Europe. I was organizing a tour of European mining operations for some American industry leaders, and in a telephone conversation with one of these men I asked, "You know, our travels will take us to Milan, Italy, home to one of the most famous opera houses in the world. Would you like me to get tickets for a performance while we are there?"

There was a long pause on the other end of the line, and then came the reply, "Look, Dr. Kochanowsky, this is going to be a business trip. We won't have time for things like that."

It was hard for me to believe that our schedule would be so tight, but it turned out he was correct. We did not have time for the opera. We were too busy going to night clubs every night until about 4 a.m. I hardly got any sleep during the whole trip.

On that same trip, however, I did force my will upon my colleagues in another way. We were scheduled to go from Italy to Germany, and my companions were going to fly, but that was just too outrageous for me to tolerate. "Are you crazy?" I asked, "We'll be going through Switzerland, the most beautiful country in the world. We have got to rent a car and make the trip by car."

They protested that it would just be a waste of time, but I insisted and would not be denied. We took the road trip, and they all were profoundly impressed by the beauty of the Swiss Alps. They thanked me in the end for insisting on the change in travel plans.

In the summer of 1967, I was invited to speak at an international mining conference in Moscow. It was to be my first trip to Russia since my departure in 1922. I took Anna along, but we left Vera in Switzerland, fearing that if the communists had my whole family within their grasp, they might prevent me from leaving the U.S.S.R. It turned out that my fears were justified.

One evening, when Anna and I returned to our hotel room after dinner, we were surprised to find three strange gentlemen in our room. All of them were wearing dark suits and ties. As soon as we stepped through the doorway each of them took out a feather duster from his jacket and pretended to be cleaning the furniture. In a few seconds they excused themselves and quickly disappeared.

The next evening I got a call just before dinner from a man I did not know. He invited me to come down to the bar for a drink, but asked me not to bring my wife. When I met him downstairs, the first thing he said was, "So, I understand that you wish to stay in Russia." He seemed disappointed when I told him such was not the case, and he became even more disappointed when I told him our daughter was still in Switzerland. He even offered me a seat on the board of the Academy of Sciences, the highest honor a Russian scientist can receive. But I was not at all interested. He kept talking to me for quite a while, trying to persuade me to change my mind. All the while, Anna stewed upstairs, worrying about what the KGB agent might be doing to me. I have to say, it was something of a relief to leave my homeland again.

Despite my discomfort during my visit to the U.S.S.R., I nevertheless remained a proud Russian through and through. This nationalistic feeling had not diminished even after five disastrous decades of communist rule in Russia. Even now, for example, I still feel patriotic indignation when I read in the newspaper about Chinese claims for territory within Siberian borders. Loyalty to Mother Russia will always burn fiercely in my heart.

In 1933 I had lost all contact with my family. Since then, all of my letters had gone unanswered, and so I assumed that everyone had died. This proved to be a false assumption, however. After my trip to Moscow in 1967, my brother Joseph, who was then living in Leningrad (now St. Petersburg again), somehow learned that I had attended the mining conference there. He began to search for me with the aid of the International Red Cross. Eight months later I received a telephone call at home in Pennsylvania with the news that my brother was looking for me. In disbelief, I first responded that I had no brother. As the Red Cross representative began explaining the circumstances behind the search, my skepticism soon turned to excitement at this amazing news.

I wanted to return to Russia immediately to visit Joseph and my sister Berta, who was also still alive, but I was advised against it because of the current tense political situation in Czechoslovakia. The next year, in 1969, I traveled to Russia again with Anna, leaving Vera behind in Switzerland once more. After forty-seven years of separation, I saw my brother Joseph and my sister Berta again in Leningrad. It was a wonderful reunion, although marked prominently by sad stories about how my parents, my other brothers, and our family friends had died. Berta and Joseph were leading drab lives, the typical existence of Soviet citizens. Joseph had retired. He and his wife, also a retired physician, had one unmarried son, Sasha, who lived with them. My sister Berta, still lively at nearly eighty years of age, had lost some of her mental capacities. She may well have been suffering from some form of dementia. Although she remembered me and many details about the old days, some of her remarks seemed quite bizarre. The four of them were living in a small apartment in a high-rise Soviet-era building. I would have liked to help them to move to the United States, so that we could all be together again, but in those years emigration from the U.S.S.R. was nearly impossible. Besides, they were elderly people now, and they had grown accustomed to their lives in the Soviet Union. I did not get the impression they were eager to start over in a new land. Although I never visited any members of my family again, I maintained a regular correspondence with Joseph until his death in 1981. Some of the gifts I mailed to him and his wife were received, others were not.

As I would travel frequently abroad and enjoy foreign hospitality, at my own home in State College I would often entertain visiting experts from all over the world. One of the most memorable of these visits was from several of my old Wülfrath colleagues, including Dr. Flachsenberg. We toured all over the country visiting American mines, and I was proud to show them the best of American industry. I was now a proud American.

Just as I had made some comical language errors as a student in Germany, my German guests made some humorous mistakes too, both involving customs and language. In one restaurant, the waiter started by suggesting a particular entrée on the menu. This was not a customary practice in German restaurants and my guest was offended. "*I* will decide what I will eat," he replied. On another occasion, in another restaurant, impatient for his meal to arrive, he asked, "Waiter, when will I become a steak?" And later he said, "Waiter, I want a piece of desert." (mispronouncing the word *dessert*). Dr. Flachsenberg, the head of one of the largest lime mines in the world, was surprised to see "lime juice" on a menu. "I have worked with lime all my life," he exclaimed, "but I have never heard of anyone drinking lime juice."

Another series of events surrounding their visit made me reflect again on the possibility of a divine plan. I had been anxious to impress my visitors, and I knew we would be traveling in my car, so I took the car, a handsome dark green 1950 Buick, to a body shop to be repainted, and to have several small dents hammered out. On the morning of my guests' arrival, I picked up my car, which looked absolutely beautiful with its new, fresh paint job. I opened both doors, to make a full inspection, and then I backed the car up just a short distance to the gas pump to fill the tank. While backing the car up, I suddenly heard a horrible crunching sound. I had left the passenger door open as I backed up the short distance to the pump, and I hadn't seen the stack of cinder blocks off to the right. The passenger door hit the stack of blocks, scratching the beautiful paint job badly, and making a small dent in the edge of the car door.

Of course I was terribly disappointed that my car would not be presentable for my guests, but there was no time to fix the damage, so I had to drive the car the way it was, and apologize for the unsightly gash. A few weeks later Anna, I, and Vera, who was only seven years old at the time, got out of the car in our driveway. Anna closed the passenger door, and unfortunately Vera's finger got in the way. It was badly hurt, and we had the finger examined by our doctor, but there was no permanent damage. There is no doubt in my mind that she escaped permanent injury only because of the dent in the edge of the door—the dent I had put there by running into the stack of cinder blocks. Because of that dent, the door did not line up evenly with the frame—there was a small gap, just large enough for a seven-year-old's finger, and that was exactly where Vera's finger had been. A half inch higher or lower, and the heavy Buick door would surely have sliced her tiny finger off. Ten years later, she would go on to study piano at the Oberlin Conservatory of Music.

After experiencing so many hardships during my life, I knew how to appreciate all the things that I now had. But most of all I treasured my wife and my daughter. I loved my wife deeply. With years of suppressed desire now free to be expressed, I could devour her with an admiring look, or crush her lovingly in my arms. I felt her presence throughout my entire being, no matter how far away I was from her. She was the woman who had lived so long in my dreams. In spirit, she had given me strength and inspiration during my years of misery, long before I met her. Because of her I had been able to stay strong, and to bear all of the ordeals and the persecutions. I had refused to tolerate thoughts of death, because I wanted to live to meet her.

Although I was an agnostic, there were several values in life I deemed sacred: freedom, peace, justice, truth, honesty, and beauty. But most holy to me was my marriage and my family. Through my wife and daughter, I felt extremely rich. Making them happy became my most important objective, my inspiration for living. A man is completely happy only when he loves and is loved. The stronger the love, the stronger he is.

I loved Anna so much that I could not deny her anything. She did not have to ask me for what she wanted. When she expressed pleasure in something, I wanted to give it to her. It made me happy to buy her the things she enjoyed. It is amazing what a man can do for a woman when she is his beloved. I was happy if she was happy.

The contentment I found in my family life inspired me and nourished my drive to succeed professionally and financially. In pursuing these goals, I experienced great satisfaction in inventing new mining methods and machinery, in continuing to lecture, to conduct research, to write and publish papers. However, all these successes made sense only in the context of my family. Money may be a symbol of success and security, but it is not an end in itself.

By the mid-1960s, after climbing to the top of my profession, I felt I had reached the summit of a tall, steep mountain. I had fulfilled all my dreams. Soon I knew I would be sixty-five years old, and because of the university's rules, I would be forced to retire. But I was not afraid of my age. A Siberian, who had come from a healthy family—my grandparents had lived into their mid-nineties—I expected to survive a long time. Siberians had been bred to endure the rough climate, with extreme temperatures ranging from 70 below zero in the winter to well over 100 degrees in the summer. They are examples of nature's principle of "the survival of the fittest."

I felt strong in all respects, and with eagerness I looked forward to my retirement, because I would then have both financial security and *time*. I planned to travel more, and take longer journeys, with Anna instead of alone. Especially when our daughter was in college, we could take a trip around the world, enjoying the different cultures of many people and the beauty of their countries. After my retirement, I could do what I liked best. I could lecture, just for pleasure. I could write and publish my memoirs. I also wanted to write a textbook on the economics of open pit mining. I would have enough time to do all these things without feeling rushed. After having accumulated a vast body of knowledge and experience, I felt my best and most important contributions would be made after my retirement.

I had been climbing mountains since I was a child. Along the way I had fallen several times and faced death repeatedly, but I had at last succeeded in reaching the top, in realizing my dreams and goals. Standing on the peak of the mountain, I felt exhilarated. I felt that I could ascend even higher. Only the sky was the limit. Up until now I had focused mainly on making my family happy and secure. From now on I would turn my attention to work which would benefit mankind.

As a final goal, I wanted to improve living conditions in the countries I had lived in, and in underdeveloped countries around the world, helping the people of the world, if I could, with my knowledge of the mining industry. Since I was internationally known as an engineer and scientist, I believed my help would be universally welcomed. I knew Anna would be interested in my goals, and would be willing to support me in such endeavors. Together we would learn about the problems of people of different nations, and if possible, try to solve some of them.

I also planned to donate money to various peaceful causes. I particularly wanted to establish fellowships for university students in the field of mining. These aims were my highest goal, my most significant dream. I had dreamed these dreams as a child in Siberia, when I had longed to follow in the footsteps of my father and my brothers Joseph and Matthew. In excellent health, possessing love and happiness within my family, having a great interest in my profession and satisfaction in my accomplishments, and now with the addition of money and *time*, I felt nothing could stop me from achieving my final goals. I faced the future and retirement with confidence and joyful anticipation.

I knew I was still a dreamer, and I liked to think of myself as one. I felt my life had been enriched by my dreams, but I was a realistically-minded dreamer too. After more than forty years in my profession, I knew that I could make tremendous contributions in the field of mining throughout the world. But at the same time, I also recognized that I had no desire to reach these goals alone. Without a wife, I knew I would feel incomplete. To be happy, I needed the companionship of someone with whom I shared a mutual respect and trust. I needed the inspiration that a good wife provides. Fortunately, I had such a wife. The long years of waiting had brought me fulfillment beyond my fondest expectations.

BORIS TEACHES A SURVEYING CLASS AT THE PENNSYLVANIA STATE UNIVERSITY

ANNA WORKS BEHIND THE COUNTER AT SCHLOW'S
DEPARTMENT STORE (1953-1956)

NEW HOUSE AND NEW CAR IN STATE COLLEGE, PENNSYLVANIA

Boris (1954)

By Dr. B. J. Kochanowsky, professor, Department of Mining, The Pennsylvania State University

*Text Reprinted from Mining Congress Journal, November, 1961

New technique holds promise
of improved blasting efficiency
at open pit and strip mines

THE ANGLE DRILLER

This photo accompanied the author's article
"Inclined Drilling and Blasting"
published in the *Mining Congress Journal*, November, 1961.

THE MOBILE CRUSHER

BORIS IN THE LAB

BORIS WITH PLEXIGLASS MODEL OF ANGLE DRILLING

ANNA AND BORIS DINING IN NEW YORK CITY (1963)

Boris and daughter Vera (1959)

Epilogue
by Vera Kochanowsky

The Shifting Tides

What fates impose, that men must needs abide;
It boots not to resist both wind and tide.

—Shakespeare, *Henry VI, Part III*

In the penultimate chapter of his memoir, my father looks forward to his retirement as a pinnacle, the fulfillment of his life's dreams. While his life did have a happy ending of sorts, it was not at all the one he expected. His memoirs, written more than twenty years before his death, end with the greatest tragedy of his life. Shortly before his retirement, in May of 1970, Anna, his wife of twenty-four years, left him, filing for divorce soon thereafter. My father did not fight the divorce and let her go without a legal struggle, but he was devastated. A mere two pages in length, his final chapter, entitled "Fall," describes the catastrophic torments he suffered as a result of losing my mother:

I have no words to describe the agony, the suffering, and the bitterness I endured as a result of the loss of my wife, whom I loved and adored deeply. To me she had always been the loveliest woman in the world. Years of persecutions could not destroy my spirit, my optimism, my will to overcome obstacles, and my enthusiasm for living. But the loss of my beloved crushed me completely. The horrible blow hit me directly in the heart, and I felt as if I were being killed. I was physically alive, but spiritually dead. My dreams, goals, and drives were destroyed, and life suddenly became empty and senseless. I felt

*like a big, strong, healthy tree, which, being cut with a single
mighty stroke, falls crashing to the earth, to lie there prostrate,
helpless, finished.*

*All my early dreams I had been able to fulfill, but this one,
the most important and precious one, I had now lost. What
Lenin, Hitler, and the infuriated mob in Belgium could not
do, the dearest person in my life did.*

The divorce became final in July. My father, newly retired and in a stupor of depression, slept for many, many hours each day. He had slowed down as a result of a massive heart attack he suffered in 1967. But now, to drown his sorrow, he began taking sleeping pills. Whenever he emerged from his room, he appeared to be nearly paralyzed. Often he would blame his deep melancholy on his Russian heritage, identifying with the pervasive sense of tragedy and hopelessness described in the works of famous Russian authors, such as Dostoyevsky and Chekov. The thought of suicide certainly crossed his mind. He would talk at length to friends, and he may have even seen a psychologist briefly, an extreme measure in those days. But I have no doubt that the person to whom he opened his troubled heart the most was me, his only child. It was a heavy burden for a thirteen-year-old. Until that time, my father had been a secondary figure in my upbringing, as he had been heavily focused on his teaching and consulting in the years leading up to his retirement. I knew he loved and cared for me deeply, but his debilitating depression made me feel frightened and uncomfortable. I listened to him, but said very little.

Around this time, my father met and befriended a fellow Russian, Vladimir (Val) de Lissovoy (1918-2009),[33] a professor at Penn State in the College of Human Development, who held a PhD in social psychology from Cornell University. His area of expertise was child development and family relationships. Valodya, as my father called him, had left Russia as a small boy and had lived with his family in Greece, Serbia, and France, before their final move to the Chicago area in 1925. The two men had much in common, and both relished their Russian cultural ancestry. Although

---

[33] Val de Lissovoy spoke at my father's funeral in 1992. The text of his speech is in the appendix.

246

he had spent much of his youth in the United States, Valodya understood the Russian mentality well. Doubtless he counseled my father a great deal on an informal basis, something my father desperately needed, but which he could not bring himself to seek elsewhere. In 1970 Val had just married his second wife, a young, charming woman named Charlotte, whom my father had met briefly many years earlier on a university sponsored trip to Europe. It was also Charlotte's second marriage. The couple welcomed my father's friendship and invited him to their home often. Charlotte, a musician herself, had begun studying Russian. My father was eager to help her, and gladly lent her some of his recordings of famous Russian operas. Now my father had before him the example of two people who had emerged intact from their first marriages, and were actively building a happy life together.

After an initial period of grieving for Anna, my father began to focus on writing his memoirs. He also resumed his consulting work. As he started working again, he gradually renewed his interest in mining and in promoting some of his earlier inventions. He worked on patents and began to travel extensively again. For a couple of months each year he would return to Wülfrath to work alongside his old colleagues. To me he would often still complain of depression and express his deep longing for my mother, but the reality of his new life was slowly dawning on him. Although he did not mention it to me at the time, he even began to date other women.

In the year following the divorce, my father began a relationship with one of the secretaries in the administrative offices of the Rheinische Kalksteinwerke, Maria Chudobba. In fact, Fräulein Homan (Ch. 5, pp. 97, 99) who had first introduced my father to then-director Paul Ludowigs in 1932, was responsible for bringing them together. She took my father aside and told him in no uncertain terms that she believed Maria would be good for him. Maria, only thirty-five years old in 1970, was still unmarried. The youngest of four children, she lived at home and took care of her aging parents in Mettmann, a small town not far from Wülfrath. Quiet but friendly, Maria may have been flattered by my father's attentions. It is likely that she had already heard about him prior to their first meeting because of my father's long association with the company and his strong friendships with the current director (Flaschenberg) and his predecessor

(Ludowigs, now retired). Fräulein Homan, who had never married, was retired now too, but she obviously still had a firm handle on what was happening within the company. The job had been her life.

Although Maria differed from my mother in both appearance and character, she possessed many positive attributes. She was unassuming and kind, and she could handle my father's occasional angry outbursts with tolerance and grace. The unwavering gentleness and patience she showed her ailing parents much impressed my father. In their conversations, she was sympathetic and lent an understanding ear to his complaints. Theirs was not a passionate affair, but a quiet relationship that blossomed slowly. Because my father only spent two months of the year in Wülfrath, their time together was necessarily brief. In between they would write and telephone. As their relationship grew more serious (by this time I was away at college), they began to take vacations together.

But my father was not eager to marry again. He was unsure of his feelings and was developing friendships with other women too. There was a real reluctance on his part to make a serious personal or financial commitment to any woman. Throughout his life, major decisions had always been a source of great stress. When such decisions were necessary, he would agonize over them endlessly. Also, it seemed clear in his conversations with me that he was still pining for my mother, hoping that she would leave her new husband and come back to him, although there was no actual indication that this was even a remote possibility.

After I started college, he began spending a couple of months in Clearwater, Florida, every winter. Sometimes he would visit me at school for a few days, always by himself. He was consistently vague about his activities. Then, on one of his business trips to a mine in the western part of the United States, he experienced another heart attack. This one was milder than the one he had had in 1967, but nevertheless it weakened him. His doctors put him on a regimen of heart medications and advised him to carry nitroglycerin pills with him at all times, in case of sudden chest pains. Gradually, he began to slow down, reducing his work load while still continuing to work in Wülfrath and take vacations in Clearwater.

After 1981, when I began work on my doctorate at Stanford University, my father would stay with me for two or three months each year to avoid the cold Pennsylvania winters. At about this time, he became concerned that his condition was worsening. Always scientifically minded, he created a chart and came up with a rating system to gauge how he was feeling each morning and evening. It showed in the course of weeks and months that he really was declining and that the medicines the doctors were prescribing were not helping him sufficiently. He had watched open-heart operations on television, in awe of the technology involved. Gradually he came to the conclusion that this was what would save his heart and allow him to live to the age of ninety, a private goal he had set for himself. None of the cardiologists in State College recommended surgery, believing instead that medicine was the best route, so my father began searching for second, third, and fourth opinions from doctors at the Stanford University Hospital during his stays with me. The cardiology department there had a stellar reputation. Finally, in 1983 he found a doctor who proposed open-heart surgery. The tests showed that my father needed a quadruple bypass. But he was already seventy-nine years old, so there was some added risk involved because of his age, and his recovery would take longer than for a younger man. But he was adamant. He said he was not at all afraid of undergoing the operation, but was actually looking forward to it as a means toward improved health.

However, in the back of his mind, he must have recognized that he would need help, certainly after the surgery, but perhaps for the rest of his life. It was at this point that he began to consider marriage as a serious option, if not a necessity. He arranged to stay with me after the surgery and for a few months while recuperating, but even he recognized that I could not take on the burden of caring for him indefinitely. He had his sights on a career for me. I had been awarded a Fulbright Fellowship and would be in Europe for a year, and after that I would return to Stanford to complete my degree.

Late in 1983, my father began bringing up the topic of remarriage with increasing frequency and seriousness. It was only at this time that I learned of his relationships with other women. At first he did not tell me their names, but only gave me thumbnail descriptions of them as he verbally weighed for me the advantages and disadvantages of each potential spouse. But the woman who had taken such good care of her parents during their declining years came up more and more often. This quality I suspect helped tip the scales in her favor. Finally, I learned her name, Maria (which, coincidently, had also been the name of Boris' own mother). After my wedding in December of 1983, my father at last made the decision to propose to her.

My father's bypass operation took place on April 27, 1984, and it was successful. Unfortunately, the bravery he had exhibited before surgery did not remain with him during his recovery, which was long and arduous. The doctors recommended a regular daily regimen of walking. My father felt weak, and was afraid of stressing his heart, so he did less and less each day, despite my urgings. Finally, after about a month, he had to return to the hospital because his lungs were filling with fluid. The doctors again told him he had to exercise to make a full recovery. Finally, and out of desperation, he began to walk daily in the large courtyard of my apartment building. At first I followed him around with a chair so that he could rest en route. Gradually he gained some strength, and by July he felt well enough to return to Pennsylvania. In September, just before my departure for Europe, my father married Maria Chudobba. Her older sister, Ina Alabaster, who resided in Wales with her husband and three daughters, was the only member of Maria's family present at the wedding. My husband and I were the only other witnesses at the ceremony.

MARIA CHUDOBBA

It took nearly a year for my father to make a full recovery. By the spring of 1985, although he had lost quite a bit of weight, he was fully mobile and able to focus on his new life with Maria. He took on no more consulting work and began a period of true retirement, relying on a comfortable pension from the university, social security, and some wise financial investments he had made in previous years.

Maria was an avid gardener. My father, who had never had much interest in gardening before, was suddenly making plans to add numerous trees and bushes, and even a fountain, to our backyard. Life became simpler. With no money problems or worries about children, they could get up every morning and plan each day as they wished. They would take walks, visit friends, go shopping, cook, enjoy the garden, and even travel. I would venture to say that I had never seen my father happier. Somehow, his depression and all the complaints and ruminations about past mistakes magically evaporated. Rarely did he speak of my mother, nor did he seem preoccupied with his own health as he had been in the past, with one exception.

His eyes were gradually deteriorating due to cataracts and the onset of glaucoma.[34] When he accidentally ran his car into a bicyclist at the end of our street, he decided to give up driving entirely. Fortunately, the bicyclist survived the impact with no serious injury. The evening sun had been in my father's eyes, and the policeman summoned to the scene did not even issue him a ticket, but nevertheless, it was the last straw and he drove no more. From that point on, Maria took charge of the car. In the last few years of his life, my father underwent numerous eye operations, some more successful than others. The two cataract operations, a relatively common procedure, went fine. The several operations he had for his glaucoma however, had mixed results. He had been ill-advised by his optometrist (not an MD), and had already lost some of his sight because of damage to the optic nerve before he visited an ophthalmologist. Both eyes were affected. The resulting loss of vision caused him much anguish because of the many activities he enjoyed which required the use of his eyes (mainly reading and writing). Incensed with what he considered the ineptitude of his

---

[34] Glaucoma can damage the optic nerve, in some cases causing blindness, due to increased pressure within the eye. Some studies have linked heart disease with glaucoma.

former optometrist, he shared his experience with many of his friends and acquaintances, beginning what was essentially an anti-optometrist crusade. He even made an appearance on a local television program highlighting the pitfalls of vision care, describing his dissatisfaction with the optometrist who had steered him wrong.

Except for his eye problems, my father enjoyed several good years between 1985 and 1989. During the late 1980's, a visiting professor from the Soviet Union, Victor Khartchenko,[35] made the acquaintance of both my father and his friend Val de Lissovoy. He was friendly with them and the three men socialized together often. Apparently Khartchenko had many excellent political connections back home. When my father expressed an interest in visiting his homeland again, and most particularly in seeing Krasnoyarsk (the town was strictly off-limits to tourists under Soviet rule), Khartchenko offered to arrange the trip and even to act as his guide. My father was thrilled with the idea, yet he did not pursue it at first. His fear of returning to communist Russia remained strong because of the experiences he had had while visiting there in the late 1960's. He followed the political events of 1989 in Eastern Europe with great interest, and was ecstatic to learn of the fall of the Berlin Wall later that year. The collapse of the Soviet Union seemed imminent. He contacted Khartchenko, who had by then returned to Russia, and began making preparations for the journey which was to take place the following August. My husband and I were to accompany him and Maria on the trip. In the meantime, Khartchenko kindly sent my father photographs of many historic buildings in Krasnoyarsk, including a picture of my father's own home (See Ch. 1, p. 31). Still known locally as the Kochanowsky Print Shop, it had remained standing all these years, as it had been solidly constructed of brick and mortar, rather than wood. Coincidentally, it was now in use as part of the local mining school.

As tantalizing as the photographs were, in the end the trip did not

---

[35] Khartchenko's various titles included: (1) State Committee of Public Education, Moscow Mining Institute: Professor, Doctor of Technical Sciences, Head of the Department of "Economic and Rational Use of the Natural Resources," Dean of the Special Faculty (2) USSR State Committee for Sciences and Technology: Higher Business School for Mining, President (3) United Nations: Natural Resources & Energy, Technical Cooperation for Development, Interregional Advisor in Coal.

take place. In June of 1990 my father experienced a major health setback. His lungs were filling with fluid and he was hospitalized for several days. His doctor adjusted his medications to try to control the problem, and at the same time he strongly advised my father not to make the journey. My father ultimately relented and cancelled the trip. He returned home from the hospital considerably weaker and sobered by his experience. Maria took excellent care of him, but this illness definitely marked the beginning of his final decline.

Concerned about my father's condition, I called his physician. This doctor had a jovial disposition and got along quite well with my father on a personal level. For many years they had enjoyed an amiable doctor-patient relationship. However, he had been one of the hometown doctors who had advised against open-heart surgery. My father, ever his own man, had proceeded with the operation, against his doctor's advice, believing that prescription medicine alone was an insufficient treatment for his condition. Now I asked the doctor directly, had he expected this fluid build-up in the lungs?

"Yes," came the answer, which genuinely surprised me. "Your father has congestive heart failure. The heart attacks he suffered in earlier years permanently damaged certain portions of the heart muscle. The operation he underwent brought better blood flow to the major vessels, but the smaller vessels and the capillaries are dying off. These will gradually undermine the efficiency of the heart's work."

The operation had bought him a few good years, but it was no cure, as my father had hoped it would be. Now it was unlikely that he would die of a major heart attack, but he would instead face an excruciatingly slow, steady decline. In that instant, I began to appreciate the philosophical wisdom of the small-town doctor. Which is better, to die quickly of a heart attack, or to dwindle away slowly over the course of several years? For me, there would be no debate: I would rather go quickly. But for him, I could not say. If he had been fully informed of the consequences beforehand, what would he have done? I would wager that he would still have chosen to undergo surgery, trusting in luck and his own indomitable persistence to pull him through. If he had not done so, he might have missed those happy years with Maria, or the birth of his only grandchild, Andrew, in 1989. Andrew's birth caused him such overwhelming happiness that he was too moved to speak to us when we called to give him the news over the telephone.

But the cost of his decision was great. His weight began to decline, making easier work for the heart, but with the loss of muscle came loss of strength. Maria had learned a lot about herbal medicine and homeopathy from her sister, Ina. She concocted and tried many recipes to help his digestion, his breathing, his mood, and his overall health, but to no avail. At best he would improve slightly for a time, only to suffer a more severe setback a few weeks later. In the last year of his life, he started needing oxygen during the day, then all the time. In the final months, he lost the ability to walk and became confined to his bed. It was difficult for all of us to watch him go like this.

My husband and I had moved with our son to the Washington DC area in the late summer of 1990. Thereafter we would make frequent trips on weekends and holidays to visit my father and Maria. He would watch Andrew play and converse with us, but eventually he became more withdrawn and spoke less and less. Maria was his main caregiver, but she eventually arranged for supplemental home care, so that she could go on errands and have a little time to herself. She was a churchgoer and the friends she found there helped her maintain some equilibrium during this very difficult time.

Once, after a particularly severe setback, my mother came to the house to pay my father a brief visit. It was quite awkward with all of us sitting in the bedroom—me, my husband Greg, Maria, and my mother. My father was lying in bed. She inquired as to how he was feeling and wished him a good recovery.

As she was about to leave, he asked "But, when shall I see you again?"

She made no response, heading for the door. But before she could reach it he said, "Then I shall see you in Paradise."

I will never forget his words, a surprising utterance coming from a confessed non-believer. Perhaps he was just being sarcastic, but I think not. His connection to her was still strong, and I believe that he could not bear the thought of never seeing her again. It was the only thing he could say to express to her his undying love.

It sometimes seemed that even the force of his character was diminishing with his physical strength. Yet during his final days in the hospital, he regularly ripped out his IVs and fought mightily with the nurses when they came to draw his blood. This continued until the last few hours, when he went into a coma-like state. He died alone in the wee hours of the morning. Maria had gone home around 2 a.m. That evening I had been packing, making preparations to return home to be at his side. But he died before I could get there, in the hour or two just before dawn, that deepest part of night that had always been the most difficult for him to get through during his long illness. Although he had come close to his goal in longevity (87 years and 7 months), his heart, the site where he felt the detrimental effects of his depression had manifested, finally gave out.

Maria called at 6:30 a.m. The news shocked me more than I expected. His decline had taken so long, it seemed interminable. Yet now he was really gone. I peered outside through my bedroom curtains. It was December 17, 1992. The weather was warmer than usual, and a heavy fog hung in the motionless air, obscuring everything around. Driving the four hours home, it seemed to me that I was in a dream, traveling through a world unnaturally suspended. Perhaps the world was in shock, just as I was, that he had departed the earth forever.

The funeral was set for two days later, December 19. It was a quiet affair. Only close friends and some professional colleagues attended the service, along with Maria, me, my husband, and his family. My mother was not there. His old friend Val de Lissovoy spoke eloquently, capturing the essence of my father's charm. (A transcription of his remarks appears in the appendix.) Years earlier, my father had selected a plot at the largest local cemetery and had made all the arrangements. The design on the grave's bronze marker was a crossed hammer and pick, a traditional mining emblem. Underneath were inscribed three words he chose from the New Testament: Faith, Hope, and Love. These qualities he had come to believe were the most crucial in life.

Being thirty years younger than my father and knowing that she would likely outlive him, Maria had made plans to move to Wales, where her sister lived, after my father's death. Indeed, he had set aside some money in his will for her to do just that. Maria changed her mind, however, and decided to remain in State College for the next ten years. Once or twice a year she would take extended trips to Europe to visit her siblings and their children.

My mother and stepfather, who had recently retired, were busy with the construction of a new lodge on some acreage they owned in the Pennsylvania wilderness. They both loved nature and felt most at peace in the midst of it. Their log home served as a kind of personal refuge for both of them. My stepfather also continued to serve on many professional committees, partly to please my mother, because the meetings frequently took place in fascinating corners of the globe. Her intense love of travel had never abated.[36] Their excursions took them to China, Russia, Algeria, Egypt, South America, as well as many lovely spots in the United States and Europe.

Upon her return from a trip to Switzerland in late October of 1999, my mother was diagnosed with stage four lung cancer. She had never been a chain smoker. I had rarely seen her smoke while I was growing up. Apparently she sometimes smoked one or two cigarettes after I went to bed and at parties I did not attend. She was always careful to keep the house free of tobacco smell. When she remarried, her second husband insisted that she give up the habit, and she did. After thirty years of smoke-free existence, she came down with the same illness that had felled her father, who had been a chain smoker all his life. Her oncologist encouraged her to undergo radiation treatment and aggressive chemotherapy, so she decided to fight. Unfortunately, the treatments were relatively ineffective, destroying her quality of life without adding appreciably to her lifespan. She died about nine months later, in August of 2000.

In 2002, when Maria was sixty-seven years old, she sensed that she was slowing down and no longer felt able to handle the demands of caring for the house and garden. Her beloved cat had died, and she decided that the time was right to move back to Germany. Although her older sister Ina had passed away two years earlier, Maria still had a brother living in Germany, as well as several nephews and nieces.

A few months after her move, Maria was diagnosed with non-Hodgkin's lymphoma and began treatment. I visited her during the summer of 2004

---

[36] Throughout her life, Anna relished traveling. She could converse easily in German, Swiss-German, French, Spanish, and English. She also studied Russian and Chinese. Her second husband, Charles Hosler, said that she turned into a different person when she traveled. She became fearless and self-confident. All traces of shyness and insecurity simply melted away.

for a few weeks. During this visit, I also had the opportunity to meet one of my father's relatives, Larysa Kapushchevska, who had moved to Neuwied, Germany from the Ukraine in 2001. Larysa was the granddaughter of my father's only sister, Berta. Her father, Valentin, had known my father and had enjoyed riding on his back as a young boy shortly before my father's departure from Russia. (Ch. 3, p. 60)

I had never met any members of my father's family before. When my parents had traveled to Russia in the late 1960's, they purposely left me behind in Switzerland as a security measure. Thereafter, I had almost no news of my Russian relatives, although my father kept up a correspondence with his brother Joseph until Joseph died in 1981. I could not speak Russian, nor did I have any knowledge of the whereabouts of any of my Russian relatives. Sometime in 2001, when Maria was still living in State College, out of the blue, Larysa telephoned Maria. Unfortunately, Maria spoke very little Russian, so their communication was severely limited, but she learned that Larysa and her husband Victor had received permission from the German government to relocate to Germany. Larysa wished to get in touch with me, and Maria gave her my telephone number. My resulting conversation with Larysa was just as difficult. However, among my acquaintances were two women who had a good command of the Russian language.[37] I invited them to my house to act as interpreters and called Larysa back a few days later. We were able to exchange addresses in this way, and we began to correspond. Fortunately, because Larysa had moved to Germany, she soon acquired enough fluency in German for us to communicate in that language.[38]

During my visit to Germany in 2004, both Maria and her older brother Johannes traveled to Neuwied with me, where we met Larysa and Victor for the first time. It was a joyous occasion. We were treated to some traditional Russian delicacies, which Larysa offered us with the generous Russian-style hospitality described by my father in the early chapters of his

---

[37] My thanks go to Anne Harrison and Theadocia Austen.

[38] Throughout my childhood my parents spoke German regularly at home, as it was the language they had spoken when they first met. During my long summer vacations in Switzerland, I had to communicate with my maternal grandparents in German because neither of them could speak any English.

memoirs. This unexpected opportunity to meet one of my father's closest relatives meant a great deal to both Maria and me.

I was planning another visit to Germany in the fall of 2005, when I received news of Maria's death only four days prior to my departure. I arrived in time to attend her funeral and was able to meet and speak with her family and several of her friends.

After attending Maria's funeral, I returned to Neuwied to visit Larysa and Victor once more. This time, I was intent upon learning more about Larysa's side of the family and asked her many questions. I discovered that her grandmother Berta, my aunt, had been a talented amateur painter. Morris, Berta's husband, had been imprisoned for over ten years (six months in 1937, and again from 1944 until 1954) by the communists. This and the many other stresses Berta faced proved to be too much for her, and she eventually developed schizophrenia. I also learned that Larysa's father, like mine, had had a gift for playing the piano.

In the course of our discussions, Larysa explained that she and her husband had been granted permission to move to Germany because of her Jewish background. I expressed some surprise. She responded that yes, she was half Jewish, and that I was too—an even bigger surprise. Apparently both of my father's parents had been Jewish, but they had kept that fact hidden from him. In order to avoid anti-Semitism, they had made an effort to blend into mainstream Russian society. In his memoirs (Ch. 6, p. 117) my father refers briefly and vaguely to some possible Jewish ancestry: "Although I knew that I had a few drops of Jewish blood in my veins, I never considered myself Jewish." He then tells of his early experiences observing blatant anti-Semitism in Siberia, but without any indication that it was, or could have been, directed at him. It may be that his parents had decided not to share the truth about their background with their youngest child for his own protection. Had my father known of his Jewish heritage, he might have handled himself with less confidence and assurance when he was confronted by the Nazi authorities. On the other hand, he might have decided to quit Germany much sooner, perhaps saving himself five years of persecution. His life story might well have taken a completely different path had he been aware of his parents' background.

His own faith had always been more in himself and in the remarkable people he encountered, many of whom he had entrusted with his life. He believed that religion was purely a human creation whose purpose was to help people face life's difficulties and to calm their fears of the unknown. When questioned about his religious beliefs, he could enjoy a good-natured debate. I remember when pairs of Mormon missionaries would come to our door. Rather than sending them away, he would invite them in and begin asking them all kinds of awkward questions: "Why does God kill babies? Why does God let millions of people starve in Africa? Why does God allow disease to destroy so many people's lives? Why doesn't God stop criminals from hurting and killing people? If God is love, how can he stand by and do nothing to help?" And so on. The missionaries would do their best to answer his questions, but their efforts at converting him never got anywhere.

While the study of the psychological implications of religion may have intrigued him, he was actually much in awe of creation itself. The beauties of the world and the complexities of life itself were a constant source of wonder to him. Art, sculpture, music, and theatre excited his passion. His love of music, particularly of classical piano music, never left him. We had two grand pianos at home during my teenage years, and we would often play duets together. His favorite pieces were the concertos he had performed in his youth, some passages of which he still had reliably in his fingers, even after so many years. While I did not share his particular taste in music, I developed an intense love of music too, as well as an enthusiasm for artistic expression through performance.

His early dreams of becoming a philanthropist lead my father to set up three scholarships in his will. Two were given to the College of Earth and Mineral Sciences at Penn State University to support students of mining. The third scholarship he established was for young pianists (ages twelve through seventeen) to be administered by the State College Music Academy, the local music school I had attended as a teenager. He named the prize after me: The Vera Kochanowsky Scholarship Award. Since 1995 the school has held the competition, which is in the form of a public recital, every other year. The winner is awarded a generous monetary prize which goes toward their future music education. Every two years I return to my hometown for this event, and in my mind I also return to my youth, to the days when I, too, was a young piano student. Each time I am amazed at the technical prowess, the depth of musical expression, and the remarkable poise of the young competitors I hear. The composers selected invariably are ones that both my father and I used to play: Beethoven, Mozart, Bach, Rachmaninoff, and Chopin, among others. Sometimes, before the competition begins, I am invited to speak. When I do, I often end with a passage I wrote to preface the original competition guidelines. It begins with the story of my father's first lessons on the piano, one of the stories he particularly liked to tell me when I was a child:

In 1913, a mother in Siberia sent her eight-year old son, Boris, to study with a local piano teacher. Two weeks later, the teacher sent young Boris back to his mother with a note saying that her son was unteachable and it was no use for him to continue to study piano. Four years later, Boris happened to hear Mendelssohn's *Piano Concerto, Op. 25 in G Minor* in the local concert hall, performed by a high school student. He was so inspired by the performance that he ran all the way home and insisted that *now* he must begin to study the piano. After initial reluctance, Boris' mother gave in to her son's overwhelming persistence. Only three years later, at the age of fifteen, Boris played the same concerto in the same concert hall.

Although his phenomenally rapid rise was short-lived, lost in the wake of the Russian Revolution, he considered his early accomplishment on the piano to be a crucial factor in the development of his self-confidence, upon which he relied to face many challenges throughout his life. His love of music never diminished. This scholarship competition is dedicated to the power of music to inspire and strengthen the human spirit.

After many years of editing and refining my father's memoirs, I am glad that they now can be read and shared by a wider audience. Like my father, I hope these pages will inspire others to pursue their dreams and seek the best things life has to offer.

Appendix

H ere follows the eulogy given by Vladimir de Lissovoy (1918-2009) at Boris Kochanowsky's funeral on December 19, 1992:

A stranger coming to know Boris will learn in no uncertain terms that Boris is a *Sibiyak*. A *Sibiyak* is a Russian, a Siberian. And *Sibir* in Mongol Tartar dialect means "sleeping land." And the stranger will quickly learn that he is originally from Krasnoyarsk, and that means "beautiful ravine." And that Boris' source of strength and energy is the Yenisei River, the name taken from Evank dialect, meaning "big river." And a big river it is, with more than a million square miles of drainage basin and 2,538 miles in length. This majestic and beautiful river discharges a gigantic figure of 302,000 cubic feet of water per second into the Arctic Ocean. In describing this river, Boris could not sit still. He would gesture with great emphasis and sprinkle his description with "Wows" and similar exclamations.

Anton Chekov, seeing the Yenisei, wrote: "Never in my life have I seen a river more magnificent than the Yenisei. While the Volga is a dressy, modest, pensive beauty, the Yenisei is a powerful, turbulent giant which does not know what to do with its enormous power and its youth." He goes on to say, "On this bank stands Krasnoyarsk, the best and most beautiful of all Siberian towns, and on the opposite bank, there rise mountains misty and dreamlike." How familiar these descriptions are to those of us who knew Boris.

His was the energy of the Yenisei, the creativity of Krasnoyarsk, and the power of the taiga forest!

This region of Siberia is rich in mineral deposits of coal and precious metals, but the real heart is green: the famous taiga. And the Siberians loved their taiga. There are fantastic, marvelous stories about it. And they all stress one point: its freedom. There is a mystic attitude toward the great forest, its enormity and stark beauty create a sense of mystery and a sense of power. Chekov noted, "the power and the enchantment of the taiga are not in its giant trees or its silence, but in the fact that only migrating birds, perhaps, know where it ends."

The most dangerous animal in the taiga is the wolf, and the least dangerous is the bear. And so our Boris came from a city 2,100 miles east of Moscow, a city established by Siberian Cossacks in 1628. At the time of his childhood it was a cultural and manufacturing center, the home of several research and teaching institutes, a conservatory of music, a theater, a concert hall, a high school, and it was a major center of tea trade.

In our years of friendship with Boris, Charlotte and I were always aware of his remarkable inventiveness and creativity. He exuded power and directness. He was the Siberian bear. His stories of mining experiences centered on his designs in blasting in the form of huge explosions. But it was not the destructive power he wanted, it was the ultimate use of this power for creative purposes, as the mountain that he leveled with such control that the mass of falling earth would form the base of a dam.

"Think of the results," he would say to me, "then the plan of how to proceed with anything is just a matter of engineering."

He would illustrate this, describing some of his inventions with a surge of enthusiasm and emphasis on the result. Since my own engineering capability and capacity is limited to the construction of bird houses from plans marked, "Very easy, you cannot go wrong" (where I inevitably went wrong), I could do little but listen in awe as I viewed the plans, the photographs, and the great models that Boris had.

This man of the Yenisei and the taiga loved music, loved music with a passion. Of course, Beethoven, with his power, was his ideal, and Rachmaninoff, close behind. And yet his gentleness was to be seen and felt in his love of beauty, in his memories of the gentle Russian mother love, and in his deep and constant love for his daughter. As a rule, he always was in control of his emotions. The only exception that I witnessed was when he described one of Vera's recitals. A tear or two was in evidence and he said, "She was so beautiful." And then, as if catching himself, he added, "Her technique was excellent; it was a wonderful recital."

Charlotte was learning Russian, and Boris was helpful and encouraging. Knowing her love of music, he gave Charlotte recordings of *Boris Godunov* and the excruciatingly beautiful opera *Eugene Onegin*. What lovely evenings we spent listening, while following the Russian text in the libretto.

It is said that there is only one human emotion greater than the ability to love, and that is the knowledge that one is loved. This blessing came to Boris in the magnificent gift of Maria. Her care, her consideration, her devotion is without parallel. Those of us privileged to know her, and to have witnessed her care before Boris' illness, as well as during those difficult days, know the meaning of love. For this we are grateful.

Thus, we celebrate the long and productive life of the man from Krasnoyarsk, with the *élan vital* of the Yenisei, this gentle power, teacher, inventor, father, husband, and our friend. Boris, we love you.

Made in the USA
Middletown, DE
15 June 2017